ETHICS UNDER CAPITAL

POLITICAL THEORY AND CONTEMPORARY PHILOSOPHY

Political Theory and Contemporary Philosophy encourages a sustained dialogue between the most important intellectual currents in recent European philosophy—including phenomenology, deconstruction, hermeneutics—and key political theories and concepts, both classical and modern. In doing so, it not only sheds new light on today's shifting political realities but also explores the previously neglected consequences of the two disciplines.

Series editor: Michael Marder

Other volumes in the series include:

Politics in the Times of Indignation: The Crisis of Representative Democracy, Daniel Innerarity (translated by Sandra Kingery)

Medialogies: Inflationary Media and the Crisis of Reality, David R. Castillo and William Egginton

Democracy and Its Others, Jeffrey H. Epstein

The Democracy of Knowledge, Daniel Innerarity (translated by Sandra Kingery)

The Voice of Conscience: A Political Genealogy of Western Ethical Experience, Mika Ojakangas

The Politics of Nihilism, edited by Nitzan Lebovic and Roy Ben-Shai

On Hegel's Philosophy of Right, Martin Heidegger (edited by Peter Trawny, Marcia Cavalcante Schuback and Michael Marder, translated by Andrew J. Mitchell)

Deconstructing Zionism, Michael Marder and Santiago Zabala

Heidegger on Hegel's Philosophy of Right, Marcia Sa Cavalcante Schuback, Michael Marder and Peter Trawny

The Metaphysics of Terror, Rasmus Ugilt

The Negative Revolution, Artemy Magun

The Voice of Conscience, Mika Ojakangas

Contemporary Democracy and the Sacred, Jon Wittrock

ETHICS UNDER CAPITAL

MacIntyre, Communication, and the Culture Wars

JASON HANNAN

BLOOMSBURY ACADEMIC
LONDON • NEW YORK • OXFORD • NEW DELHI • SYDNEY

BLOOMSBURY ACADEMIC
Bloomsbury Publishing Plc
50 Bedford Square, London, WC1B 3DP, UK
1385 Broadway, New York, NY 10018, USA
29 Earlsfort Terrace, Dublin 2, Ireland

BLOOMSBURY, BLOOMSBURY ACADEMIC and the Diana logo are trademarks of
Bloomsbury Publishing Plc

First published in Great Britain 2020
Paperback edition published 2021

Copyright © Jason Hannan, 2020

Jason Hannan has asserted his right under the Copyright, Designs and Patents Act, 1988, to be identified as Author of this work.

For legal purposes the Acknowledgments on p. vi constitute an extension of this copyright page.

All rights reserved. No part of this publication may be reproduced or transmitted in any form or by any means, electronic or mechanical, including photocopying, recording, or any information storage or retrieval system, without prior permission in writing from the publishers.

Bloomsbury Publishing Plc does not have any control over, or responsibility for, any third-party websites referred to or in this book. All internet addresses given in this book were correct at the time of going to press. The author and publisher regret any inconvenience caused if addresses have changed or sites have ceased to exist, but can accept no responsibility for any such changes.

A catalogue record for this book is available from the British Library.

A catalog record for this book is available from the Library of Congress.

ISBN: HB: 978-1-3500-8060-7
PB: 978-1-3502-5953-9
ePDF: 978-1-3500-8059-1
eBook: 978-1-3500-8061-4

Series: Political Theory and Contemporary Philosophy

Typeset by Deanta Global Publishing Services, Chennai, India

To find out more about our authors and books visit www.bloomsbury.com and sign up for our newsletters.

CONTENTS

Acknowledgments vi
Prologue: A Metaphor for the Age viii

Introduction 1

1   Crisis of Communication 21

2   Roots of the Culture Wars 45

3   Emotivism on Steroids 67

4   Why Not Deliberative Democracy? 101

5   Why Not Agonistic Pluralism? 125

6   Ground of Fire 149

7   The Ship at Sea 177

Epilogue: Reason as Resistance 203
Index 214

ACKNOWLEDGMENTS

This book began as my doctoral dissertation, which examined the place of dialogue and communication in the thought of Alasdair MacIntyre. Although I had happily met the expectations of my dissertation committee, I had some difficulty imagining a worthwhile book on so narrow a topic. I therefore put the project on hold until I could find a suitable angle from which to write a book about MacIntyre and communication. That changed after the 2016 US presidential election. The sheer insanity of American politics and public discourse, both leading up to and following the 2016 general election, gave me a newfound appreciation for MacIntyre's political thought. It also gave me the angle I was looking for to reconceive this project. How successful the final product is will be for the reader to decide.

I am grateful to Michael Dorland, Chris Dornan, and Marc Furstenau for their guidance, patience, and support during every stage of the dissertation process. I am also grateful to Maurice Charland, who was a spirited and engaged external examiner. Graduate school is a nightmare for many. Thanks to my committee, I can confidently look back upon it as a wonderfully positive experience.

I also wish to thank a number of very kind and generous friends and colleagues for their feedback and support in the course of reconceiving this project: Kelvin Knight, Neil Davidson, Paul Blackledge, Robert Hariman, Peter Ives, Matthew Flisfeder, and Jaqueline McLeod Rogers. When I was a mere postdoc, Alasdair MacIntyre took time out of his incredibly busy schedule to answer several of my questions about his work. I greatly appreciate his patient, thorough, and eloquent responses, which confirmed for me that this book had to be written. Richard Raber very graciously read the entire manuscript in meticulous detail and offered many excellent suggestions for improving it. I owe him an exceptional debt of gratitude. The University of Winnipeg has been extremely supportive of every aspect of my academic career. This includes the freedom to teach whatever I want. My course Rhetoric in a Pluralistic Society has given me the opportunity to teach MacIntyre to undergraduate students and to apply his ideas to contemporary case studies. That course has been extremely helpful in thinking through much of the material in this book. I wish to thank my students from the many iterations of that course for their critical engagement with MacIntyre's ideas and for patiently working their way through a text as challenging as *After Virtue*.

Bloomsbury has been a truly exemplary publisher. I am grateful to Liza Thompson, Frankie Mace, Lisa Goodrum, and Lucy Russell for their assistance, patience, and professionalism throughout every stage of the publication process. I also wish to thank Michael Marder, an outstanding philosopher, for including this book in his wonderful series with Bloomsbury.

Some of the material in this book has been published previously. I would like to acknowledge the various publishers for permission to reproduce that material here, in some cases in revised form. Portions of Chapter 4 have previously appeared in "Moral Discourse Without Foundations," *Communication Theory*, 26.1(2015): 21–40 and "A Blind Spot in Political Theory: Justice, Deliberation, and Animals," *Journal of Animal Ethics*, 9.1(2019): 27–38. Portions of Chapter 5 have previously appeared in "Truth as First Casualty" in *Truth in the Public Sphere*, Lanham, MD: Lexington, 2016. Portions of Chapter 6 have previously appeared in "Alasdair MacIntyre's Contribution to Communication Theory," *Empedocles: European Journal for the Philosophy of Communication* 4.2 (2012): 183–98. I wish to thank Bloomsbury and University of Notre Dame Press for permission to reprint excerpts from Alasdair MacIntyre, *After Virtue: A Study in Moral Theory*, London, UK: Bloomsbury, 2013, and University of Notre Dame Press for permission to reprint excerpts from Alasdair MacIntyre, *Whose Justice? Which Rationality?* Notre Dame, IN: University of Notre Dame Press, 1988 and *Three Rival Versions of Moral Enquiry: Encyclopaedia, Genealogy, and Tradition*, Notre Dame, IN: University of Notre Dame Press, 1991.

PROLOGUE: A METAPHOR FOR THE AGE

Imagine a parallel universe like the one you know, but dark, cold, and desolate. You can walk down the same streets. You can see the same houses. You can even enter your own home. When you open the door, everything inside—the tables and chairs, the books on the shelf, the pictures on the wall—is exactly as you left it. It appears to be a perfect replica of your home. It even seems to bear the print of your touch, as if you were just there. Yet, it also looks and feels abandoned. You are surrounded by an unsettling silence and stillness. Everyone you know is missing. Your friends, family, and neighbors are nowhere to be found. No one can be seen walking the streets. Even the animals have disappeared. The only life appears to be the tendrils and membranes of some vast plant, one with no beginning and no end. The plant envelops every object in sight, as if to keep it in place. As you walk through this dark world, you can hear a faint echo of familiar voices. You sense the real world is close by, perhaps just behind a wall. But you can find no doorway, no portal, leading back to it. You face the terrifying thought that you're forever trapped in this shadow world. You ask yourself whether this is just a dream. You wonder if you will ever awaken from what feels like a nightmare. You begin to question your sanity. Soon, you realize you are not alone. This dark world, it turns out, is home to bloodthirsty creatures that feed on human bodies. You recognize among the bodies the faces of family and friends, all of them unconscious, all of them wrapped in the tendrils of the all-encompassing plant. Not wanting to face the same fate, you run and hide. You do what you can to survive. You cling to the hope that you will soon return to reality. You cling to the hope that the world you remember is real. Welcome to the Upside Down.

A recurring theme in the Netflix television series *Stranger Things*, the Upside Down is an alternate dimension of reality that resembles something very much like hell. While it is unclear whether the writers intended any symbolism behind it, some commentators have playfully suggested that the Upside Down is a fitting metaphor for the real world.[1] And it might as well be. The state of American democracy today appears to have become an alternate dimension—a kind of twilight zone in which our institutions remain the same, in which we go through the same formalities and perform the same rituals, but in which madness reigns supreme.

As of this writing, Donald Trump has been president for just over two years. The man who launched his political career with a shockingly racist tirade against Mexican immigrants no longer shocks and scandalizes us anymore. His pathological lying, vicious insults, incessant trolling, public buffoonery, and trashy behavior were once the stuff of intense public discussion. Students began paying attention to politics. Teachers like myself found endless material for lectures and classroom discussion. Trump was also a gift to late night comedians, who merely had to quote him to generate endless laughter. He made their jobs easier. The jokes wrote themselves.

Most importantly, Trump was a gift to the American news media. They capitalized on his every word and deed to produce an endless sewer of sensational coverage. Major news channels like CNN, MSNBC, ABC, and CBS were perfectly happy to shed any pretense of serious journalism to take up the mantle of tabloid news, as long as it meant cheap and easy ratings. They were willing and eager to be Trump's punching bag, happy to play the part of the hapless victim, even as they implicitly cheered him on through unceasing coverage. They gave him what he wanted—the spotlight—which only further fed his ego and fueled his drive to do the one thing he knows best: stay in that spotlight. Despite all appearances to the contrary, the relationship between Trump and the new media has been symbiotic.

Early in Trump's presidency, it had become a kind of sport for respectable news outlets to document the man's every lie, misstatement, and distortion.

Releasing official lists of Trump's lies were hailed as a sort of journalistic achievement, a way of keeping the mad king in check, taming his recklessness with the power of impersonal fact-checking.[2] No matter how much he lied, the idea was, such lists would provide an anchor to reality. They served as solid pillars of objectivity, a means of keeping our balance amidst the chaos. Political commentators found a new sense of mission and purpose. They coined new terms to capture the spirit of the age. The most prominent of these terms was "post-truth," selected by *Oxford Dictionary* as its 2016 word of the year.[3] As with late night comedy and the news media, Trump provided ample material for the world of political commentary, which experienced a rebirth of sorts after the launch of his presidential campaign. Suddenly, everyone and their uncle had become a political commentator. In this theater of the absurd, no opinion seemed any more or any less valid than the next.

But the value of keeping track of Trump's lies and offering yet more political commentary seems to have worn out. The more these lists are updated and the more that commentators reflect on Trump, the more banal and meaningless it all becomes. The lists and the commentary have dissolved into white noise. Trump has shown himself to possess a special kind of power over the media and our political discourse. He has shown himself to be a master of shock and awe rhetoric. Much like its counterpart on the battlefield, this type of rhetoric bombards our minds with outrageous displays of mendacity, tastelessness, shamelessness, and sheer viciousness. At some point, the constant shock and awe gave way to numbness and futility. It became clear that the mad king could not be tamed. It felt pointless to try. It became easier to accept that he firmly held the reins of our public discourse, determining every news cycle, driving every political debate. His pathological lying and wild conspiracy theories are no longer shocking. His trashiness, his embarrassing behavior before foreign dignitaries, his incompetence about the laws and institutions of the very country he runs, no longer scandalize us. We have grown accustomed to it all. We now passively accept news of his lies like we do the weather report. The madness has become normalized. "Trump was outrageous in Michigan. So where's the outrage?" asks *The Washington Post* with sincere incredulity.[4] The only shocking thing is that anyone is still shocked by Donald Trump. What was once outrageous now mostly passes without comment. We seem to have completed our transition to a parallel universe. We appear to inhabit our own version of the Upside Down, a simulacrum of democracy.

What is reality like inside of our Upside Down? In 2018, Donald Trump was nominated for the Nobel Prize.[5] Many prominent figures seriously believed Trump was a peace broker, despite taunting North Korea's Kim Jong Un on Twitter, childishly calling him "Rocket Man," and threatening nuclear war.[6] After comedian Michelle Wolf delivered a scathing performance at the 2018 White House Correspondents Dinner, in which she spoke the brutal truth about politicians and the media, both conservatives and liberals severely criticized her for crossing a line—for being too merciless in her assertion of the truth.[7] In our version of the Upside Down, a comedian who speaks the truth is held to a higher standard of public decorum than the president of the United States, who lies and insults with every breath he takes.

Gun violence has become another index of the inversion of reality. After the mass shooting at Marjory Stoneman Douglas High School in 2018, student survivors of the shooting spoke out about gun violence. They did interviews. They gave speeches. They spoke before lawmakers. They took it upon themselves to organize the historic March for Our Lives, as if it really needed to be said that children deserve to be able to go to school without the fear of being gunned down by a classmate.[8] For this, they became the target of conservative ire. They were accused of being "crisis actors."[9] They were smeared on social media. They were sent death threats.[10] But the backlash wasn't limited to anonymous trolls online. Leslie Gibson, a Republican candidate for Maine's House of Representatives, attacked student survivors Emma González and David Hogg on Twitter. Gibson called González a "skinhead lesbian" and Hogg a "bald-faced liar."[11] Kevin Sabo, a Trump official at the Department of the Interior, compared Hogg to Nazis.[12] Jamie Allman, former host of a nightly show on KDNL in St. Louis, threatened to sexually assault Hogg with a "hot poker."[13] Laura Ingraham, one of the most prominent talk show hosts at Fox News, mocked Hogg on Twitter for being rejected by four colleges.[14] Hogg's younger sister appropriately responded to Ingraham on Twitter: "Coming from a 14 year old, please grow up."[15] In our Upside Down, children have more maturity and good sense than adults.

Living in the Upside Down can be confusing, dispiriting, frustrating, infuriating. The sheer absurdity of it all is only compounded by the realization that it's not just conservatives who seem to have lost their grip on truth and reality. Liberals, too, have reinforced the illogic of this topsy-turvy universe by embracing political figures once regarded as monsters. The rehabilitation of George W. Bush is a case in point. Bush, it should never be forgotten, is the man who lied his way into the Iraq War, a foreign policy disaster that took the lives of 100,000 Iraqi civilians, cost over $1 trillion, sparked the rise of ISIS, destabilized the Middle East, and created the Syrian refugee crisis. Bush established the notorious detention camp in Guantanamo Bay, imprisoning captives of war and subjecting them to torture, all without trial. He shredded civil liberties and established a military state in the name of protecting the nation from an ill-defined foreign enemy. He oversaw the slow and appallingly inept response to Hurricane Katrina, resulting in over 1,800 deaths and the displacement of 400,000 people, most of them poor and African American. His aggressive push for deregulation played a large role in the 2008 financial crisis, which led to the Great Recession, the effects of which we are still experiencing today. In short, Bush was a nightmare for human rights, civil liberties, and the economy. He was—and remains—a war criminal. He was also deeply unpopular, not just with liberals, but even with conservatives, especially libertarians who opposed the invasion of Iraq.

Following the conclusion of his spectacularly failed presidency in 2008, Bush disappeared from the public spotlight.[16] He was conspicuously missing from his brother Jeb's presidential campaign in 2015.[17] He was nowhere to be seen at the Republican National Convention in 2016.[18] It was widely understood that Bush was toxic to Republican candidates and therefore ought to be kept in political quarantine.

Then, in early 2017, Bush reemerged from hiding to go on a national tour to promote his newfound purpose in life: art.[19] The war criminal had discovered the paintbrush. Liberals welcomed his return with open arms—literally. First, he was pictured hugging Hillary Clinton.[20] Then, he was pictured hugging Michelle Obama, whose husband's presidential campaign was defined against the entire Bush legacy.[21] Bush later appeared on *The Ellen DeGeneres Show*, where he was pictured hugging DeGeneres, a notable liberal and gay rights icon.[22] The man once reviled by American liberals managed, after a mere few years in hiding, to reinvent himself as a harmless, irresistible teddy bear. His responsibility for destroying millions of human lives, creating lasting geopolitical instability in the Middle East, mismanaging one of the worst natural disasters in American history, and overseeing the worst economic crisis since the Great Depression appears to have been completely erased from public memory.

In our version of the Upside Down, monsters can become teddy bears. For those who have not become entrapped in the tendrils of the all-encompassing plant, an apt metaphor for the stupefying effects of popular culture and social media, this is where the truly disturbing implication lies: if George W. Bush can be rehabilitated, there is no reason not to expect that Donald Trump himself will one day be rehabilitated, too.

* * *

How do we make sense of this madness? How did we come to inhabit the Upside Down? How do we survive within it? Can we ever escape it? More to the point, how do we not fall into the trap of offering more empty commentary that risks dissolving into more white noise? This book is about a prophetic figure who offers answers to these questions. Over thirty years ago, Alasdair MacIntyre warned us of "the coming ages of barbarism and darkness." What he described then very much resembles the Upside Down recounted above. He provided the conceptual tools for diagnosing a widespread, but largely unseen, cultural crisis.

He also offered a way to survive that crisis. Some of his critics took offense at his harsh critique of our culture. They dismissed his warning as the ramblings and exaggerations of a bitter pessimist. They labeled him a reactionary. They reasserted their faith in liberal democracy. There is no crisis, they assured us. All is well.[23] Yet, here we are, in the Upside Down, with Donald Trump in the White House. The premise of this book is that MacIntyre was right all along.

Notes

1. See, for example, Michael Morelli, "We're All Living in the 'Upside Down': 'Stranger Things' Is a Show about the Internet's Dark Sides," *Salon*, September 2, 2016. https://www.salon.com/2016/09/01/were-all-living-in-the-upside-down-stranger-things-is-a-show-about-the-internets-dark-sides/ (accessed January 13, 2019); and Anna Leskiewicz, "How Stranger Things 2 Explores Ordinary and Extraordinary Suffering," *The New Statesman*, October 30, 2017. https://www.newstatesman.com/culture/tv-radio/2017/10/how-stranger-things-2-explores-ordinary-and-extraordinary-suffering (accessed January 13, 2019).

2. See, for example, David Leonhardt and Stuart A. Thompson, "Trump's Lies," *The New York Times*, December 14, 2017. https://www.nytimes.com/interactive/2017/06/23/opinion/trumps-lies.html (accessed January 13, 2019).

3. https://en.oxforddictionaries.com/word-of-the-year/word-of-the-year-2016 (accessed January 13, 2019).

4. James Downie, "Trump Was Outrageous in Michigan. So Where's the Outrage?" *The Washington Post*, April 30, 2018. https://www.washingtonpost.com/blogs/post-partisan/wp/2018/04/30/trump-was-outrageous-in-michigan-so-wheres-the-outrage (accessed January 13, 2019).

5. "Donald Trump Formally Nominated for a Nobel Prize for 'his tireless work to bring peace to our world,'" *The Telegraph*, May 4, 2019. https://www.telegraph.co.uk/news/2018/05/03/donald-trump-formally-nominated-nobel-peace-prize-tireless-work/ (accessed April 1, 2019).

6. Stephen Treloar, "Two Norwegian Lawmakers Nominate Trump for Nobel Peace Prize," *Bloomberg*, June 13, 2018. https://www.bloomberg.com/news/articles/2018-06-13/trump-nominated-for-peace-prize-by-norwegian-lawmakers-nrk-says (accessed January 13, 2019).

7. David Smith, "White House Correspondents' Dinner: Michelle Wolf Shocks Media with Sarah Sanders Attack," *The Guardian*, April 29, 2018. https://www.theguardian.com/us-news/2018/apr/29/white-house-correspondents-dinner-michelle-wolf-stuns-media-with-sarah-sanders-attack (accessed January 13, 2019).

8. Michael D. Shear, "Students Lead Huge Rallies for Gun Control across the U.S.," *The New York Times*, March 24, 2018. https://www.nytimes.com/2018/03/24/us/politics/students-lead-huge-rallies-for-gun-control-across-the-us.html

9. Mack DeGeurin, "We Met With Crisis Actor Conspiracy Theorists and the Victims They Baselessly Attack," *Vice*, April 12, 2018. https://motherboard.vice.com/en_us/article/qvxxew/rise-of-the-crisis-actor-conspiracy-theory (accessed January 13, 2019).

10. Lisa Ryan, "Parkland Shooting Survivors Aren't Letting Death Threats Stand in the Way of Activism," *The Cut*, March 19, 2018. https://www.thecut.com/2018/03/parkland-survivors-emma-gonzalez-60-minutes-death-threats.html (accessed January 13, 2019).

11. Matt Stevens, "'Skinhead Lesbian' Tweet about Parkland Student Ends Maine Republican's Candidacy," *The New York Times*, March 18, 2018. https://www.nytimes.com/2018/03/18/us/politics/maine-republican-leslie-gibson.html (accessed January 13, 2019).

12. Avery Anapol, "Interior Official Compared Parkland Students to Nazis: Report," *The Hill*, April 9, 2018. https://thehill.com/homenews/administration/382264-interior-official-compared-parkland-students-to-nazis-report (accessed January 13, 2019).

13. Elliott C. McLaughlin, "Sinclair TV Host Resigns after Making Vulgar Comment about Parkland Student David Hogg," *CNN*, April 10, 2018. https://www.cnn.com/2018/04/10/us/sinclair-commentator-resigns-jamie-allman-david-hogg/index.html (accessed January 13, 2019).

14. Benjamin Fearnow, "Conservative Radio Host Laura Ingraham Mocks Parkland Survivor David Hogg For College Rejections," *Newsweek*, March 28, 2018. https://www.newsweek.com/laura-ingraham-david-hogg-colleges-ucla-uc-santa-barbara-twitter-parkland-864992 (accessed January 13, 2019).

15. Ed Mazza, "Parkland Survivor Slams Fox News Host: 'Coming From A 14-Year-Old, Please Grow Up,'" *HuffPost US*, March 29, 2018. https://www.huffingtonpost.ca/entry/lauren-hogg-laura-ingraham_us_5abc7654e4b06409775d0d2c (accessed January 13, 2019).

16. Paul Waldman, "The Strange Disappearance of George W. Bush," *The American Prospect*, April 24, 2012. https://prospect.org/article/strange-disappearance-george-w-bush (accessed January 13, 2019).

17. Cathleen Decker, "In Jeb Bush's Foreign Policy Speech, George W. Bush Goes Missing," *Los Angeles Times*, August 12, 2015. https://www.latimes.com/nation/politics/la-na-jeb-bush-analysis-20150812-story.html (accessed January 13, 2019).

18. Jessica Taylor, "Dumpster Fires, Fishing and Travel: These Republicans Are Sitting Out the RNC," *NPR*, July 18, 2016. https://www.npr.org/2016/07/18/486398726/dumpster-fires-fishing-and-travel-these-republicans-are-sitting-out-the-rnc (accessed January 13, 2019).

19. Eli Watkins and Jamie Gangel, "George W. Bush Discovers His 'inner Rembrandt' in Homage to Veterans," *CNN*, February 27, 2017. https://www.cnn.com/2017/02/27/politics/george-w-bush-paintings/index.html (accessed January 13, 2019).

20 Rebecca Savransky, "Photo Shows Hillary Clinton, George W. Bush Together at Reagan's Funeral," *The Hill*, March 14, 2016. https://thehill.com/blogs/ballot-box/272869-photo-shows-hillary-clinton-george-w-bush-together-at-reagans-funeral (accessed January 13, 2019).

21 Corky Siemaszko, "Michelle Obama Embraces George W. Bush: Why That Photo Was So Moving," *NBC News*, September 26, 2016. https://www.nbcnews.com/news/us-news/michelle-obama-embraces-george-w-bush-why-photo-was-so-n654451 (accessed January 13, 2019).

22 Erin Jensen, "George W. Bush Talks That Inauguration Day Poncho, Putin and Michelle Obama on 'Ellen,'" *USA Today*, March 2, 2017. https://www.usatoday.com/story/life/entertainthis/2017/03/02/george-w-bush-ellen-degeneres-show-putin-press-michelle-obama-poncho/98626090/ (accessed January 13, 2019).

23 See, for example, Jeffrey Stout, *Democracy and Tradition*. Princeton, NJ: Princeton University Press, 2004, 118–39.

Introduction

If crisis begets opportunity, then we are living in the midst of what the Greeks called *kairos*, an opportune moment. The devastating financial crisis of 2008 ignited a fierce political awakening and a hunger for radical change that shows no signs of being satiated. An entire generation has lived through the aftermath of the Great Recession. Those who were not fortunate enough to have been born into great wealth have had to contend to one extent or another with a rigged economic system. They have witnessed the injustice of that system all around them. They have felt its destructive effects. They live it every day in the new gig economy, where they are forced to work multiple jobs just to survive. Some have decided to become homeless to pay for college. Others have given up the dream of a college education altogether. Millennials have been scolded for being financially incompetent, for being too entitled, and for indulging in too much avocado toast. While some have answered the call of right-wing ideologues who blame minorities and immigrants, others have taken a more critical view of the political economic order. They wish to understand the nature of capitalism, the dynamics of class conflict, the machinations of power, and the lure of ideology. More than at any other time in recent memory, a younger generation is questioning the very foundations of the liberal capitalist order.

Marx and Engels are currently undergoing a lively rebirth.[1] Sales of *Capital* and *The Communist Manifesto* have risen dramatically.[2] Thomas Piketty's *Capital in the Twenty-First Century* became an international best seller.[3] Students have turned in large numbers to David Harvey, Naomi Klein, Noam Chomsky, Arundhati Roy, Michael Hardt, and Antonio Negri to understand the nature of the global capitalist order. Marxist theory is fashionable once again, some of its more notable figures being Fredric Jameson, Terry Eagleton, Jacques Rancière, Jodi Dean, Slavoj Žižek, and Silvia Federici.[4] New magazines such as *Jacobin, Current Affairs, n+1,* and *The Baffler* are to the present moment what *Dissent, The New Reasoner,* and *The New Left Review* were to an earlier one.

The spirit of resistance has also gone digital. The wildly popular podcast *Chapo Trap House* and the YouTube channel *The Young Turks* have disseminated critical commentary to cult followings in the millions online. Membership in the Democratic Socialists of America is surging. And Bernie Sanders and Alexandria Ocasio-Cortez, two self-styled socialists and relentless critics of Wall Street and the billionaire class, are among the most popular politicians in America, a land where socialism is no longer exclusively a dirty word.[5] If the 2008 financial crisis opened a window, it looks as if that window will not be closing any time soon.

This book addresses this window, what can be called a *kairotic* moment. It offers a new reading of the political philosopher Alasdair MacIntyre, one that might serve those looking to make sense of our volatile time and to craft a meaningful politics suitable to the present condition. MacIntyre is one of the best guides we have for understanding and resisting the ideology of liberal capitalism. He offers invaluable conceptual tools that enable us to see the logic of the free market at play in our public discourse. He helps us navigate through that discourse by making sense of the confusing cacophony of disparate voices. Most importantly, he proposes a model of public communication that resists the toxic hostility so characteristic of today's digitally mediated culture wars. He shows us how to disagree with each other without falling back upon a politics of instrumental will and power. His voice is urgently needed in an age of online trolling and pathological incivility. Unfortunately, MacIntyre's work has been subjected to grotesque misinterpretation, some of it by critics, much of it by would-be admirers. Tragically, this invaluable critical theorist has largely been relegated to the sidelines of today's debate about the ravages of our neoliberal age.

MacIntyre is best known for his 1981 book, *After Virtue: A Study in Moral Theory*. When it was first published, *After Virtue* created something of a firestorm in the Anglophone world. MacIntyre had argued that something was deeply wrong with our culture—that the way we talk to one another about ethics and politics was "in a grave state of disorder."[6] He traced the source of that disorder to the Enlightenment, charging it with failure. He leveled a harsh critique against the dominant moral philosophies of our age.

MacIntyre took aim in particular against liberalism, the philosophical foundation of the Western world. He further called for a return to Aristotle and the virtues. He proposed a powerful theory of narratives, traditions, and practices as the basis for moral identity and practical reason. In the book's dramatic final chapter, he set up an ultimate showdown between Nietzsche and Aristotle, and an unlikely alliance between Trotsky and St. Benedict, the founder the Benedictine order. MacIntyre closed with a warning that we were entering our own Dark Ages and admonished us to preserve the virtues of civility in the face of impending cultural chaos.

As far as works of moral philosophy go, *After Virtue* was an unusually eloquent and hyperintelligent thrill ride. It read like a suspenseful novel in which the reader discovered that she was a character caught up in an ominous historical drama. Many readers fell in love with the book without necessarily understanding it. Some enjoyed it simply for the sheer elegance of MacIntyre's writing style. Others loved it because of his deeply prophetic voice; certain that he was saying something important, uncertain of what that actually was. *After Virtue* is not an easy text to read. It contains numerous arcane references and cryptic allusions that require extensive background reading to appreciate properly. It is also written in a distinctly dialectical style, recognizable to those with a deep familiarity with Marx and Hegel, but not so recognizable to those with no such familiarity. At once a difficult and provocative book that took aim at the idols of the age, *After Virtue* was bound to be misunderstood by many.

That misunderstanding stems in large part from MacIntyre's harsh critique of liberalism. In our everyday political discourse, "liberalism" means something like today's Democratic Party of the United States, a politically centrist party with a limited commitment to equality, social welfare, and the environment. Liberalism in this popular sense is associated with Hollywood celebrities, late night comedians, the ACLU, the NAACP, Amnesty International, and the Sierra Club. It is a mix of neoliberal economic policies and tepid gestures toward social justice. To conservative ears, any critique of "liberalism" will naturally sound like music, the voice of a kindred spirit at war against cultural elites and the guardians of political correctness. Thus, conservatives are liable to see MacIntyre as an ally in their war against the Left. To liberal ears, any critique of liberalism will inevitably come across as a form of reactionary conservatism, the voice of an intransigent bellyacher resolutely opposed to social progress. Liberals are thus liable to see MacIntyre as the enemy, an opponent of civil rights and gender equality, perhaps even a forerunner of the so-called intellectual dark web.[7] Neither the conservative nor the liberal interpretation could be more disastrously incorrect.

When MacIntyre sets his sights on liberalism, what he has in mind is *classical* liberalism, the political philosophy that focuses upon the rights and freedoms of the individual, privileging this abstraction above all else.[8] Among these rights and freedoms is the right to private property, one of the core precepts of free market ideology. For MacIntyre, the individualism encoded into the right to private property *is* the ideological root of injustice. When some people own land, natural resources, real estate, and the means of production, they hold a decided advantage over those who own none of these things. Private property enables exploitation.

This exploitation is itself the source of alienation, the inability of the poor and propertyless to decide their future. By advocating the right to private property, liberalism fosters asymmetrical relations between people, a division between capitalist and worker, thus necessarily creating hierarchy and inequality. Liberalism also imposes the right to private property upon Indigenous cultures, whose languages do not necessarily include the concept of a natural right to private property.[9] By dressing up private property in the false rhetoric of natural rights, liberalism thus becomes an instrument for European power and domination over Indigenous cultures. Worst of all, liberalism creates a social universe in which human relationships are governed by instrumental reasoning, destroying the bonds of human community and social solidarity.

If this all sounds so very Marxist, it is because MacIntyre was for two decades one of the leading Marxist intellectuals of the British New Left. Early on in his intellectual career, MacIntyre internalized Marxist categories of analysis and Marxism's antipathy toward liberalism and bourgeois morality. That antipathy has remained with him ever since. MacIntyre's indebtedness to Marx, however, is lost upon those readers who approach him as if he had not written anything before 1981. While *After Virtue* is undoubtedly his most important book, it cannot be understood in isolation from his other writings, both earlier and later. When seen in that broader light, it becomes clear that *After Virtue* is an extension of, and an advancement upon, MacIntyre's formative engagement with Marxism.[10]

The Marxist MacIntyre

MacIntyre's engagement with Marxism goes back to the beginning of his intellectual career. As an undergraduate student in Classics at Queen Mary College, University of London in the late 1940s, MacIntyre joined the Communist Party of Great Britain.[11] At the age of twenty-three, he published his first book, a remarkable work entitled, *Marxism: An Interpretation*.[12] This book explored the parallels between Marxism and Christianity, making the case that the former had adopted the structure and function of the latter.

Of the many themes of the book, two stand out in particular. The first is the fall of humanity into a state of alienation. While Christianity might have told the more dramatic story of the fall, Marxism did the better job of describing the nature of alienation. In a capitalist order, workers necessarily live in a state of separation, not just from the products of their labor, but from themselves and from the world. If the mission of Christianity is to save humanity after the fall, the mission of Marxism is to emancipate workers from the oppression of capitalism. If Christianity offers hope for salvation in the next world, Marxism offers hope for emancipation in this world. It is clear from MacIntyre's words that the goal of emancipation and the dialectical mode of critique were permanently etched into his bones at an early age.

Following the 1956 revelations of Stalin's crimes against humanity, MacIntyre left the Communist Party. He remained a Marxist, albeit without a political organization to call home. He began publishing in prominent New Left journals, including *Universities and Left Review* and *The New Reasoner*.[13] He soon gained prominence in the British New Left, a movement whose leading lights included Perry Anderson, Stuart Hall, Charles Taylor, Dorothy Thompson, Edward Thompson, and Dorothy Wedderburn. In 1957, Edward Thompson attempted to address the crisis of Western Marxism that followed the horrifying revelations about Stalin.[14] Thompson suggested that Western Marxists had developed a "split mentality," since they drew intellectual and political inspiration from Marx and Engels, yet failed to acknowledge that Stalin had done much the same. Against this split mentality, Thompson argued for a humanist reading of Marx and Engels that opposed the depravities of both Stalinism and capitalism alike.

MacIntyre took up this same theme in 1958 with this landmark essay, "Notes from the Moral Wilderness."[15] He criticized some of his comrades for condemning the crimes of Stalin by appealing to liberal humanism. This move, he pointed out, made little sense. Liberalism notably divorced morality from desire and history, thereby depriving itself of any moral authority other than that of the individual. More to the point, Marxism was founded precisely in opposition to classical liberalism. To reinvent Marxism through a liberal humanist frame was thus to lapse into incoherence. Between the "barren opposition of moral individualism and amoral Stalinism," MacIntyre suggested an alternative basis for moral judgment: the Marxist conception of human nature.[16] This conception reconnected morality to desire and history.

It thereby gave Marxists a viable ground on which to critique Stalin while remaining committed to revolutionary praxis.

In the late 1950s, many British Marxists believed it was possible to establish socialism without revolution. MacIntyre strongly disagreed. His reading of Lenin reaffirmed his conviction that revolution not only was absolutely necessary but also could not come about without revolutionary organization. In 1959, he joined the Socialist Labour League, a group that took its inspiration from Trotsky, Stalin's primary political rival, and had become a refuge for Marxists who had abandoned the Communist Party.[17]

The Socialist Labour League offered MacIntyre the opportunity to put into practice his vision of revolutionary politics. He celebrated the solidarity between members of different class backgrounds and advocated for radical democratic equality between the members of the league. He wrote for the *Labour Review*, *The Listener*, and the league's main outlet, *The Newsletter*. He frequently appeared on BBC radio, making an eloquent and impassioned case for the revolutionary cause.[18] During this time, he published his essay, "Freedom and Revolution" in *Labour Review*.[19] He argued that freedom could not be achieved individually or through capitalism. Freedom meant revolution. Revolution meant organization. Organization meant democratic discipline. Unfortunately, MacIntyre did not find this democratic discipline in the Socialist Labour League, whose partisan politics and authoritarian leadership he found unbearable.[20]

MacIntyre found a new home in International Socialism, a smaller organization that was more democratic, more politically broad-minded, and more intellectually lively and rigorous. During this time, he published numerous essays in *International Socialism*, *Socialist Review*, *Encounter*, *The New Listener*, and *The New Statesman*. He offered socialist perspectives on the Cold War, nuclear disarmament, the dismantling of the welfare state, and the fragmentation and depoliticization of the working class. He wrote intellectual profiles and reviews of Raymond Williams, Jean-Paul Sartre, C. Wright Mills, György Lukács, Herbert Marcuse, and Lucien Goldmann. MacIntyre regarded

Goldmann in particular with rather high esteem. He described Goldmann as "the finest and most intelligent Marxist of the age."[21] A critic of the economic determinism and scientific pretension of orthodox Marxism, Goldmann argued in *The Hidden God* for replacing a rationalist view of the human condition with a tragic one, a condition marked by risk and uncertainty. As Goldmann put it, "Risk, possibility of failure, hope of success and the synthesis of these three in the form a faith which is a wager are the essential constituent elements of the human condition."[22] On this view, a socialist revolution was not the historical inevitability that orthodox Marxism made it out to be. Rather, any such revolution hinged entirely on the proletariat.

By 1964, MacIntyre had already accepted Goldmann's tragic view of the human condition. In his essay, "Prediction and Politics," MacIntyre argued that Marxism is not a natural science like physics or chemistry.[23] Unlike the physical world, the social world is not subject to impersonal laws of motion. He took issue with Engels's scientific rendition of Marx, which replaced a dialectical conception of history with a mechanistic one. On the mechanistic view, the capitalist class would remain clueless about the volatility of the market system. The working class would develop a revolutionary consciousness, a critical understanding of the system, and a desire to overthrow it. Following a major economic downturn, a socialist revolution would inevitably follow. This chain of events could all be predicted like so much clockwork.

Against this mechanistic picture of society, MacIntyre pointed out two unfortunate realities. The first was that the capitalist class had developed a critical understanding of the nature of the system. They found ways to stabilize the economy. They turned to technological innovation to create new markets and continue economic expansion. They also realized the long-term benefit of compromising with the trade union movement. The second unfortunate reality was that the working class had not, in fact, moved toward a revolutionary consciousness. Poverty, it turned out, did not radicalize workers. Worse, the trade unions and social democratic parties had convinced the working class that the only way to improve their lot in life was through the market system. The path to revolution thus did not naturally flow in the manner and direction that scientific Marxism had predicted. MacIntyre thus drew a sharp distinction between Marx and Marxism. As he put it, "Marx was not a post-Engels classical Marxist."[24] Marx offered an invaluable analysis of capitalism. Classical Marxism, developed by Engels and subsequent theorists, fell prey to scientific pretension. The value of the one, MacIntyre asserted, should not be implicated by the failures of the other. A socialist revolution was still possible. However, it depended upon the self-understanding of committed political revolutionaries and a deeper integration with the working class.[25]

By 1965, MacIntyre had taken a different view of socialist organizations and the idea of a vanguard party, primarily on the influence of Socialisme ou Barbarie, a French Marxist organization whose leading voices included Guy DeBord, Gérard Genette, Claude Lefort, Jean-François Lyotard, and especially Cornelius Castoriadis, who at the time wrote under the pseudonym Paul Cardan. MacIntyre had accepted Castoriadis's critique of socialist organizations, though not necessarily his spontaneist view of socialist revolution.

Inspired by Rosa Luxembourg, the spontaneist view held that a socialist revolution should come from below, without the paternalism of a vanguard party. While this view did not give reason to abandon socialist organizations, it nonetheless severely diminished their importance. In 1965, MacIntyre participated in a public debate with Castoriadis on the future of socialist politics. MacIntyre represented International Socialism, and Castoriadis, Socialisme ou Barbarie. But instead of a disagreement, MacIntyre largely agreed with his interlocutor. He accepted Castoriadis's critique of the doctrine of revolution from above. In doing so, MacIntyre angered his fellow members of International Socialism.[26]

By 1967, MacIntyre no longer believed that the Marxist conception of human nature was a viable foundation for moral judgment. In *A Short History of Ethics*, he offered a lightning tour of the history of moral philosophy from the ancient world to the present day.[27] He pointed out the shortcomings of each moral theory—why it failed to provide a rational basis for moral judgment.

But in doing so, MacIntyre exposed a glaring self-limitation: On what moral basis did he critique these different moral theories? He acknowledged that he had no answer. For the young political philosopher, this would prove to be an acute problem.

His last hope for a foundation for moral judgment and for a socialist revolution lay in the practice and consciousness of the proletariat. Unfortunately, he had come to see the working class as too fragmented to unite and overthrow the system he had grown so passionately to despise. MacIntyre thus faced Goldmann's wager once again. As Goldmann wrote, life "becomes a wager that God, Humanity, or the Proletariat exists and will triumph."[28] If the wager took the form of faith, then MacIntyre no longer had faith in the proletariat. And if Marxism did not offer a reliable blueprint for revolution, then he no longer had reason to remain Marxist. In 1968, he therefore left International Socialism, never again to be seen at its meetings.[29]

After Virtue and after

While MacIntyre continued to endorse Marx's analysis of capitalism, his rejection of political Marxism prompted the search for an alternative basis for morality and revolutionary praxis. MacIntyre spent the next decade searching for answers. He learned from the works of Hegel, Elizabeth Anscombe, Thomas Kuhn, Imre Lakatos, and Hans-Georg Gadamer. Most of all, he learned from Aristotle, in whom he found the key to the big riddle of how to ground morality. The result of this lengthy period of intense investigation and philosophical soul-searching was *After Virtue*, a wide-ranging work that presents a dramatic and fundamental rethinking of morality from the ground up. *After Virtue* is notably divided into two parts: diagnostic and constructive.

The first part identifies a profound crisis in Western culture. MacIntyre observes that our public communication is disordered, fragmented, and shrill—a phenomenon best illustrated by the extreme vitriol of today's culture wars, campus wars, and battles over free speech. We disagree with each other. That's hardly new. But now, the more we engage with each other, the further we dig in our heels and the more hardened and dogmatic we become. We have reached an impasse, one that is now morphing into violence and social chaos. So, how did we get here? Relying upon Hegel's historicist theory of knowledge, MacIntyre provides an illuminating answer to this question, tracing the roots of the problem back to the Enlightenment, an argument that bears a distinct echo of Theodor Adorno and Max Horkheimer's *Dialectic of Enlightenment*.[30]

In the second part of *After Virtue*, MacIntyre solves the puzzle that had been teasing him for so long: How to provide a rational basis for morality and politics. MacIntyre makes a compelling case for a return to Aristotle and the tradition of virtue ethics. To a younger generation today, especially those shaped by the contemporary idiom of social justice, this answer is liable to seem quaint, perhaps even hopelessly so. Why should the answer to the riddle of morality be a return to an ancient thinker, especially one who endorsed slavery and patriarchy? But to revive the tradition of the virtues, as MacIntyre shows, is not to revive everything associated with Aristotle. Many contemporary women philosophers, for example, have also argued for a revival of virtue ethics.[31] We can take the good and leave the bad. The virtue of virtue ethics is that it enables us to make rational moral judgments about our everyday world, including arguments *against* slavery and patriarchy.

By rooting those judgments in desire and history, they differ sharply from the sanctimonious preaching of moralizing blowhards. So, what, then, is the secret? How might the virtues be grounded in desire and history? At the heart of MacIntyre's case for the virtues are social practices, traditions, and narratives—the building blocks of human communities. These building blocks, MacIntyre contends, are as basic as it gets. They are the normative core of human thought, speech, and action. To deny this core is to undermine one's ability to deny anything at all. MacIntyre thus also found a powerful response to Friedrich Nietzsche, for whom *all* morality is ultimately a form of nonrational power. In the narrative of *After Virtue*, it thus boils down to a contest between

Aristotle and Nietzsche, between a rationalist and an anti-rationalist politics. This is not a choice, but a showdown, one from which Aristotle emerges as the preeminent victor.

And yet, *After Virtue* is incomplete. By locating morality in traditions, it raises the problem of rival and competing traditions. If justice is a tradition-bound concept, then what happens when two very different traditions of justice clash? How do we talk between traditions? On whose terms? How do we decide between different conceptions of justice? These are some of the driving questions behind *Whose Justice? Which Rationality?* MacIntyre depicts a social universe in which conflict between traditions is basic and inescapable. He therefore envisions a politics of communication and dialectical engagement between traditions in conflict. This communicative politics is one of MacIntyre's most important, yet least recognized, contributions to political thought. The primary aim of this book is to make that contribution explicit.

An Aristotelian Marxist?

How, then, should we classify MacIntyre's thought? What label, if any, should we apply to it? In his review of *After Virtue*, the cultural theorist Fredric Jameson writes, "MacIntyre's is far and away the most important and the most brilliant reformulation of the question of the ethical in recent years, a book with which any statement on the subject must necessarily come to terms."[32] As a Hegelian Marxist and an astute dialectical critic, Jameson instantly recognizes the influence of both Hegel and Marx upon MacIntyre's thinking. When MacIntyre challenges the moralism of abstract rules, when he locates the ethical in the historical world of social practice, he walks in the footsteps of Hegel and Marx. For this reason, Jameson writes, "MacIntyre's is therefore a Hegelian Aristotelianism, and finally a Marxian one, insofar as Marx everywhere in this book constitutes the richest ultimate source for MacIntyre's vision of history and social life."[33] Jameson regards *After Virtue* as an invaluable resource for the Marxist tradition. As he puts it, MacIntyre "offers the most probing and devastating analysis of the reifications of moral categories under capital that we possess."[34]

Yet, for all this high praise, Jameson acknowledges the force of MacIntyre's critique of Marxist politics, a critique that he takes very seriously. While Jameson neither explicitly accepts nor rejects that critique, he sees it as reenacting a debate internal to the history of Marxism itself. That is, Jameson does not see a crisis of Marxism per se, but rather a crisis of Leninism. He observes that "Marxist ideology has everywhere singularly abandoned any attempt to project politically and socially gripping visions of a radically different future."[35] For Jameson, MacIntyre's souring on political Marxism does not necessarily constitute a break from Marxism in toto. Within Jameson's expansive and ecumenical frame, it appears that MacIntyre is not just a kindred spirit, but still very much a comrade.

While it would be stretching it too far to label MacIntyre a Marxist, there is no question that his philosophical project builds upon his formative engagement with Marxism. It should be understood that Marxism has two core components: theory and praxis. Marxism is, in the first instance, a systematic theory and critique of capital. Secondly, Marxism is a revolutionary politics. MacIntyre remains committed to the critique of capital. He continues to share the bulk of Marx's understanding of the historical dynamics and destructive effects of capital. He also remains committed to the downfall of capital. In this, he has not broken with Marxism one scintilla. Rather, his primary disagreement with Marxism concerns its politics: its lack of a genuine ethics and its utopianism of the future—the promise of a better world whose actual structure and design have yet to be spelled out with any degree of consensus.

According to MacIntyre, this gaping hole glaring accounts for Marxism's historical pattern of falling back upon the private moral authority of bureaucratic individualism whenever it advances toward political power.[36] In distancing himself from that bureaucratic individualism, MacIntyre does not abandon the struggle against capital. Rather, he takes a more grassroots and democratic approach. In this respect, MacIntyre is closer to the left communism of Rosa Luxemburg, Sylvia Pankhurst, and Anton Pannekoek, a tradition that Lenin famously dismissed as an "infantile disorder."[37]

In the world of radical thought and politics today, MacIntyre fits squarely within the anti-capitalist movement. This movement consists of communists, socialists, anarchists, Indigenous communities, various social justice movements, radical environmentalists, and even animal liberation activists. Despite their different theoretical and political frameworks, despite their different motivating impulses, these groups nonetheless share a commitment to the struggle and resistance against capital and the creation of a humane and ecologically sustainable world.

Some of the most prominent faces of this movement include Naomi Klein, Yanis Varoufakis, Noam Chomsky, Slavoj Žižek, Angela Davis, Antonio Negri, Arundhati Roy, George Monbiot, Cornel West, and Chris Hedges. Many of these thinkers draw from Marx to one extent or another. They are not, however, all Marxists. For the purposes of this book, what matters in making sense of MacIntyre's thought is not whether or not he is a Marxist, but rather that he shares a militant opposition to a common enemy, namely, capitalism.

The aim and scope of this book

This book is written for those interested in MacIntyre's relevance for the anti-capitalist movement. The primary focus of the book is his analysis of ethics under capital. This analysis has two dimensions: critical and constructive. The critical dimension concerns the corrosion and perversion of ethics under capital, the way in which the free market shapes our moral language, our categories of thought, and the nature and structure of our public discourse. A major theme of the book is what the sociologist James Davison Hunter termed *the culture wars*: the battle between conservatives and liberals for the heart and soul of the Western world.[38] The culture wars can be understood as the state of social chaos to which the market logic of liberal individualism inevitably leads. MacIntyre helps us understand why we are in a culture war and how we can navigate it without becoming consumed by it.

The constructive dimension of MacIntyre's project concerns the possibility of a genuine ethics under capital. Mere opposition to capital is insufficient. We need a rational framework to guide our praxis, lest we fall into the trap of becoming the very monster we wish to fight. If capital at its core is instrumental and manipulative, it will not do to resort to an instrumental and manipulative politics in turn. Capital must be fought and resisted through a social and ethical framework, not the private and arbitrary judgments of a small and exclusive leadership. One of MacIntyre's achievements is to spell out what a genuine ethical framework looks like.

That framework can help guide the project of resistance and revolution. It can also help guide our public discourse in the face of the culture wars. Many political theorists have proposed models of public discourse for a world of moral conflict and radical disagreement. Three of the most influential theorists in this respect are John Rawls, Jürgen Habermas, and Chantal Mouffe. Rawls and Habermas represent a deliberative approach to democracy; Mouffe, an agonistic approach. One of the aims of this book is to draw a contrast between MacIntyre, on the one hand, and Rawls, Habermas, and Mouffe, on the other. As I will argue, MacIntyre avoids certain critical pitfalls intrinsic to their conceptions of public communication. By making explicit his alternative conception, I hope to provide a corrective to those critics who falsely construe MacIntyre as some sort of reactionary, irrationalist, and isolationist conservative.[39]

This book is ultimately a small contribution to a growing literature on MacIntyre. In recent years, a number of scholars have produced important studies on different aspects of MacIntyre's thought. Some of these studies have attempted a synthesis of his philosophical oeuvre, emphasizing the internal structure and coherence of this thinking. Others trace the trajectory of his intellectual career. Others still seek to highlight the lasting relevance of his thought and to defend him against the misrepresentation of his critics.[40] In my own discipline of rhetoric and communication studies, MacIntyre has left a lasting impact. His theory of narrative was the definitive basis for the "narrative paradigm," a prominent model of communication.[41] A great number of communication scholars have also welcomed MacIntyre's call for reviving virtue ethics.[42] However, he is not generally regarded as a communication theorist in his own right.[43]

While this book is about Alasdair MacIntyre, its primary purpose to apply his ideas to contemporary politics and communication, to show what we can *do* with his ideas. Hence, this book is directed first and foremost to those interested in radical political thought. Although MacIntyre was one of the most prominent voices of the British New Left, he has since sadly faded from the public limelight. In the rich and lively discourse on resistance and opposition to capital today, MacIntyre's ideas are conspicuously missing. His name is rarely mentioned, except as a relic from the past. By offering a new reading of his work, this book is intended to appeal to both, an older generation familiar with his intellectual legacy and a younger generation unfamiliar with MacIntyre, but likely to find enormous value in his analysis of ethics under capital.

Notes

1 Stuart Jeffries, "Why Marxism Is on the Rise Again," *The Guardian*, July 4, 2012. https://www.theguardian.com/world/2012/jul/04/the-return-of-marxism (accessed January 13, 2019).

2 C.W. "An engrossing account of the life of Karl Marx," *The Economist*, November 3, 2015. https://www.economist.com/prospero/2017/11/03/an-engrossing-account-of-the-life-of-karl-marx (accessed January 13, 2019); Alison Flood, "Communist Manifesto Sales Rise Up as Penguin Releases Bargain Classics," *The Guardian*, March 4, https://www.theguardian.com/books/2015/mar/04/communist-manifesto-tops-best sellers-penguin-little-black-classics (accessed January 13, 2019).

3 Heidi Moore, "Why Is Thomas Piketty's 700-Page Book a Bestseller?" *The Guardian*, September 21, 2004. https://www.theguardian.com/money/2014/sep/21/-sp-thomas-piketty-bestseller-why (accessed January 13, 2019).

4   Relevant classic and recent works, by no means exhaustive of their thought, include Fredric Jameson, *Marxism and Form: Twentieth Century Dialectical Theories of Literature*. Princeton, NJ: Princeton University Press, 1971; Fredric Jameson, *The Political Unconscious: Narrative as a Socially Symbolic Act*. Ithaca, NY: Cornell University Press, 1981; Fredric Jameson, *Postmodernism, or the Cultural Logic of Late Capitalism*. Durham, NC: Duke University Press, 1991; Fredric Jameson, *Representing Capital: A Reading of Volume One*. London, UK: Verso, 2011; Terry Eagleton, *Marxism and Literary Criticism*. Berkeley, CA: University of California Press, 1976; Terry Eagleton, *Criticism and Ideology: A Study in Marxist Literary Theory*. London, UK: New Left Books, 1976; Terry Eagleton, *Ideology: An Introduction*. London, UK: Verso, 1991; Terry Eagleton, *After Theory*. New York, NY: Basic Books, 2003; Terry Eagleton, *Why Marx Was Right*. New Haven, CT: Yale University Press, 2011; Terry Eagleton, *Materialism*. New Haven, CT: Yale University Press, 2016; Louis Althusser, Étienne Balibar, Roger Establet, Pierre Macherey, and Jacques Rancière, *Reading Capital: The Complete Edition*. London, UK: Verso, 2015; Jacques Rancière, *Proletarian Nights: The Workers' Dream in Nineteenth-Century France*. London, UK: Verso, 2012; Jodi Dean, *Democracy and Other Neoliberal Fantasies: Communicative Capitalism and Left Politics*. Durham, NC: Duke University Press, 2009; Jodi Dean, *The Communist Horizon*. London, UK: Verso, 2012; Jodi Dean, *Crowds and Party*. London, UK: Verso, 2016; Jodi Dean, *Comrade*. London, UK: Verso, 2019; Slavoj Žižek, *The Sublime Object of Ideology*. London, UK: Verso, 1989; Slavoj Žižek, *Tarrying With the Negative*. Durham, NC: Duke University Press, 1993; Slavoj Žižek, *The Ticklish Subject*. London, UK: Verso, 1999; Slavoj Žižek, *The Parallax View*. Cambridge, MA: MIT Press, 2006; Slavoj Žižek, *Less Than Nothing: Hegel and the Shadow of Dialectical Materialism*. London, UK: Verso, 2012; Slavoj Žižek, *The Relevance of the Communist Manifesto*. Cambridge, UK: Polity Press, 2019; Silvia Federici, *Caliban and the Witch: Women, The Body, and Primitive Accumulation*. Brooklyn, NY: Autonomedia, 2004; Silvia Federici, *Revolution at Point Zero: Housework, Reproduction, and Feminist Struggle*. Oakland, CA: PM Press, 2012.

5   Arwa Mahdawi, "Socialism Is No Longer a Dirty Word in the US—and That's Scary for Some," *The Guardian*, July 29, 2018. https://www.theguardian.com/commentisfree/2018/jul/29/socialism-no-longer-dirty-word-us-scary-for-some (accessed April 21, 2019).

6   MacIntyre, Alasdair, *After Virtue: A Study in Moral Theory*. Notre Dame, IN: University of Notre Dame Press, 1984, 2.

7   Jacob Hamburger, "The 'Intellectual Dark Web' Is Nothing New," *Los Angeles Review of Books*, July 18, 2018. https://lareviewofbooks.org/article/the-intellectual-dark-web-is-nothing-new/ (accessed April 7, 2019).

8   The classic statement of the liberal doctrine of individual property rights is John Locke's *The Second Treatise of Government*. See Lock, *Two Treatises of Government*, Peter Laslett, ed. Cambridge, UK: Cambridge University Press, 283–446.

9   MacIntyre addresses the problem of moral and linguistic incommensurability, with particular attention to the European imperial encounter Indigenous cultures in his essay, "Relativism, Power, and Philosophy," *Proceedings and Addresses of the American Philosophical Association* 59.1 (1985): 5–22.

10 As Kelvin Knight and Paul Blackledge remark, "MacIntyre's turn to Aristotle since his break with the Marxist left in the 1960s is best understood not as not as conservative rejection of modernity, but as an attempt to deepen insights inherited from Marx's critique of capitalism." See Kelvin Knight and Paul Blackledge, eds. *Virtue and Politics: Alasdair MacIntyre's Revolutionary Aristotelianism*. Notre Dame, IN: University of Notre Dame Press, 2011, 2.

11 Blackledge and Davidson, "Introduction: the Unknown Alasdair MacIntyre," in Paul Blackledge and Neil Davidson, eds. *Alasdair MacIntyre's Engagement with Marxism*. Chicago, IL: Haymarket Books, 2009, xx.

12 MacIntyre, *Marxism: An Interpretation*. London, UK: SCM Press, 1953. The book was later revised and republished as *Marxism and Christianity*. New York, NY: Schocken Books, 1968.

13 Blackledge and Davidson, "Introduction," xxiii.

14 E. P. Thompson, "Socialist Humanism," in *E. P. Thompson and the Making of the New Left: Essays and Polemics*. New York, NY: Monthly Review Press, 2017, 49–88.

15 MacIntyre, "Notes from the Moral Wilderness," in Paul Blackledge and Neil Davidson, eds. *Alasdair MacIntyre's Engagement with Marxism*. Chicago, IL: Haymarket Books, 2009, 45–69.

16 Ibid., 52.

17 Blackledge and Davidson, "Introduction," xxvii.

18 Ibid., xxiv–xxx.

19 MacIntyre, "Freedom and Revolution," in Paul Blackledge and Neil Davidson, eds. *Alasdair MacIntyre's Engagement with Marxism*. Chicago, IL: Haymarket Books, 2009, 123–34.

20 Blackledge and Davidson, "Introduction," xxvii.

21 MacIntyre, "Pascal and Marx: on Lucien Goldman's Hidden God," in Paul Blackledge and Neil Davidson, eds. *Alasdair MacIntyre's Engagement with Marxism*. Chicago, IL: Haymarket Books, 2009, 208, n. 6.

22 Lucien Goldman, *The Hidden God: A Study of Tragic Vision in the Pensées of Pascal and the Tragedies of Racine*. London, Verso: 2016, 302.

23 MacIntyre, "Prediction and Politics," in Paul Blackledge and Neil Davidson, eds. *Alasdair MacIntyre's Engagement with Marxism*. Chicago, IL: Haymarket Books, 2009, 249–62.

24 Ibid., 258.

25 Ibid., 261.

26 Ibid., xli–xlii.

27 Alasdair MacIntyre, *A Short History of Ethics: A History of Moral Philosophy from the Homeric Age to the Twentieth Century*. London, UK: Routledge, 1998.

28 Goldman, *The Hidden God*, 301.

29 Blackledge and Davidson, "Introduction," xliii.

30 Max Horkheimer and Theodor W. Adorno, *Dialectic of Enlightenment: Philosophical Fragments*. Stanford, CA: Stanford University Press, 2002.

31 See, for example, G. E. M. Anscombe, "Modern Moral Philosophy," *Philosophy* 33.124 (1985): 1–19; Philippa Foot, *Virtues and Vices and Other Essays in Moral Philosophy*. Berkeley, CA: University of California Press, 1978; Martha C. Nussbaum, *The Fragility of Goodness: Luck and Ethics in Greek Tragedy and Philosophy*. Cambridge, UK: Cambridge University Press, 1986; Cynthia A. Freeland, ed. *Feminist Interpretations of Aristotle*. University Park, PA: The Pennsylvania State University Press, 1998; and Sarah Borden Sharkey, *An Aristotelian Feminism*. Basel, Switzerland: Springer, 2016.

32 Fredric Jameson, "Morality versus Ethical Substance; or Aristotelian Marxism in Alasdair MacIntyre," *The Ideologies of Theory: Essays 1971–1986, Volume 1, Situations of Theory*. Minneapolis, MN: University of Minnesota Press, 1988, 181.

33 Ibid.

34 Ibid., 182.

35 Ibid., 183.

36 MacIntyre, *After Virtue*, 261.

37 For a useful account of the distinction between left-communism and Leninism, see Ian D. Thatcher, "Left-Communism: Rosa Luxemburg and Leon Trotsky Compared," in Daryl Glaser and David M. Walker, eds. *Twentieth Century Marxism: A Global Introduction*. New York, NY: Routledge, 2007.

38 James Davison Hunter, *Culture Wars: The Struggle to Define America*. New York, NY: Basic Books, 1991.

39 See, for example, Martha Nussbaum, "Recoiling from Reason," *The New York Review of Books* 36.19 (1989); Hillary Putnam, "Pragmatism, Relativism, and the Justification of Democracy," in John Arthur and Amy Shaprio, eds. *Campus Wars: Multiculturalism and the Politics of Difference*. Boulder, CO: Westview Press, 1995, 268; and Stout, *Democracy and Tradition*, 118–39.

40 Bruce W. Ballard, *Understanding MacIntyre*. Lanham, MD: University Press of America, 2000; Paul Blackledge, *Marxism and Ethics: Freedom, Desire, and Revolution*. Albany, NY: SUNY Press, 2012; Paul Blackledge and Neil Davidson, eds. *Alasdair MacIntyre's Engagement with Marxism*. Chicago, IL: Haymarket Books, 2009; Jason Blakeley, *Alasdair MacIntyre, Charles Taylor, and the Demise of Naturalism: Reunifying Political Theory and Social Science*. Notre Dame, IN: University of Notre Dame Press, 2016; Keith Breen, *Under Weber's Shadow: Modernity, Subjectivity and Politics in Habermas, Arendt and MacIntyre*. New York, NY: Routledge, 2016. Lawrence Cunningham, ed. *Intractable Disputes about the Natural Law: Alasdair MacIntyre and Critics*. Notre Dame, IN: University of Notre Dame Press; Thomas D. D'Andrea, *Tradition, Rationality, and Virtue: The Thought of Alasdair MacIntyre*.

Surrey, UK: Ashgate, 2006; John Gregson, *Marxism, Ethics and Politics: The Work of Alasdair MacIntyre*. New York, NY: Palgrave MacMillan, 2018; John Horton and Susan Mendus, eds. *After MacIntyre: Critical Perspectives on the Work of Alasdair MacIntyre*. Notre Dame, IN: University of Notre Dame Press, 1994; Kelvin Knight, ed. *The MacIntyre Reader*. Notre Dame, IN: University of Notre Dame Press, 1998; Kelvin Knight, *Aristotelian Philosophy: Ethics and Politics from Aristotle to MacIntyre*. Cambridge, UK: Polity, 2007; Knight and Blackledge, eds. *Virtue and Politics*; Christopher Stephen Lutz, *Tradition in the Ethics of Alasdair MacIntyre: Relativism, Thomism, and Philosophy*. Lanham, MD: Lexington Books, 2004; Christopher Stephen Lutz, *Reading Alasdair MacIntyre's After Virtue*. London, UK: Continuum, 2012; Peter McMylor, *Alasdair MacIntyre: Critic of Modernity*. London, UK: Routledge, 1994; Jeffery L. Nicholas, *Reason, Tradition, and the Good: MacIntyre's Tradition-Constituted Reason and Frankfurt School Theory*. Notre Dame, IN: University of Notre Dame Press, 2012; Emile Perreau-Saussine, *Alasdair MacIntyre: Une Biographie Intellectuelle*. Paris, France: Presses Universitaires France, 2005; Fran O'Rourke, ed. *What Happened in and to Moral Philosophy in the Twentieth Century? Philosophical Essays in Honor of Alasdair MacIntyre*. Notre Dame, IN: University of Notre Dame Press, 2013; Anthony Rudd and John Davenport, eds. *Kierkegaard after MacIntyre: Freedom, Narrative, and Virtue*. Chicago, IL: Open Court, 2001.

41 Walter Fisher, *Human Communication as Narration: Toward a Philosophy of Reason, Value, and Action*. Columbia, SC: University of South Carolina Press, 1987. See also Thomas B. Farrell, 'Narrative in Natural Discourse: On Conversation and Rhetoric', *Journal of Communication* 35.4 (1985): 109–27; Thomas S. Frentz, "Rhetorical Conversation, Time, and Moral Action," *Quarterly Journal of Speech* 71.1 (1985): 1–18; John L. Lucaites and Celeste Michelle Condit, "Re-Constructing Narrative Theory: A Functional Perspective," *Journal of Communication* 35.4 (1985): 90–108; Michael Calvin McGee and John S. Nelson, "Narrative Reason in Public Argument," *Journal of Communication* 35.4 (1985): 139–55; William F. Lewis. "Telling America's Story: Narrative Form and the Reagan Presidency," *Quarterly Journal of Speech* 73.3 (1987): 280–302.

42 Celeste Michelle Condit, "Crafting Virtue: The Rhetorical Construction of Public Morality," *Quarterly Journal of Speech* 73.1 (1987): 79–97; Thomas B. Farrell, *Norms of Rhetorical Culture*, New Haven, CT: Yale University Press, 1993; James Herrick, "Rhetoric, Ethics, and Virtue," *Communication Studies* 43.3 (1992): 133–49.

43 For my modest attempts to change this, see "Alasdair MacIntyre's Contribution to Communication Theory," *Empedocles: European Journal for the Philosophy of Communication*, 4.2 (2012): 183–98; "Moral Discourse Without Foundations: Habermas and MacIntyre on Rational Choice," *Communication Theory*, 26.1 (2015): 21–40; "Alasdair MacIntyre: Tradition and Disagreement," in Jason Hannan, ed. *Philosophical Profiles in the Theory of Communication*, New York, NY: Peter Lang, 2012.

1

Crisis of Communication

Thirty-six-year-old Josh Dukes has the rare distinction of being the first victim of gun violence under the presidency of Donald Trump. Dukes suffered a near-fatal gunshot wound during violent clashes at the University of Washington's Seattle campus on January 20, 2017, the day of Trump's inauguration. The clashes were the outcome of a campus visit by Milo Yiannapolous, the former Breitbart writer and right-wing troll, who was scheduled to give the final talk of his "Dangerous Faggot Tour." Tensions had already been high on campus, with student-led workshops on resistance and protest in the Trump era. Indeed, tensions had been high all over the country ever since Trump won the general election just two months prior. But Milo's scheduled appearance attracted hundreds of his supporters eager to hear him speak and an even larger number of protestors determined to stage an intervention against the rise of fascism in America. The anti-fascist protestors were made up largely of socialists and anarchists. Many of the anarchists, known by the moniker Antifa, came dressed in their signature black clothes and black masks. They came prepared for physical confrontation.

The verbal war of words began as Milo's fans lined up outside the auditorium where he was scheduled to speak. Things escalated after the doors opened and members of Antifa moved to block the entrance. While hundreds of ticket holders made it into the auditorium, dozens were left outside. The heated verbal exchanges soon gave way to physical pushing and shoving. Then the first punches were thrown. Josh Dukes was one of the anti-fascist protestors without a mask. He came with the intention of participating in a peaceful demonstration.

At one point, Dukes intervened to break up a fight. He shielded a fellow protestor with his body. One of Milo's supporters then took out a gun and shot Dukes in the abdomen. In the midst of the noise and chaos, no one had heard the gunshot. Dukes fell to the ground, bleeding profusely. He was eventually rushed to the hospital. The bullet had gone straight through his body. It cost him his gallbladder and part of his colon. He suffered a damaged liver and diaphragm. Dukes now lives with a long and nasty scar running down his stomach, a painful reminder of one of the most violent episodes of the campus wars in recent memory.[1]

One of the claims of this book is that Alasdair MacIntyre predicted this event—or, at least, events like it. This is admittedly a bold claim, but it can be supported through a careful reading of his most important work, *After Virtue*. The best place to start is with MacIntyre's diagnosis of a contemporary communication crisis in Western democracies. In the unforgettable first chapter of *After Virtue*, MacIntyre asks us to imagine an apocalyptic nightmare straight out of dystopian fiction. A fanatical group of Know Nothings go on a wild rampage against science. They carry out a mass killing of scientists and destroy scientific books, journals, and libraries, effectively wiping out all knowledge of science. But a later generation seeks to restore this lost discipline called science. Amidst the ruins, they find bits and pieces of scientific literature and attempt to stitch a knowledge of science back together. Yet what they produce resembles nothing like science. They use scientific terminology, but in a very strange, arbitrary, jumbled, and pointless way. They then get into arguments about science, as if there were a logical conclusion to their debates. From their graves, the dead scientists would not so much be rolling over as just plain mystified, for all they would hear is white noise.

This is when MacIntyre makes a provocative and controversial claim that has generated so much opposition and resistance. For MacIntyre, this dystopian nightmare is a good analogy for the state of moral and political rhetoric today. As he puts it,

> The hypothesis which I wish to advance is that in the actual world which we inhabit, the language of morality is in the same state of grave disorder as the language of natural science in the imaginary world which I described. What we possess, if this view is true, are the fragments of a conceptual scheme, parts which now lack those contexts from which their significance derived. We possess indeed *simulacra* of morality, we continue to use many of the key expressions. But we have—very largely, if not entirely—lost our comprehension, both theoretical and practical, of morality.[2]

We moderns, according to this argument, are like the wannabe scientists in the dystopian nightmare. We use moral terminology like "good" and "bad," "right" and "wrong," but in a very preachy, finger-wagging sort of way that would have been quite strange to premodern ears. This starting claim trips up many of MacIntyre's readers and critics, to whom it sounds as if he looks to the past as a kind of Garden of Eden of morality, a time when everything was fine and well, and from which we have since fallen. This interpretation lends itself to regarding MacIntyre as a conservative, even regressive, thinker. But his claim is not about the *content* of morality, which he observes differs from across time and culture, but rather the *form* of morality.

Here, it might be useful to draw a distinction between *morality* and *moralism*. The first, as he conceives it, is grounded in desire and history. Morality is uncontroversial. It does not feel like verbal sticks and carrots. It makes instinctive sense, because its validity is based on everyday practice. The second is the sort of preaching and finger-wagging that we find so insufferable, unless it is us doing the preaching and finger-wagging. MacIntyre's point is that our culture has undergone a paradigm shift from morality to moralism, a shift that has gone unrecognized.

We moderns like to believe that we have some grasp of morality, when in fact we do not. This is not a general claim about everyone who inhabits the modern world. Rather, it's a claim about a specific figure, the modern liberal individual, the embodiment of the liberal ethos. Those who have thoroughly internalized the logic of liberal individualism will be the moralistic counterparts to the wannabe scientists in the dystopian nightmare recounted above. They will use moral language in the same confused and disordered way, to the same pointless end. But how plausible is this claim? How fair is the comparison? The evidence, MacIntyre argues, lies right before us, in our everyday moral rhetoric. MacIntye puts the point as follows:

> The most striking feature of contemporary moral utterance is that so much of it is used to express disagreements; and the most striking feature of the debates in which these disagreements are expressed is their interminable character. I do not mean by this just that such debates go on and on and on—although they do—but also that they apparently can find no terminus. There seems to be no rational way of securing moral agreement in our culture.[3]

We can illustrate MacIntyre's claim through the example of free speech, one of the key battleground issues in the contemporary culture wars. Few issues incite such intense passion and provoke such strong opinions as the debate over free speech. Just about everyone has something to say about trigger warnings, safe spaces, hate speech, no-platforming, and flag burning. Like so many other battles in the culture wars, the battle over free speech has come to be seen as a kind of ultimate showdown, where something grave and fundamental is at stake: truth, freedom, justice, human dignity, even Western civilization itself. Any compromise is framed as a concession to the enemy. Hence, a certain absolutism and uncompromising militancy is de rigueur. Yet, for all of the intense passions and strong opinions, the loudest voices are remarkable for their inconsistency and arbitrariness.

Although free speech was formerly one of the pillars of liberal politics, in recent years it has become a rallying cry for conservatives. Denouncing the menace of liberal political correctness, conservatives have rebranded themselves as the new champions of free speech. They zero in on policies like trigger warnings and safe spaces as evidence of liberal tyranny on college campuses. They sanctimoniously deride liberal "snowflakes" for being weak, fragile, sensitive, and immature.

Against the exaggerated image of liberal fragility, conservatives present themselves as tough-minded and thick-skinned adults who possess the maturity to handle the grown-up world of clashing ideas. Indeed, Milo's campus tour in the fall of 2017 was framed as a celebration and defense of free speech. An entire legion of conservative talking heads, including David Horowitz, Ann Coulter, Michelle Malkin, Ben Shapiro, Ezra Levant, and Dinesh D'Souza, have seized on this theme to recast conservatives as the saviors of free speech and Western civilization.[4]

Yet, in 2016, when Colin Kaepernick decided to kneel on the field during the national anthem to protest police brutality and institutional racism against African Americans, that same legion of sanctimonious conservatives refused to defend his right to free speech. Instead, they led the attack against Kaepernick for disrespecting the national anthem.[5] Donald Trump called on the NFL to "get that son of the bitch off the field."[6] Under pressure from Trump, the NFL created a new policy banning players from kneeling on the field during the national anthem. The NFL did, however, give players the option of waiting in the locker room.[7] In an interview, Trump said, "I don't think people should be staying in the locker rooms. . . . You have to stand proudly for the national anthem. Or you shouldn't be playing, you shouldn't be there. Maybe you shouldn't be in the country."[8]

When Nike decided in 2018 to capitalize on the kneeling controversy by recruiting Kaepernick for one of their advertisements, American conservatives protested by cutting up their Nike socks and burning their Nike shoes.[9] As far as they were concerned, kneeling during the national anthem is a grave and unforgivable offense. Somehow, conservatives managed to move seamlessly between defending free speech on campus in the name of individual liberty to opposing free speech on the field in the name of patriotism and love of country.

Though it is tempting to conclude that this glaring inconsistency is unique to conservatives, that conclusion would be mistaken. Many prominent liberals exhibit a similar pattern. When Hillary Clinton was asked about Kaepernick's decision to kneel during the national anthem, she replied, "That's not against our anthem or our flag." Clinton went on to say that kneeling "is a very reverent position" that "demonstrate(s) in a peaceful way against racism and injustice in our criminal system."[10] Yet, in a speech delivered at the 2016 American Israel Public Affairs Committee (AIPAC) convention, Clinton vowed to dismantle the Boycott, Divestment, and Sanctions (BDS) movement aimed at pressuring Israel to comply with international law and to withdraw from the Occupied Territories.[11] More recently, a group of liberal politicians have taken Clinton's vow a step further. Senators Chuck Schumer, Kirsten Gillibrand, Ron Wyden, and Richard Blumenthal are pushing for legislation criminalizing public speech and activism against Israel. The Israel Anti-Boycott Act (S. 720) would make such speech and activism punishable by up to $1 million and twenty years in prison.[12] Liberal politicians are able to move seamlessly between defending free speech on the ground of individual rights and liberties to opposing political speech in the name of a strategic political alliance. The debate over free speech thus reveals the uncanny ease with which conservatives and liberals alike can switch their stances and premises in full public view without the slightest controversy. Switching premises has become a normalized feature of our moral rhetoric.

But this is only one problem. Another is the problem of incommensurability. We can illustrate this second problem through the debate over gun rights. In the United States, proponents of gun rights will, as a matter of reflex, invoke the Second Amendment to defend their right to keep an unlimited cache of guns at home, to carry a concealed weapon in public, and even to carry a semiautomatic rifle to bars, churches, shopping malls, and college campuses. They will insist upon the right to self-defense—against home intruders, bad guys with guns, and a government that oversteps its bounds. "Guns are good," they will say. "Guns save lives." "An armed society is a polite society." "The only way to stop a bad guy with a gun is to have a good guy with a gun." And so on. Even in the face of almost daily reports of mass shootings all across the country, proponents of gun rights will stand by the Second Amendment. Mass shootings may be tragic, but they're "the price of freedom."[13] Nothing, not even the blood of innocent children, can be allowed to compromise this God-given right to keep and bear arms.

Proponents of gun control, on the other hand, are justifiably frustrated with the obstinacy of Second Amendment fundamentalism. They will point to the examples of other Western nations, such as Canada, Great Britain, Australia, and Japan, which have strict gun laws and dramatically lower rates of gun violence. Fewer guns, they will point out, mean fewer deaths. Proponents of gun control will also invoke alternative rights. In a viral Facebook post, filmmaker and activist Michael Moore called for replacing the Second Amendment with a new amendment that protects "the primary right of all people to be free from gun violence."[14] After the horrific mass shooting at Marjory Stoneman Douglas High School in Parkland, Florida, many student survivors invoked "right to be able to go to school and not fear for our lives." They also invoked the right of teachers to be able to teach without having to become human shields for their students.[15]

The gun debate is a good case study in moral incommensurability. Each side rests on premises not shared by the other: the right to keep and bear arms versus the right to live, study, and teach; and a hypothetical claim about government tyranny versus an empirical claim about the public good. To a proponent of gun control, talking to a proponent of gun rights is like talking to an alien from another universe. It can seem baffling that anyone could value guns more than human lives. But in the moral universe of Second Amendment fundamentalism, guns *are* more valuable than human lives. The sheer callousness toward victims of gun violence is the clearest possible indication of the hierarchy of guns over people within that twisted universe. To Second Amendment fundamentalists, the call for gun control is a call for government tyranny, something to be resisted—with guns.

MacIntyre's observes that moral disagreement today falls into this general pattern of premise versus premise, assertion versus counter-assertion. When challenged about our views, we have a habit of falling back upon our starting premises. But when those starting premises are in turn challenged, we have nothing deeper on which to fall back. A common instinct at that point is to reassert our starting premises, but in an angrier, more defiant, and forceful way, as if anger, defiance, and forcefulness somehow strengthened our case.

The instinct to fall back upon reactionary emotion is the defining characteristic of noxious right-wing media personalities like Sean Hannity and Bill O'Reilly, for whom anger is a perfectly acceptable substitute for rational argument. Both Hannity and O'Reilly built their reputations by shouting at the camera and shouting further at their liberal guests. Their rhetorical style is premised on the futility of dispassionate reasoning and the necessity of macho bravado and uncompromising assertiveness. They conflate logic with adrenaline and testosterone.

Emotivism as a semantic theory

In the face of irresolvable disagreement, it is tempting to succumb to some form of skepticism about morality. One common form of such skepticism is that of the Vienna Circle, the early twentieth-century society of logical positivists, whose members included Rudolph Carnap, Kurt Gödel, Otto Neurath, and Moritz Schlick. In keeping with their empiricist worldview, the Vienna Circle famously rejected morality as a legitimate object of study, since moral claims cannot be verified empirically. They therefore consigned moral philosophy, along with metaphysics, theology, and aesthetics, to the dustbin of false disciplines. As far as the Vienna Circle was concerned, the only relevant and interesting question about morality was a linguistic one: the meaning of moral claims.

One of the students of the Vienna School was the British analytic philosopher A. J. (Freddie) Ayer, whose book, *Language, Truth, and Logic* first introduced the emotivist theory of language.[16] A few years later, the American analytic philosopher Charles L. Stevenson developed emotivism into a more systematic and elaborate theory.[17] At its core, emotivism is the thesis that moral claims are not arguments at all since they are not *about* anything in the first place.

On the emotivist view, to say, "This gun weighs 6 pounds," or "That gun is made of steel," is to say something empirically verifiable about a specific object. But, according to Ayer and Stevenson, to say, "Guns are good" does not say anything about guns, but about oneself—a mere expression of personal will, desire, and preference. It amounts to saying, "I love guns!" Similarly, to say, "Guns are evil," is merely to say, "I hate guns!" On the emotivist view, moral claims can also function as commandments. So, "Guns are evil," could just be another way of saying, "Ban guns!" According to Ayer and Stevenson, there is nothing more to moral claims than these expressions of personal preference. Superficially, emotivism seems like a plausible theory, not just for the meaning of moral claims but also for the intractability of moral disagreements. If moral disagreements are nothing more than a clash of wills, desires, and preferences, then it's little wonder they cannot be rationally resolved.

But MacIntyre poses a challenge for emotivism: if moral claims are indeed mere expressions of personal preference, then it should be possible in practice to substitute moral claims with corresponding expressions of preference. That is, we should be able to conduct a debate about guns using expressions like "Hooray for guns!" and "I hate guns!" But such a conversation could never get off the ground. There's something conspicuously disappointing about a moral debate consisting of a clash of mere preferences. We would immediately recognize that a crucial element is missing. "I love guns!" and "I hate guns!" are qualitatively different statements from "Guns are good" and "Guns are bad." The latter two statements appeal to impersonal standards, something *beyond* personal will, desire, and preference. As a theory of meaning, then, emotivism must be false.[18] The empirical theory fails the empirical test. But what about emotivism as a theory of human relationships?

Emotivism as a social theory

If emotivism is reconceived as social theory, then it rests on some picture of the social world, some idea of the nature of human relationships. MacIntyre wonders, then, what such a world would look like. How would the inhabitants of that social world relate to one another, talk to one another, engage one another, persuade one another? MacIntyre here introduces one of the most provocative insights of *After Virtue*.

The core of emotivism, he says, is "the obliteration of any genuine distinction between manipulative and non-manipulative social relations."[19] MacIntyre invokes Kant to illustrate this distinction. In his ethics, Kant famously contrasts treating others as an end from treating them as a means to one's own end. The first entails a view of others as intelligent and rational minds, as possessing a unique moral integrity, and as capable of independent thought and judgment. As unique, intelligent, and rational minds, others are entitled to objective reasons for our moral claims and arguments. They are entitled, that is, to appeals to higher standards that go beyond personal will, desire, and preference. They may reflect on these reasons and appeals. They may exercise skepticism. They may agree or disagree, or have no opinion at all. Whatever their final judgment, it cannot be coerced. It must be respected as free and voluntary.

But to treat others as a means to one's own end presupposes a very different view of the social world: a vast collection of individuals, each pursuing an idiosyncratic agenda, each agenda determined by personal desire and preference, everyone in competition with each other, everyone out to manipulate each other through so many sticks and carrots, with the ultimate aim of manipulating others to bend to one's will. To treat others as a means to one's own end necessarily entails a view of others as unintelligent and irrational, as incapable of independent thought and judgment. Everyone sees themselves as manipulators and everyone else as manipulable. There is no appeal to higher standards, because there are no higher standards. There is nothing to mediate social relationships but individual will, cunning, and power. In the clash of wills, whoever possess greater cunning and power necessarily prevails. Social life is thus a competition of stratagem. According to MacIntyre, this bleak universe is sadly the one we now inhabit, the universe of capitalist modernity, with its cult of the individual.

Like the melancholy Jacques from Shakespeare's *As You Like It*, who says, "All the world's a stage, and all the men and women merely players," MacIntyre concieves of the world as a stage, one large social drama acted out against the backdrop of liberal capitalism. As with certain genres of theater, known for their familiar characters and recurring storylines, MacIntyre sees the social drama of modernity as enacted by certain stock characters. What is so distinctive about these characters, what makes them so unique to our culture, is how thoroughly they have internalized and embodied the manipulative ethos of emotivism.

In the first edition of *After Virtue*, MacIntyre identifies three stock characters who epitomize that manipulative ethos: the aesthete, the therapist, and the manager. These are not marginal figures, but rather the moral representatives of our culture. They are the ideals and archetypes, the exemplars and paragons, to whom the rank and file of an emotivist culture aspire.

The aesthete

The first of these stock characters, the aesthete, is the apotheosis of bourgeois values. Following the American literary critic William Gass, MacIntyre points to Gilbert Osmond from Henry James's *Portrait of a Lady* as the consummate fictional expression of the aesthete.[20] Osmond is the product of extreme wealth and leisure. Never having had to struggle for anything in his life, he lives for no purpose, goal, or ambition other than his ego. In this respect, Osmond is a late nineteenth-century precursor to Paris Hilton and Kim Kardashian. The only focus of his energies is himself. He sees himself as a work of art, an object for the awe and admiration of others. He therefore carries himself to that end, speaking, dressing, and dining in such a way as to convey the highest standards of style and taste. That style and taste, however, are insincere. Everything he says and does is calculated for effect: the flattering of his ego.

The extreme nature of Osmond's bourgeois personality is not limited to the consumption of expensive clothes, gourmet food, and fine art. He is also a consumer of people. Osmond sees others only in relation to his ego, as either instruments or obstacles to his quest for self-glorification. He marries Isabel because of her style, taste, and wealth, not because of any genuinely loving feelings for her. She is a mere showpiece, another object to fortify his public image, just like the clothes he wears, the food eats, and the art he buys. That Isabel possesses an independence of mind and judgment is a threat to his existence, something to be crushed and eradicated under the relentless force of his calculating will. Osmond exerts his power over Isabel, forcing her into dutiful submission and obedience. He does the same with his daughter, who is raised as a kind of mindless adulator. Within the domain of their home, Osmond wields the authority of a minor tyrant. In treating his own wife and daughter as objects of consumption, he effectively eviscerates their autonomy and selfhood. Osmond is, in a phrase, a malignant narcissist. Although MacIntyre doesn't make it explicit, narcissism is not an aberration, but a feature of the self-oriented culture of emotivism.

The therapist

The second stock character in the drama of modernity is the therapist.[21] Here, MacIntyre critiques, not Freud or psychoanalysis per se, but rather the uncritical role of therapy in a liberal capitalist system, which produces widespread alienation, neurosis, and ennui. In such a culture, the role of the therapist is to alleviate the symptoms of mental illness, but without any critical reflection on the nature of the political and economic order. The pathological is rendered personal.[22] The job of the therapist is to rehabilitate the mentally ill back into the very system that induced their mental illness in the first place. The therapist thus substitutes therapeutic technique for psychological truth.[23] All that matters is feeling better, not insight or understanding.

Because of its apolitical nature, therapy has become an integral part of our cultural landscape, even an industry unto its own. Perhaps the greatest testament to MacIntyre's observations about the triumph of the therapeutic is the superstardom of Dr. Phil, a television conman who shamelessly capitalizes upon mental illness and social dysfunction for the sake of his television show. Our therapeutic culture is also evident in the dizzying popularity of a practice like yoga. Although yoga originated in ancient India as a spiritual practice predicated upon material renunciation, it has been appropriated, commodified, and marketed in the Western world as form of therapy for everyone, including the rich and powerful. Yoga has proven to be exceptionally popular among Wall Street bankers, hedge fund managers, and traders, who require an effective stress reliever to thrive in the hyper-competitive world of finance capital.[24] In the United States, yoga is now a $16 billion industry.[25]

The manager

The third major stock character in the drama of modernity is the manager.[26] Because of the omnipresence of large-scale organizations, which require expert management for their success and survival, the manager is the most familiar and prominent of all the stock characters of our culture. The key to managerial excellence is a demonstration of a mastery of technique and efficiency in realizing the goals of the organization. Managers specialize in the bottom line. In the case of the corporation, this bottom line is the maximization of shareholder value. In the case of the political party, it's the maximization of political power. Thus, the manager who demonstrates a stronger record of delivering the bottom line naturally wields greater authority and commands greater respect.

In an emotivist social universe, which values technique and efficiency above all else, the most successful managers hold the status of sages and prophets. The culture looks up to them for hope, purpose, meaning, and guidance. Their goals serve as the highest goals to which our culture aspires, because we lack higher goals, a higher social purpose. The limits of the managerial agenda thus represent the limits of our culture's moral imagination. Lee Iacoca, Jack Welch, Bill Gates, Richard Branson, Steve Jobs, Mark Zuckerberg, Elon Musk, Jeff Bezos—these are the sages and prophets of a liberal capitalist society. They are the most successful managers. They built their reputation upon a mastery of management and technique. They must, so the logic goes, possess some special moral and philosophical insight. Moral authority is thus established by managerial success.

The ruthlessness by which the manager pursues the bottom line—paying workers abysmally low wages, dodging taxes, fighting regulation—is ultimately excused, overlooked, and justified by that success. Holding the manager accountable to a higher standard carries no moral weight. Condemning the manager for paying workers cutthroat wages, while accumulating unprecedented sums of private wealth, only falls on deaf ears.

Perhaps the most deplorable example of our culture's fawning deference for the manager is the cultural prominence of Jeff Bezos, the founder and CEO of Amazon. As of this writing, Bezos has a net worth of over $136 billion.[27] He makes $230,000 per minute and makes more in ten seconds than the median Amazon employee makes in an entire year.[28] Hundreds of Amazon employees rely on food stamps for their survival.[29] In Arizona, that's one in three Amazon workers. Bezos has also neurotically deployed surveillance technology to monitor every micro-movement of Amazon's warehouse employees in the name of maximizing efficiency and stamping out human error. This technology effectively reduces warehouse employees to human robots.[30] A recently implemented logistics app, aimed at meeting aggressive delivery targets, has resulted in warehouse employees falling asleep the wheel, urinating in bottles, and defecating in plastic bags.[31]

Yet, for all his obvious greed, his totalitarian drive for power and control, his sociopathic pursuit of profit, and his complete lack of compassion for workers, Human Rights Campaign, one of the most prominent civil rights organizations in the United States, awarded Bezos their National Equality Award in 2017.[32] In a culture that values efficiency above all else, an efficient despot is revered as a moral hero.

The primacy of sophistry

As the main characters in the drama of modernity, then, what the aesthete, the therapist, and the manager hold in common is their capacity to bend others to their will. That capacity, again, requires the dissolution of several critical distinctions: manipulative versus non-manipulative social relationships; the consumption of objects versus the consumption of people; technique versus truth; and managerial success versus moral authority. For the purposes of this study, we can identify one more key distinction that gets dissolved in an emotivist culture: rational versus nonrational persuasion.

The primary mode of rhetoric in an emotivist culture is sophistry, what Socrates in the *Gorgias* describes as serving up the verbal equivalent of pastries—dazzling words that secure assent, not because of their rational content, but merely because of their ornamental style.[33] Emotivism thrives on what Edward Bernays termed the "engineering of consent," which presupposes the irrationality, gullibility, and manipulability of humanity.[34] Socrates, with his nagging quest for truth and his demand for analytical rigor, would be an outsider to our culture. In our culture, we debate strategy, not truth. We debate means, not ends. We are free to pick from any number of ends, but only in a purely arbitrary way. We have no way of debating ends, of weighing them against each other, of rationally comparing them, of judging some ends to be superior to others.

Moral debate in our culture is a matter of rhetorical technique, of effective sophistry between the proponents of rival and competing ends. Debate about a higher purpose is categorically shunned. Emotivism, put simply, is the triumph of instrumental reason. Seen through an emotivist lens, certain disturbing aspects of our culture and politics can be understood, not as aberrations, but rather as the logical outcome of instrumentalism. These include the tribal nature of contemporary democracy and the appearance of a toxic new character in our digitally mediated culture: the troll.

American democracy as instrumentalism

In a short essay for *HuffPost* entitled, "Stop Treating Political Parties like Sports Teams," writer and film producer James Di Fiore expresses his immense frustration with the tribal nature of democratic politics.[35] Di Fiore sees contemporary democracies as a game of winning and politics as "the art of managing hypocrisy." He takes issue with our habit of condemning certain political leaders for their conduct, while excusing others for the same conduct. "Sometimes," he says, "this hypocrisy is so blatant, so pronounced, that it surprises me to know that most of us never see it."[36] The essence of the political game is to "protect your own, politics be damned." Worse, the game doesn't appear to be ending any time soon. "It's a cycle that feeds each side through hate and a sense of superiority," he says, "and it is probably responsible for a society stagnating in its own slung mud." De Fiori wants us to imagine a politics in which we do not treat elections like the Super Bowl. He wants us to stop treating political parties like football teams, to be either cheered or booed, depending on which side we happen to support. Rather, he calls for a politics in which we debate the issues, not blindly follow political personalities.

A recent example illustrates Di Fiore's very real concern. The 2016 Republican primaries were an appalling display of brazen and shameless political tribalism. The entire field of Republican candidates campaigned on a purely negative platform: their resolute determination to undo Obamacare; their almost fanatical opposition to Hillary Clinton; their demonization of "liberals" and "progressives"; their hysterical fear-mongering about socialism; their hostility to regulations of any kind; and their defiant rejection of climate science.[37] Conspicuously missing from Republican campaign rhetoric was any clear statement of what sort of world they actually wanted to create, any positive and substantive blueprint of a better society. The goal of winning the general election was treated as a given. The only question was about the means, about determining the strongest candidate to defeat the enemy. The perfect emptiness of their political platforms served as a blank screen on which conservative voters projected their fantasies of the future.

At first, the idea of candidate Trump, the trashy game show host with fake hair and a bombastic, over-the-top personality, was a source of great entertainment. Trump was seen as a political clown at best and a political disaster at worst. But Trump shrewdly campaigned on his record as a businessman and his status as a billionaire. He boasted of his many successful businesses and the many jobs he allegedly created. That his record was marred by corruption, lawsuits, scandals, and bankruptcies proved to be of little consequence. His image as a rich, powerful, and successful businessman, carefully crafted over several decades, established his political credibility and expertise to Republican voters.

He deftly pushed the emotivist logic that if he can manage so many successful businesses, then not only can he defeat the enemy but he can also manage the greatest business of all, the United States.[38] The logic was cringe-worthy. But it worked. When confronted by his rivals at the Republican presidential debates about his obnoxious language and reckless conduct, Trump consistently fell back on the one talking point he knows best: to emphasize his great wealth, his business success and acumen, and his role as a job creator. This talking point, however dubious its veracity, consistently shut down his rivals.[39] It was so powerful and effective that it carried him to victory.

Critics of the Republican primaries would have been wrong to think that their Democratic counterparts were somehow free of the curse of moral instrumentalism. On the contrary, the Democratic primaries were an egregious case study in instrumental logic. From the moment Hillary Clinton announced her intention to run for president, to her humiliating defeat at the hands of Donald Trump, to her pathetic and resentful explanation for why she lost the election, the spirit and psychology of moral instrumentalism were on full display.

Hillary's announcement video was a bizarre pastiche of feel-good lines and images.[40] It featured women, minorities, young couples, interracial couples, same-sex couples, and seniors, all making bland and pointless announcements about their personal plans in life: growing tomatoes, moving to a new neighborhood, starting a new business, getting married, getting ready for retirement. This meaningless storyline was then followed by Clinton's announcement for her own plans: running for president. What was so remarkable about this mind-numbingly dull and uninspiring video was its glaring lack of a political message. It looked like a human resources video about workplace diversity. Like her Republican rivals, she, too, had no positive vision of a better society.

Her campaign was about her. It smacked of royal entitlement, as if she were the rightful heir to the throne. The narcissism behind her campaign was best captured in the hashtag #imwithher. She banked on her identity and legacy to secure political victory. She thought she could endear herself to reliable voting blocs through effortless messaging, presenting herself as the natural choice for the job. She thought, for example, she could secure the Latinx vote by patronizing the Latinx community, listing the many ways in which she was just like "your abuela."

This clumsy and presumptuous attempt at voter outreach was widely ridiculed on social media. The Latinx community was justifiably outraged by her "Hispandering." They responded on Twitter by listing the many ways in which Hillary was precisely *not* like anyone's abuela, from being a white woman of white privilege, to her vast personal wealth, to her support for war and drone strikes, to her aggressive push to send Central American child refugees back to the violence-ridden countries from which they fled.[41]

Clinton's plans to sail smoothly into the White House were, to her great irritation, further disrupted by the sudden and dramatic rise of Senator Bernie Sanders onto the political scene. An outsider to the Democratic Party, Sanders campaigned on a positive and substantive platform of universal healthcare, tuition-free public college, making billionaires and mega-corporations pay their fair share, regulating Wall Street, and aggressively taking on the fossil fuel industry. Clinton was forced into the awkward dance of dismissing Sanders's platform as so much naïve and wishful progressive dreaming, while somehow still claiming for herself the coveted mantle of progressivism.

She further sought to discredit Sanders on the grounds that he wasn't a true Democrat, that he wasn't loyal to the party agenda, as if party loyalty were the equivalent of political credibility.[42] For all her red-baiting of Sanders, her talk of party loyalty bore a disturbing resemblance to the rhetoric of Bolshevism. Out of arguments, she fell back on the one talking point she knows best. She positioned herself, not as a candidate with a positive and substantive vision for the country, but rather as the candidate who best represents the party agenda and the best chance to defeat the Republican enemy.[43] She fell back, that is, on instrumental logic.

That Clinton managed to secure the Democratic nomination on so transparently vacuous a political platform is a testament to just how thoroughly Democratic voters had internalized the instrumentalism of the Democratic Party. But this open contempt and disregard for political substance in favor of a cold and calculating Machiavellian will to power was precisely what led to Clinton's defeat. She chose to play the game of thrones. She lost to a madman who played it better.[44]

In looking back upon the 2016 general election, we still feel utterly mystified and speechless that a television game show host lied so brazenly and pathologically straight into the White House. Watching it all in real time, it seemed like a bad movie, a train wreck so severe that it surely marked a radical break from the past. We felt that something was terribly amiss, that Trump was a very different sort of candidate, one with no historical precedent. But in truth, Trump's habitual lying did not mark a radical break of any kind. Rather, his political style was the continuation of an existing pattern, one set long before he ever decided to run for public office.

In framing Trump as some sort of unique historic evil, we have forgotten that his Republican predecessor was also a brazen and shameless liar. We have forgotten that George W. Bush lied his way into invading Iraq, falsely claiming that Iraq possessed weapons of mass destruction, even going so far as to fabricate the evidence. Indeed, the idea of a post-truth world, an idea so prominent in contemporary political commentary, did not originate with the Trump era, but rather with Bush era. Several commentators had already been talking of our "post-truth era," "post-truth politics," and "post-truth journalism." The presidency of George W. Bush had already been labeled a "post-truth presidency."

We lament our post-truth world today, but we had already been living in one for quite some time.[45] If Trump's lying revealed anything, it was that lying is perfectly at home American democracy. He revealed that the distinction between rational and nonrational persuasion had long been dissolved, and that truth had long ceased to be a normative ideal. Trump merely exploited that dissolution, blurring the line between truth and falsehood, taking it to its most extreme conclusion. He made explicit through his actions what had long been implicit in political practice: that American democracy is not about truth and reason, but rather the victory of will, cunning, and power.

Trump is the logical culmination of emotivism, the embodiment of a culture of individualism, consumption, technique, and efficiency—in all its extraordinary ugliness, hideousness, and rapaciousness. He is, in a very real sense, an aesthete and a manager rolled into one. He is a vulgar version of Gilbert Osmond, accompanied by a vulgar version Isabel, Melania Trump, who by all observations lacks a genuine personality and a genuine self beneath all of that expensive clothing and makeup. Yet, Trump is something more. He is also a troll, a new character in our social drama, a new symbol of the rot of the culture of emotivism.[46]

Notes

1. David Neiwert, "Alt-Right Event in Seattle Devolves Into Chaos and Violence Outside, Truth-Twisting Inside," *Southern Poverty Law Center*. https://www.splcenter.org/hatewatch/2017/01/23/alt-right-event-seattle-devolves-chaos-and-violence-outside-truth-twisting-inside (accessed January 13, 2019); Julia Carrie Wong, "'I Refuse to Be Like Them': Why the Man Shot While Protesting Milo Yiannopoulos Doesn't Want Revenge," *The Guardian*, April 4, 2017. https://www.theguardian.com/world/2017/apr/04/man-shot-milo-yiannopoulos-protest-seattle-trump-interview (accessed January 13, 2019).

2. MacIntyre, *After Virtue*, 2, emphasis added.

3. Ibid., 6.

4. Adam Liptak, "How Conservatives Weaponized the First Amendment," *The New York Times*, June 30, 2018. https://www.nytimes.com/2018/06/30/us/politics/first-amendment-conservatives-supreme-court.html (accessed January 13, 2019).

5. Jason Wilson, "Take a Knee: How Conservative Media Is Reacting to NFL Protesters," *The Guardian*, September 25, 2017. https://www.theguardian.com/us-news/2017/sep/25/take-a-knee-how-conservative-media-is-reacting-to-nfl-protestors (accessed January 13, 2019).

6. Bryan Armen Graham, "Donald Trump Blasts NFL Anthem Protesters: 'Get that son of a bitch off the field,'" *The Guardian*, September 23, 2017. https://www.theguardian.com/sport/2017/sep/22/donald-trump-nfl-national-anthem-protests (accessed January 13, 2019).

7. Adam K. Raymond, "New NFL Anthem Rule: Players Must Stand or Stay in Locker Room," *New York Magazine*, May 23, 2018. http://nymag.com/intelligencer/2018/05/nfl-anthem-rule-players-must-stand-or-stay-in-locker-room.html (accessed January 13, 2019).

8. Veronica Stracqualursi, "Trump: NFL Players Who Don't Stand during National Anthem Maybe 'shouldn't be in the country,'" *CNN*, May 24, 2018. https://www.cnn.com/2018/05/24/politics/trump-nfl-national-anthem/index.html (accessed January 13, 2019).

9. Hilary Weaver, "Conservatives Are Chopping Up Their Gym Socks Over Nike's Colin Kaepernick Campaign," *Vanity Fair*, September 4, 2018. https://www.vanityfair.com/style/2018/09/conservatives-react-to-colin-kaepernick-nike-campaign (accessed January 13, 2019).

10 Jacqueline Thomsen, "Clinton on NFL Players Who Kneel: 'That's not against our anthem or our flag,'" *The Hill*, October 16, 2017. https://thehill.com/blogs/blog-briefing-room/news/355588-clinton-on-nfl-players-who-kneel-thats-not-against-our-anthem (accessed January 13, 2019).

11 Alex Emmons, "Hillary Clinton Attacks Israel Boycott Movement in AIPAC Speech," *The Intercept*, March 22, 2018. https://theintercept.com/2016/03/22/clinton-attacks-israeli-boycott-movement-in-aipac-speech/ (accessed January 13, 2019).

12 Glenn Greenwald, "U.S. Lawmakers Seek to Criminally Outlaw Support for Boycott Campaign against Israel," *The Intercept*, July 19, 2017. https://theintercept.com/2017/07/19/u-s-lawmakers-seek-to-criminally-outlaw-support-for-boycott-campaign-against-israel/ (accessed April 3, 2019).

13 Jessica Roy, "Bill O'Reilly Calls Mass Shootings 'the price of freedom,'" *Los Angeles Times*, October 2, 2015. https://www.latimes.com/nation/la-las-vegas-shooting-live-updates-bill-o-reilly-calls-mass-shootings-the-1506980448-htmlstory.html (accessed January 13, 2019).

14 Stav Ziv, "Change the Constitution and Restrict Gun Rights, Says Michael Moore," *Newsweek*, October 5, 2017. https://www.newsweek.com/change-constitution-and-restrict-gun-rights-says-michael-moore-678634 (accessed January 13, 2019).

15 PBC NewsHour, "'We do have a right to go to school and not fear for our lives,' Say Florida Shooting Survivors," *PBS NewsHour*, February 19, 2018. https://www.pbs.org/newshour/show/we-do-have-a-right-to-go-to-school-and-not-fear-for-our-lives-say-florida-shooting-survivors (accessed January 13, 2019).

16 A. J. Ayer, *Language, Truth, and Logic*. London, UK: Penguin, 1936, 33–35.

17 C. L. Stevenson, *Ethics and Language*. New Haven, CT: Yale University Press, 1944.

18 MacIntyre, *After Virtue*, 19–20.

19 Ibid., 23.

20 Ibid., 24–25.

21 Ibid., 30–31.

22 I am grateful to Richard Raber for this phrase.

23 This argument about the function of therapy is similar to Howard Waitzin's political economic analysis of the function of the healthcare system in a capitalist economy. See Waitzkin, *The Second Sickness: Contradictions in Capitalist Health Care*. Lanham, MD: Rowman & Littlefield, 2000.

24 Seema Mody, "Wall Street Yoga: Finance Gets Its Downward Dog On," *CNBC*, August 24, 2015. https://www.cnbc.com/2014/08/25/yoga-on-wall-street-big-time-bankers-seek-edge-on-the-yoga-mat.html (accessed January 13, 2019).

25 Alice G. Walton, "How Yoga Is Spreading In The U.S.," *Forbes*, March 15, 2016. https://www.forbes.com/sites/alicegwalton/2016/03/15/how-yoga-is-spreading-in-the-u-s (accessed January 13, 2019).

26 MacIntyre, *After Virtue*, 25–27.

27 https://www.bloomberg.com/billionaires/profiles/jeffrey-p-bezos/ (accessed January 13, 2019).

28 Brad Tuttle, "Jeff Bezos Is Now Making an Astonishing $230,000 Every Minute," *Business Insider*, March 9, 2018. https://www.businessinsider.com/jeff-bezos-is-now-making-an-astonishing-230000-every-minute-2018-3 (accessed January 13, 2019).

29 H. Claire Brown, "Amazon Gets Tax Breaks While Its Employees Rely on Food Stamps, New Data Shows," *The Intercept*, April 19, 2018. https://theintercept.com/2018/04/19/amazon-snap-subsidies-warehousing-wages/ (January 13, 2019).

30 Olivia Solon, "Amazon Patents Wristband That Tracks Warehouse Workers' Movements," *The Guardian*, February 1, 2018. https://www.theguardian.com/technology/2018/jan/31/amazon-warehouse-wristband-tracking (accessed January 13, 2019).

31 Chris Pollard, "Amazon Workers Pee into Bottles to Save Time: Investigator," *New York Post*, April 16, 2018. https://nypost.com/2018/04/16/amazon-warehouse-workers-pee-into-bottles-to-avoid-wasting-time-undercover-investigator/ (accessed January 13, 2019); Charlotte England, "Amazon Delivery Drivers 'feel compelled to defecate in vans' to Save Time," *The Independent*, November 12, 2016. https://www.independent.co.uk/news/uk/home-news/amazon-minimum-wage-delivery-drivers-illegal-hours-have-to-defecate-urinate-in-vans-a7411001.html (accessed January 13, 2019).

32 https://blog.aboutamazon.com/working-at-amazon/human-rights-campaign-honors-jeff-bezos-with-2017-equality-award (accessed January 13, 2019).

33 This becomes explicit during the exchange between Socrates and Polus. *Gorgias* 462a–481a.

34 Edward L. Bernays, "The Engineering of Consent," *The Annals of the American Academy of Political and Social Science* 250.1 (1947): 113–20.

35 James Di Fiore, "Stop Treating Political Parties Like Sports Teams," *HuffPost Canada*, November 2, 2016. https://www.huffingtonpost.ca/james-di-fiore/partisan-politics_b_12748638.html (accessed January 13, 2019).

36 Ibid.

37 Tom Rogan, "From Bright Young Things through Defeated Former Hopefuls to Rank Outsiders, Here Are the Republicans Seeking to Run against Hillary Clinton in the Next Presidential Election," *The Telegraph*, May 6, 2015. https://www.telegraph.co.uk/news/worldnews/us-election/11357233/Meet-the-candidates-20-Republicans-who-are-vying-to-run-for-president-in-2016.html (accessed January 13, 2019).

38 Wendy Brown has compellingly argued that neoliberalism has effectively colonized democratic culture. Following her argument, Trump can be seen, not as an aberration, but rather the fulfillment of a neoliberalized democracy. See her book *Undoing the Demos: Neoliberalism's Stealth Revolution*. Cambridge, MA: MIT Press, 2015.

39 Philip Elliott and Zeke Miller, "Why Trump Can't Lose," *Time*, February 26, 2016. http://time.com/4238371/republican-debate-donald-trump-won-lost/ (accessed January 13, 2019).

40 Hillary Clinton's "2016 Presidential Campaign Announcement (OFFICIAL)," *ABC News*, https://youtu.be/N708P-A45D0 (accessed January 14, 2019).

41 Sam Sanders, "#MemeOfTheWeek: Hillary Clinton, Not Quite An Abuela," *NPR*, December 26, 2015, https://www.npr.org/2015/12/26/461116160/-memeoftheweek-hillary-clinton-not-quite-an-abuela (accessed January 14, 2019).

42 Josh Vorhees, "Hillary Clinton Says She's 'Not Even Sure' Bernie Sanders Is Actually a Democrat," *Slate*, April 6, 2016. https://slate.com/news-and-politics/2016/04/hillary-clinton-not-even-sure-bernie-sanders-is-a-democrat.html (accessed January 14, 2019).

43 Jim Newell, "Hillary Clinton: I'm a Loyal Democrat. (Hint, Hint.)," *Slate*, April 3, 2016. https://slate.com/news-and-politics/2016/04/hillary-clinton-speech-i-m-a-loyal-democrat.html (accessed January 14, 2019).

44 It is in fairness worth noting the role of gerrymandering, voter suppression, and the Electoral College in propelling Trump to victory.

45 Jason Hannan, "Truth as First Casualty in American Politics," in Jason Hannan, ed. *Truth in the Public Sphere*. Lanham, MD: Lexington Books, 2016, xi–xxxvi.

46 Jason Hannan, "Trolling Ourselves to Death? Social Media and Post-Truth Politics," *European Journal of Communication* 33.2 (2018): 214–26.

2

Roots of the Culture Wars

When MacIntyre says that we have "lost our comprehension, both theoretical and practical, of morality," he makes a rather categorical distinction between what morality is and is not.[1] Again, this is a statement about the form of morality, not its content; the genus, not the species. To put the question plainly, what exactly *is* morality? What is its form, nature, and structure? MacIntyre asserts that, at its most basic, morality *qua* morality is teleological: ends-based practical reasoning. MacIntyre's model for this conception of morality is Aristotle's *Nichomachean Ethics*.[2]

The keys to making sense of Aristotle's teleological paradigm are *function* and *purpose*.[3] This paradigm can be illustrated through mundane objects from our everyday lives. A clock, for instance. If we ask what purpose a clock serves, we would say, to tell time. If we ask what the difference is between a good clock and a bad clock, we might say, a good clock tells time accurately, while a bad clock does not. If we ask what purpose a kitchen knife serves, we might say, to cut and chop ingredients in preparation for cooking. If we ask what the difference is between a good kitchen knife and a bad one, we might say that a good kitchen knife has a sharp blade and cuts and chops finely, while a bad kitchen knife has a dull blade and cuts and chops poorly.

We can ask the same questions about people performing social roles. If we ask what purpose a teacher serves, we might say, to teach students. If we ask what the difference is between a good teacher and bad teacher, we might say, a good teacher conveys the relevant subject matter in a clear and memorable way. She has the ability to break down complex ideas into simple terms. She inspires a love of learning. She treats students equally. A bad teacher, on the other hand, does none of these things. If we ask what purpose a doctor serves, we might say, to heal the sick. If we ask what the difference is between a good doctor and a bad one, we might say, a good doctor listens to her patients, provides an accurate diagnosis, and prescribes an effective course of treatment. A bad doctor, because of either incompetence or negligence, does not perform this function well or at all.

These mundane examples, so familiar to us all, capture the essence of the teleological paradigm. Teleology makes positive and negative judgments in the light of some function and purpose. It determines virtues and vices in that same light. Virtues are simply those qualities, traits, features, or habits that enable something or someone to fulfill their *telos*. Vices are those that obstruct that fulfillment. In light of a specific purpose and function, making positive and negative judgments, creating lists of virtues and vices, is thus a rational, factual, and uncontroversial affair. Few people would disagree that a clock that tells time unreliably is a bad clock. Few people would disagree that a teacher who fails to teach students is a bad teacher or that a doctor who fails to heal patients is a bad doctor.

For a general ethics, applicable to humanity regardless of their personal occupations or social roles, the teleological model posited a natural *telos*, based on what MacIntyre calls Aristotle's "metaphysical biology."[4] According to this view, the same way that the natural *telos* of an apple seed would be to blossom into an apple tree, the *telos* of a human being would be to develop into a flourishing person, a person who lives well, with all that flourishing and living well entail. This might include good health, a rich social life, meaningful work, and so on. Aristotle regarded the general *telos* of humanity to be flourishing, or *eudemonia*.

In the light of this *telos*, certain virtues, such as courage, patience, and truthfulness, are necessary for human flourishing, while certain vices, such as cowardice, impatience, and deceit undermine the aim of flourishing. In the

Aristotelian paradigm, moral injunctions about what one ought and ought not to do are not forms of coercive rhetoric or browbeating, but rather sensible and rational judgments justified and grounded by the practical aim of living well. Aristotle did not see ethics as a matter of mere rule-following. Rather, he conceived of it as a form of practical education aimed at teaching us what it means to live well and how to achieve our natural *telos*. The teleological paradigm, then, consisted of three components: a human *telos*, a state of unfulfilled natural human potential, and a practical education in rational ethics. These three components fit together into one coherent whole.[5]

Historically, teleological ethics assumed two distinct variations: classical and theistic. The difference is temporal. The ends of a classical teleology are *this*-worldly: personal and social flourishing. The ends of a theistic teleology, by contrast, are *other*-worldly: salvation in the afterlife. MacIntyre observes that the theistic variation, which incorporated classical elements, came to prevail in medieval Europe from the twelfth to the fifteenth centuries.[6] The theistic variation established for European culture a shared Christian moral paradigm, what Charles Taylor calls a social imaginary—a normative conceptual background for thought, speech, and action.[7]

Beginning with the Protestant Reformation in the sixteenth century, however, this social imaginary began to fracture and unravel. The theological disagreements that led to the Wars of Religion eventually sparked a movement for secular reason to replace the moral authority of Christian theology. That movement was the Age of Reason, otherwise known as the Enlightenment.

What MacIntyre calls "the Enlightenment project" of moral philosophy was the attempt to develop a secular paradigm of morality to replace its theistic predecessor.[8] That is, it sought to provide "a shared background and foundation for moral discourse and action."[9] In MacIntyre's analysis, the great historical figures of this project were Denis Diderot, David Hume, Adam Smith, and Immanuel Kant. MacIntyre also takes into consideration Søren Kierkegaard, whose thought signaled a philosophical crisis in the Enlightenment project.

The Enlightenment project proposed two distinct approaches to secular morality: the first based on natural instinct, desire, and passion; the second, on transcendental reason. According to MacIntyre, both of these paradigms proved to be failures. That is, they failed to provide the European world with a secular counterpart to the Christian paradigm that had fractured and had lost its authority. It is in this historical failure that the seeds for the modern problem of moral disagreement—and for the culture wars today—may be found.

Instinct, desire, and passion

The Enlightenment project of moral philosophy was driven by the following questions: How do we ground morality after the fall of religious power and authority? How do we know which way to act? How do we decipher right from wrong? If not by appeal to scripture or to a natural *telos*, then what? One way to answer these questions was to appeal to natural instincts, desires, and passions. This was the approach of Diderot, Hume, and Smith.

MacIntyre analyzes both Diderot and Hume at some length but takes Hume to be an especially revealing case. In Book II of *A Treatise of Human Nature*, Hume puts forth a conception of morality rooted in the passions, not reason. This move was part of Hume's empiricist critique of his rationalist predecessor René Descartes. Hume conceives of the passions as sense impressions. He divides these sense impressions into two types: original and secondary. Original sense impressions are physical pleasures and pains. Secondary sense impressions are passions and emotions that resemble pleasures and pains. Passions include pride and humility, love and hatred—four passions that Hume describes at great length in the *Treatise*.

After his analysis of the passions, Hume contends that reason has no connection to the passions. Rather, reason pertains to an altogether different type of impression: ideas. Reason determines the logical relations between ideas. It separates true ideas from false ones. Reason can assist us in the pursuit of pleasure and the aversion of pain. But on its own, reason is powerless to produce actions and moral judgments. Because they concern different types of impression, reason and the passions belong two different faculties. Hence, the tension between reason and the passions is a philosopher's myth. The proof of reason's impotence to conclude in an action lies in the disconnect between statements of *is* and statements of *ought*. As Hume puts it,

> I cannot forbear adding to these reasonings an observation, which may, perhaps, be found of some importance. In every system of morality, which I have hitherto met with, I have always remark'd, that the author proceeds for some time in the ordinary way of reasoning, and establishes the being of a God, or makes observations concerning human affairs; when of a sudden I am surpriz'd to find, that instead of the usual copulations of propositions, *is*, and *is not*, I meet with no proposition that is not connected with an *ought*, or an *ought not*. This change is imperceptible; but is, however, of the last consequence.[10]

According to Hume's well-known formulation, no *ought* can ever be logically derived from an *is*. This means that the distinction between right and wrong, between virtues and vices, is "not founded merely on the relations of objects, nor is perceiv'd by reason."[11]

How, then, do we account for moral judgments? How do we explain their order and consistency, if there is order and consistency at all? The answer, according to Hume, lies in the natural and universal passions of humanity. In *An Enquiry Concerning the Principles of Morals*, Hume writes,

> The notion of morals, implies some sentiment common to all mankind, which recommends the same object to general approbation, and makes every man, or most men, agree in the same opinion or decision concerning it. It also implies some sentiment, so universal and comprehensive as to extend to all mankind, and render the actions and conduct, even of the persons the most remote, an object of applause or censure, according as

they agree or disagree with that rule of right which is established. These two requisite circumstances belong alone to the sentiment of humanity here insisted on.[12]

Thus, beneath the superficial differences in morals from one culture to the next lies a universal structure of instinct, desire, and passion that unites the whole of humanity, a structure self-evident to everyone, if only they would look within their own hearts.

Hume recognized that the multiplicity of the passions—pride, humility, love, hatred, and so on—posed a certain problem. Lest we be pulled by different passions into chaos, we require some guiding or overarching passion to keep ourselves ordered and focused, a meta-passion by which to organize all other passions. This meta-passion, Hume claimed, was to be found in sympathy. Through sympathy with others, we tame our pursuit of pleasure and are able to live with each other in rational order.[13]

Yet, as MacIntyre points out, Hume strongly objected to the passions and the actions of the Levellers, the seventeenth-century proto-socialist English movement that fought for radical equality, popular representation, and the franchise.[14] The Levellers posed a threat to the landed gentry. They posed a headache to Oliver Cromwell. Against the established political economic order, they sought to redistribute land and property along egalitarian lines. Hume attacked the idea of radical equality and redistribution of property as illogical in theory and dangerous in practice. As he put,

> But historians, and even common sense, may inform us, that, however specious these ideas of *perfect* equality may seem, they are really, at bottom, *impracticable*; and were they not so, would be extremely *pernicious* to human society.... The most rigorous inquisition too is requisite to watch every inequality on its first appearance; and the most severe jurisdiction, to punish and redress it. But besides, that so much authority must soon degenerate into tyranny, and be exerted with great partialities; who can possibly be possessed of it, in such a situation as is here supposed? Perfect

equality of possessions, destroying all subordination, weakens extremely the authority of magistracy, and must reduce all power nearly to a level, as well as property.[15]

Hume attributed social and economic inequality to "men's different degrees of art, care, and industry."[16] He thus saw the radical redistribution of property as dangerous and inevitably fated to devolve into tyranny. Hence, contrary to his rhetoric about a "sentiment common to all mankind," Hume gives preferential treatment to the sentiments of the propertied over the propertyless. He treats the passions of a very specific and privileged social class in the England of his time as the universal nature of humanity. MacIntyre therefore writes,

> Thus the appeal to a universal verdict by mankind turns out to be the mask worn by an appeal to those who physiologically and socially share Hume's attitudes and *Weltanschauung*. The passions of some are to be preferred to the passions of others. Whose preferences reign? The preferences of those who accept the stability of property, of those who understand chastity in women as a virtue only because it is a useful device to secure that property is passed only to legitimate heirs, of those who believe that the passage of time confers legitimacy upon what was originally acquired by violence and aggression. What Hume identifies as the standpoint of universal human nature turns out in fact to be that of the prejudices of the Hanoverian ruling elite.[17]

MacIntyre raises precisely this kind of objection about those who profess to have discovered the universal content of morality either through a supposedly universal human nature or through a supposedly transcendental and universal reason.

Transcendental reason

A second approach for theorizing a secular and universal foundation to morality was transcendental reason. This was the approach of the premier intellectual giant of the German Enlightenment, Immanuel Kant. In *The*

Groundwork of the Metaphysics of Morals, Kant presents reason as a higher faculty that can deliver timeless and universal moral truth. Reason, on this view, operates not unlike a machine—a computer program or algorithm that generates unbiased, neutral, objective, and impartial results.

Accordingly, the judgments of reason are valid for all times, places, and circumstances. Reason is pure, clean, abstract, formal, consistent, singular. Reason is unsullied by the messiness, inconsistency, and contradiction of the mundane world, the world of the local, the contingent, the particular. Reason is free of the whims, caprice, and arbitrariness of ordinary people. Reason, in other words, is Godlike.

If reason rises above the mundane world into a higher realm of abstract perfection, then to appreciate reason, to grasp its logic and judgments, is to be someone who belongs to that higher realm: a rational agent. Rational agents are the key to understanding how abstract reason can deliver moral truth. In Kant's famous formulation, a moral maxim is valid only if it can be willed into a universal law, only if all rational agents can accept it.[18] This simple test yields such universal moral duties as always telling the truth, while categorically eliminating all exceptions. Rational agents, so the argument goes, would never accept the maxim that you can lie when it suits you. To do so would be to allow whim, caprice, and arbitrariness. The substantive content of reason thus rests on the consensus of the universal community of rational agents.

But what about a maxim such as "Always act out of self-interest"? It's conceivable that this maxim would pass the test of universalizability and enjoy consensus among the community of rational agents. But a world in which everyone acted out of self-interest would be a cold, cruel, and inhumane world. The point of morality, presumably, is to create a better world than that. How, then, to prevent a descent into coldness, cruelty, and inhumanity? Kant introduces a second test, the meta-maxim to treat everyone as an end, never as a means. The principle of universalizability thus finds its balancing counterpart in the principle of humanity.[19]

Superficially, it might seem that Kant's conception of transcendental reason can provide the long sought after secular foundations for a universal morality.

But that impression would be mistaken. MacIntyre points out something curious about Kant's system: the leap of logic between the universalizability and humanity principles. It is perfectly conceivable that a rational agent would reject the humanity principle to treat others as an end rather than a means. There is no rational necessity to accept it. In which case, the humanity principle doesn't pass the test of universalizability. Rather, it functions as a kind of bandage to hold together an unworkable system, one whose foundation is arbitrary. MacIntyre also notes that the actual substance of Kant's morality, the list of maxims that make up his universal moral law, just happens to conform to the morality of his community, the Lutheran Pieti of eighteenth-century Königsberg, Prussia.

If Hume's moral philosophy functioned as an ideological mask for bourgeois class interests, can the same be said of Kant's? Although MacIntyre does not discuss it explicitly, we find precisely this contention in Marx and Engels. In *The German Ideology*, they describe Kant as "the whitewashing spokesman" of the German middle class, who were driven by bourgeois class interests. When Kant speaks of the "will" of rational agents, it is "a will that was conditioned and determined by the material relations of production."[20]

On Marx and Engels's reading, Kant's moral philosophy functions as a cover for the marketplace. His rational agents are abstracted out of their class positions and class antagonisms. Rational agents agree on the content of morality, regardless of their class position. Thus, two rational agents—a member of the super-rich and a member of the super-poor—would miraculously be united in their moral will and judgment. Rational agents, as Marx and Engels observe, are thus ideological fictions that mask relations of exchange. It is very likely that this analysis influenced MacIntyre's own critique of Kant.

Radical choice

As MacIntyre observes, the fatal problems in the empiricist turn to human nature and the idealist turn to transcendental reason were not lost upon shrewd and discerning eighteenth-century observers. Søren Kierkegaard was one of the first modern European thinkers to spot the fundamental flaws of the Enlightenment project of moral philosophy. Kierkegaard was acutely aware that the dominant schools of Enlightenment thought had not, and could not, establish for themselves secular and universal foundations. He took issue in particular with the school of German idealism, which he thought deified reason at the expense of the individual. Although not commonly labeled a counter-Enlightenment thinker, Kierkegaard is, in a very real sense, one of the Enlightenment's harshest critics—the author, as MacIntyre puts it, of the "epitaph" to the Enlightenment project.[21]

Kierkegaard understood that abstract reason cannot do the hard work of filling the giant void left by the demise of religious power and authority. The philosophical systems built by abstract reason were too full of holes and contradictions. What was presented as clean, seamless, and coherent was riddled with arbitrariness. The gaps and limits of reason thus betrayed a certain absurdity to the human condition. Given this view, Kierkegaard is often described as the father of existentialism. It is worth nothing that he is also known as a philosophical irrationalist.

Kierkegaard illustrates the existential nature of the human condition through his two-volume *Either/Or*, widely regarded as a masterpiece of existentialist thought.[22] Written under the guise of two pseudonymous authors, and collected under the guise of a pseudonymous editor, *Either/Or* presents the modern subject with a choice between two very different ways of life. The first is the aesthetic life, a life motivated by the pursuit of feeling. The aesthetic life as described in *Either/Or* is not quite the same as the narcissistic life of consumption of Gilbert Osmond. The aesthetic person may well be a decent and respected member of society. But when faced with the option to pursue marriage, meaningful friendships, and public office, the aesthetic person shuns all three, simply because to do so would be to compromise the ability to pursue a life of feeling. The aesthetic person thus shuns duty and obligation wherever possible.

The second way of life is the ethical way of life. We learn that to be a properly ethical member of society is to get married, pursue meaningful friendships, and public office. To be ethical, in other words, is to live a life of duty and obligation at the expense of the pursuit of feeling. The ethical life is internally meaningful and consistent. It is composed of a clear system of duties and obligations, maxims and principles, that constitute a universal law. The ethical person is the living embodiment of universal law, the universal made flesh and blood.

But there is a caveat to the ethical life. While it is, from within itself, preferable to the aesthetic life, there are no external reasons to embrace it. We thus face a choice between the aesthetic and the ethical life from the outside, with no recourse to external criteria. The decision is ultimately an act of sheer will, a decision for which Judge Wilhelm, the pseudonymous author of the second volume of *Either/Or*, can give us no good reasons, simply because there can be no good reasons from the outside.

Either/Or is an invitation to make a radical leap into the ethical world, not unlike a leap of faith. This caveat to the ethical life, MacIntyre points out, is a two-sided coin.[23] If there is no rational reason to embrace the ethical life, then neither is there any rational reason not to reject it. Kierkegaard's attempt to vindicate the ethical life, to argue for something for which no argument can be given, is thus ultimately incoherent. The incoherence at the heart of *Either/Or* is an epitaph, not just to the Enlightenment project, but also to Kierkegaard's own.

Aftermath of the Enlightenment

One of the most provocative contentions of *After Virtue* is that the failure of the Enlightenment project sowed the seeds for today's culture of moral instrumentalism. The misguided attempts to provide a secular framework for morality only managed to leave a glaring void. That void was filled by the institution of individual rights, the paradigms for which were the English Bill of Rights, the French Declaration of the Rights of Man and Citizen, and the United States Bill of Rights, which have their philosophical roots in the thought of John Locke. Encoded into the doctrine and institution of rights is a conception of humanity as a collection of sovereign individuals. According to this conception, the individual answers to no one but himself. His moral authority lies within. Yet, this creates a certain dilemma, for he holds moral beliefs and values that require an impersonal foundation. Without such a foundation, moral arguments necessarily appear subjective. According to MacIntyre, the need for some semblance of impersonal foundations explains the appeal of both utilitarianism and natural rights.

Utilitarianism

Utilitarianism is the quintessentially British moral tradition of Jeremy Bentham, John Stuart Mill, and Henry Sidgwick. It consists of the view that morality is to be measured in terms of utility and that justice is the maximization of pleasure for the greatest number of people. At the heart of utilitarianism is a view of individual human psychology and motivation according to which each of us is driven by the desire for pleasure and the aversion to pain. (Somehow, we also supposedly desire the greatest pleasure for the greatest number, though this second desire is arbitrarily tacked on.)

MacIntyre's critique of utilitarianism concerns the nature of pleasure and pain. How exactly are we to understand these psychological categories, given how decisive they are to the utilitarian calculus? John Stuart Mill was acutely aware of the vagueness of the concept of pleasure. In his short book, *Utilitarianism*, he divides pleasure into lower and higher types. The lower type is base and appetitive; the higher type, intellectual and aesthetic.[24] This distinction supposedly provides a rational and impartial criterion for distinguishing right from wrong in our laws, policies, and actions. But

MacIntyre points out that this weak and meaningless distinction does nothing to illuminate the idea of pleasure.[25]

Contrary to Mill, pleasure can be of many types. For example, the pleasure of a bourgeois lifestyle of endless consumption is very different from the pleasure of an ascetic life of material renunciation. The pleasure of a sadist who delights in inflicting suffering upon others is different from that of an altruist who finds meaning and joy in eliminating suffering. There are no qualitative or quantitative standards for classifying and measuring pleasure. This betrays the manipulative potential behind the very idea of pleasure as a criterion of morality. As MacIntyre puts it,

> To have understood the polymorphous character of pleasure and happiness is of course to have rendered those concepts useless for utilitarian purposes; if the prospect of his or her own future pleasure or happiness cannot . . . provide criteria for solving the problems of action in the case of each individual, it follows that the notion of the greatest happiness for the greatest number is a notion without any clear content at all. It is indeed a pseudo-concept available for a variety of ideological uses, but no more than that.[26]

This is a clear echo of Marx and Engels, who, as contemporaries of John Stuart Mill, were highly critical of utilitarianism as the reigning moral ideology of English bourgeois culture. In *The German Ideology*, Marx and Engels write,

> The apparent stupidity of merging all the manifold relationships of people into the *one* relation of usefulness, this apparently metaphysical abstraction arises from the fact that, in modern bourgeois society, all relations are subordinated in practice to the one abstract monetary-commercial relation. . . . Now these relations are supposed not to have the meaning *peculiar* to them, but to be the expression and manifestation of some third relation introduced in their place, the *relation of utility or utilization*.[27]

By evaluating moral choices in terms of utility, whether defined as pleasure or satisfaction, utilitarianism erases relationships of power between people:

capitalists and workers, men and women, white and nonwhite, colonizer and colonized. All that matters is the vague and imprecise ideals of pleasure, happiness, and satisfaction. Also, by defining pleasure and happiness in individual terms, utilitarianism presupposes the social atomism at the heart of the free market system. It is not *collective* happiness or *social* well-being that matters, but rather the aggregate of individual happiness. Regardless of what Bentham, Mill, and Sidgwick intended, utilitarianism functions as another mask for the ideology of the marketplace.

In *Ethics and the Conflicts of Modernity*, MacIntyre subjects the contemporary obsession with happiness to further critical scrutiny. Happiness, he notes, is now one of the primary units of moral currency among advertisers, politicians, therapists, and self-help gurus. Happiness has become a commodified emotion. An entire field of psychology is devoted to the study of happiness, defined in the utterly banal terms of "feeling good" and "enjoying life."[28] MacIntyre points out that happiness as an ill-defined end in itself—happiness divorced from a larger conception of social flourishing—becomes an impossibly abstract, meaningless, and unachievable ideal. Happiness as an end in itself becomes happiness for no reason, happiness by any means necessary. This empty and free-floating conception of happiness as the ultimate good, with no reference to a meaningful *telos*, becomes a perfect tool for commercial and therapeutic purposes.[29]

Natural rights

As with his critique of utilitarianism, MacIntyre's critique of natural rights follows in the tradition of Marx. In his essay, "On the Jewish Question," Marx mercilessly scrutinizes the logic behind *The Declaration of the Rights of Man and Citizen*, the seminal political document of the French Revolution. He specifically zeroes in on the Declaration's idiosyncratic concept of liberty. Article IV of the Declaration reads in part, "Liberty consists in the freedom to do everything which injures no one else." Marx observes that this impoverished idea of liberty conceives of "man as an isolated monad, withdrawn into himself."[30] Liberty, according to the Declaration, is based "not on the association of man with man, but on the separation of man from man."[31] For Marx, the material implication of this anti-social conception of liberty is encapsulated in the right to private property.

Article XVII of the Declaration describes private property as "an inviolable and sacred right," of which "no one can be deprived of private usage." As Marx observes, the right to private property reflects the value of self-interest: the right to enjoy private property to the complete exclusion, disregard, and alienation of others. The antisocial right to private property thus becomes the key institution of post-revolutionary French civil society, in which each individual sees others, not as a means, but rather as a barrier, to freedom. Marx writes,

> Therefore not one of the so-called rights of man goes beyond egoistic man, man as a member of civil society, namely an individual withdrawn into himself, his private interests and private desires, and separated from the community. In the rights of man... society appears as a framework extraneous to the individuals, as a limitation of their original independence. The only bond which holds them together is natural necessity, need and private interest, the conservation of their property and their egoistic persons.[32]

Marx found it disheartening that a people liberating themselves from centuries of brutal monarchical rule, a people who so admirably and courageously succeeded in demolishing long-standing oppressive social barriers, should tragically erect a new set of oppressive barriers between themselves. The rights enshrined in the Declaration are not natural, but rather the values of bourgeois power and ownership.

MacIntyre follows Marx by exposing natural rights as moral fictions. According to one popular line of modern thought, with origins in Locke and Hobbes, all people are endowed with an inviolable set of natural and universal rights by virtue of being persons, beings who possess certain rational capacities. This conception of natural rights betrays a tension between the universal and the historical.

Rights, as MacIntyre points out, are a distinctly historical concept. To claim a right presupposes a moral language possessing the concept of rights, and social institutions recognizing rights. But any such moral language and any such social institution are necessarily historical and contingent developments. They did not always exist. If rights are natural and universal, then did they exist before we even had a language to talk about them, before we had social institutions to recognize them? In a society without the language of rights and their accompanying institutions, "the making of a claim to a right would be like presenting a check for payment in a social order that lacked the institution of money."[33] For MacIntyre, "the truth is plain: there are no such rights, and belief in them is one with belief in witches and unicorns."[34]

Like Marx, MacIntyre observes that rights presuppose a fundamental atomism and social division at the heart of society. In *Three Rival Versions of Moral Enquiry*, he writes:

> The arrival upon the scene of conceptions of right, attaching to and exercised by individuals, as a fundamental moral quasilegal concept ... always signals some measure of loss of or repudiation of some previous social solidarity. Rights are claimed *against* some other person or persons; they are invoked when and insofar as those others appear as threats.[35]

None of this, of course, means that either Marx or MacIntyre would oppose the great movements for social justice, like the women's movement, the abolition movement, and the civil rights movement. They would, however, use different language. As Isaiah Berlin writes in his eloquent biography of Marx, "Socialism does not appeal, it demands; it speaks not of rights, but of the new form of life."[36] For his part, MacIntyre fully recognizes that "in many situations appeals to human rights ... have played an important part in securing the rights of the deprived and oppressed individuals and groups." While there are "better arguments for doing what justice and the common good require," the effectiveness of the rhetoric of rights "is at once to be welcomed and yet subjected to critical scrutiny."[37]

MacIntyre holds that the proliferation of rights talk reflects a fundamental social division—the individualism and instrumentalism of modern liberal society. While natural rights can be invoked for the social good, they also can be and are invoked for asocial and even antisocial reasons; natural rights invoked *in spite* of the common good. In an emotivist culture with no shared morality—a culture of sovereign individuals, each seeking to exercise personal will and power over others—the appeal to natural rights becomes one of the most powerful and effective forms of moral instrumentalism. Put simply, rights are rhetorical weapons.

One of the most disturbing, yet least recognized, examples of the instrumental nature of rights is the century-long battle for corporate personhood in America. When we think of civil rights, we typically think of the women's movement, the abolition movement, the civil rights movement, the LGBTQ movement, the disability rights movement, and the like. But as Adam Winkler shows in his book, *We The Corporations: How American Businesses Won Their Civil Rights*, the campaign for corporate personhood is the most successful civil rights movement in modern history.[38] Most successful, because corporations in America today now enjoy more rights than human beings.

When Mitt Romney, in response to a group of hecklers at the 2011 Iowa State Fair, condescendingly said, "Corporations are people, my friend," he expressed a nefarious political philosophy that has long guided numerous Supreme Court decisions granting rights and entitlements to corporations.[39] As Winkler shows, American corporations strategically resorted to the very same tactics of the more well-known civil rights movements to advance their quest for power, including civil disobedience, test cases, and the introduction of radically new legal claims designed to remake American law.

In some cases, corporations turned to existing progressive legislation—including the Fourteenth Amendment, which protected the rights of former slaves—to argue for the recognition of corporate personhood and for greater corporate rights. Thus, while rights have undoubtedly been powerful rhetorical tools in the historic struggle for social justice, equality, and liberation, they are the same rhetorical tools used by corporations in their twisted mission for greater power and domination. In their pursuit of profit, corporations have sought more rights and entitlements to shield themselves from the very laws and regulations designed to protect human beings, such as those pertaining to the environment.

If we regard the very idea of corporate rights with a dismissive attitude, then it should not be difficult to understand Marx's and MacIntyre's warning. If rights are weapons, then they are open for anyone to use for any purpose whatsoever.

Protesting and unmasking

MacIntyre identifies two other rhetorical weapons in the arsenal of moral instrumentalism. One is the speech-act of protest, with its defining emotions of indignation and outrage. In a liberal society based on the ideals of individual liberty, freedom, and happiness, the expression of indignation and outrage takes on a peculiar significance. These emotions become powerful tools of social coercion and control, a way of getting the upper hand in social conflict.

In such moments, what matters is not right and wrong, but who expresses greater indignation and outrage. In the culture wars today, liberals and conservatives alike have mastered the strategic expression of these powerful emotions, and perfected the performance of victimhood, of fragility without vulnerability. Each now has its own outrage machine, designed to process the right input while directing fire and brimstone at selected targets. Each side, that is, has developed a complex stimulus-response system, which can be triggered by increasingly trivial offenses with almost predictable results. This is not to say that protesting isn't sometimes justified and necessary.[40] But like rights, protesting is not inherently progressive. It is one more instrument that can be wielded in any political direction.

The last rhetorical weapon that MacIntyre identifies is the act of unmasking others, of exposing "the unacknowledged motives of arbitrary will and desire which sustain the moral masks of modernity."[41] For MacIntyre, the paradigmatic figure for the act of unmasking is Freud, whose theory of unconscious motives has provided generations of cultural critics with a powerful tool for critiquing the dominant culture. In addition to psychoanalysis, cultural critics have turned to Marxism, feminist theory, postcolonial theory, and various schools of continental philosophy for cultural critique. These schools have provided the tools for unmasking racism, sexism, classism, and cultural imperialism, among other forms of power and domination.

But the act of unmasking hidden motives has evolved from a narrow genre of cultural criticism into a more overt ideological weapon in the culture wars. Unmasking is also a political tactic for undermining the moral credibility of social and political actors, exposing them as the enemy, and revealing for the rest of the world the enemy's covert intentions, schemes, and machinations. Unmasking has become a vicious cycle on both the Right and the Left, devolving into out-and-out paranoia in the era of social media. The next chapter explores the role of protesting and unmasking in the online culture wars.

Notes

1 MacIntyre, *After Virtue*, 2.

2 Ibid., 52.

3 Ibid., 58.

4 Ibid. In *After Virtue*, MacIntyre rejects Aristotle's metaphysical biology and affirms that virtue ethics can be practiced and defended on purely social terms. He later revised this view. Although he continues to reject the bulk of that biology, he now maintains that the practice of the virtues requires some basic "metaphysical grounding." He goes even further and argues that it requires a biological grounding. This metaphysical and biological grounding he provides in *Dependent Rational Animals*.

5   MacIntyre, *After Virtue*, 53.

6   Ibid.

7   Charles Taylor, *Modern Social Imaginaries*. Durham, NC: Duke University Press, 2003.

8   MacIntyre, *After Virtue*, 36.

9   Ibid., 50.

10 David Hume, *A Treatise of Human Nature*, edited by David Fate Norton and Mary J. Norton. Oxford, UK: Oxford University Press, 2000 (3.1.2), 302.

11 Ibid.

12 David Hume, *Enquiries Concerning Human Understanding and Concerning the Principles of Morals*, edited by L. A. Selby-Bigge, revised by P. H. Nidditch, 3rd edn. Oxford: Clarendon Press, 1975, 272.

13 Ibid., 229, 234.

14 MacIntyre, *After Virtue*, 230–31.

15 Hume, *Enquiries*, 194 (emphasis in the original).

16 Ibid.

17 MacIntyre, *After Virtue*, 231.

18 Immanuel Kant, *Groundwork of the Metaphysics of Morals*, translated and edited by Mary Gregor and Jens Timmermann. Cambridge, UK: Cambridge University Press. 4.432, 44.

19 Kant, *Groundwork of the Metaphysics of Morals*, 4.429, 43.

20 Karl Marx and Frederick Engels, *The German Ideology*, edited with an introduction by C. J. Arthur. New York, NY: International Publishers, 1970, 99.

21 MacIntyre, *After Virtue*, 39.

22 Søren Kierkegaard, *Either/Or: A Fragment of Life*. London, UK: Penguin.

23 MacIntyre, *After Virtue*, 42–42.

24 John Stuart Mill, *Utilitarianism*, 2nd edn. Indianapolis, IN: Hackett, 9–11.

25 MacIntyre, *After Virtue*, 63–64.

26 Ibid., 77.

27 Marx and Engels, *The German Ideology*, 109.

28 Alasdair MacIntyre, *Ethics in the Conflicts of Modernity: An Essay on Desire, Practical Reasoning, and Narrative*. Cambridge, UK: Cambridge University Press, 2016, 195.

29 Ibid., 196–202.

30 Karl Marx, "On the Jewish Question," in Ricardo Blaug and John Schwartzmantel, eds. *Democracy: A Reader*. Edinburgh, UK: Edinburgh University Press, 2001, 269.

31 Ibid.

32 Ibid., 269–70.

33 MacIntyre, *After Virtue*, 68–69.

34 Ibid., 70.

35 Alasdair MacIntyre, *Three Rival Versions of Moral Enquiry: Encyclopaedia, Genealogy, and Tradition*. Notre Dame, IN: University of Notre Dame Press, 1990, 185.

36 Isaiah Berlin, *Karl Marx*. Princeton, NJ: Princeton University Press, 2013, 8.

37 MacIntyre, *Ethics in the Conflicts of Modernity*, 78.

38 Adam Winkler, *We The Corporations: How American Businesses Won Their Civil Rights*. New York, NY: Norton, 2018.

39 James Oliphant, "Romney in Iowa: 'Corporations are people' Too," *Los Angeles Times*, August 11, 2011. http://articles.latimes.com/2011/aug/11/news/la-pn-romney-state-fair-20110811 (accessed January 14, 2019).

40 Though he is not exactly very forthcoming about his political views today, MacIntyre notably defended the necessity of civil disobedience against American militarism in Vietnam. Writing in 1968, he argued that "in Vietnam, war crimes are being committed and that resistance to the Vietnam War by acts of civil disobedience is therefore not a right, but a duty" (quoted in Blackledge and Davidson, *Alasdair MacIntyre's Engagement with Marxism*, xlvii).

41 MacIntyre, *After Virtue*, 72.

3

Emotivism on Steroids

After Virtue was first published in 1981, long before the phrase "the culture wars" entered our academic lexicon to refer to the ideological battle between liberals and conservatives for the heart and soul of the Western world. In a very real sense, MacIntyre had described the meta-historical and meta-ethical roots of that battle. But MacIntyre's analysis does more than just trace those roots. He also provides the conceptual tools for making sense of the culture wars. Building on his analysis, I argue in this chapter that the moral instrumentalism of liberal modernity gave rise to the new culture wars: a social conflict of warring ideological camps, each seeking to impose its will on the other, each fiercely resisting the will of the other. An analysis of the culture wars reveals a new set of rhetorical weapons in the arsenal of moral instrumentalism. It also reveals something more basic: the perverse nature of ethics under capital. The culture wars are not an aberration from capital. Rather, they are the inevitable cultural expression of capital. Put simply, capital thrives on the culture wars. When MacIntyre claimed we needed to preserve the virtue of civility, he may not have realized just how bad the problem would become.

The old culture wars

The culture wars are often traced to the 1960s counterculture movement. This was the revolutionary period in which an entire generation rose up to challenge unjust forms of power, authority, and tradition. Martin Luther King Jr. and Malcolm X led the civil rights movement. Angela Davis became the voice of the Black Power movement. Betty Friedan published *The Feminine Mystique*, launching second-wave feminism. In New York's Greenwich Village, the Stonewall riots marked a historic turning point for the gay liberation movement. The sexual revolution shattered traditional attitudes and rules about sexual relationships. Millions of Americans protested the Vietnam War, effectively solidifying an anti-war sentiment among large segments of the American public. Inspired by the civil rights movement, the Free Speech Movement was born on the campus of the University of California at Berkeley. Experiments in musical and artistic styles were complemented by experiments in fashion and recreational drug use. In short, the counterculture movement brought about a radical transformation in politics, values, style, and taste. In some sense, we have been living in the shadows of the 1960s ever since.

This cultural sea change, of course, was horrifying to many Americans. They strongly resisted the subversion of the old social order. They wished for blacks to remain in the back of the bus, subservient to whites. They wished for women to remain in the home, subservient to their husbands. They cringed at the idea of homosexuality, let alone the sight of it. They despised the new musical and artistic fashions. They regarded the entire counterculture movement as the moral decay of the West. They aggressively clung to the old ways. They became bitter in the process and have remained bitter ever since.

Over the next two decades, conservatives began building a counterrevolutionary movement. Their goal was nothing less than a return to the old social order. Two of the most important figures in the early days of the counterrevolutionary movement were William F. Buckley and Phyllis Schlafly. These two conservative writers and public intellectuals would spend the rest of their lives fighting to reclaim America.

By the 1990s, American conservatives had built a formidable ideology machine. They aggressively pushed the conservative cause through books, magazines, radio shows, think tanks, clubs, associations, and charitable foundations. Several conservative writers saw college campuses as the principal site of the culture wars. Allan Bloom published *The Closing of the American Mind*, in which he took aim at the supposed relativism and nihilism of the academic left, an idea that has since become something of a pathological obsession among conservative intellectuals.[1] Roger Kimball published *Tenured Radicals*, in which he similarly argued that certain schools of literary and cultural theory were undermining the Western canon and the very foundations of Western identity.[2] Kimball's principal targets included Louis Althusser, Walter Benjamin, Homi Bhabha, Jacques Derrida, Franz Fanon, Stanley Fish, Michel Foucault, Fredric Jameson, Martha Nussbaum, Richard Rorty, Edward Said, Barbara Herrnstein Smith, and Cornel West. He criticized the rise of emergent disciplines such as African American studies and women's and gender studies. He criticized queer theory, postcolonialism, new historicism, and reader-response theory. The university, Kimball argued, had been almost completely infiltrated by left-wing ideologues. Under the protection of tenure, these ideologues had brainwashed American college students with corrosive ideas.

In a similar vein, Dinesh D'Souza published *Illiberal Education*, in which he harshly criticized feminism, affirmative action, and multiculturalism, arguing that colleges and universities were being transformed by a culture of victimhood.[3] According to D'Souza, women and minorities had established a new form of tyranny on college campuses, unfairly subjecting white men to harsh and unfair treatment. Perhaps most controversially, Richard Herrnstein and Charles Murray published *The Bell Curve*, in which they drew a link between genetics and intelligence.[4] *The Bell Curve* was a rather blatant exercise in scientific racism that targeted affirmative action policies for African Americans.

By the 1990s, several conservative organizations such as Focus on the Family, Concerned Women for America, the American Family Association, and the Alliance for Defending Freedom targeted the women's movement and the LGBTQ movement in the name of defending "family values." The family, they argued, was the most basic unit of society. It therefore had to be protected from the destructive effects of feminism and homosexuality. Think tanks such as the Cato Institute, the Discovery Institute, the Heartland Institute, and the Heritage Foundation recruited conservative intellectuals and pundits, creating a kind of conservative alternative to the university system. These think thanks conferred prestigious titles upon their recruits, offered them lavish salaries, commissioned studies and reports, and dispatched them to speak on national television and public radio to parrot a conservative worldview.[5]

The conservative message was further disseminated through magazines such as *The American Conservative*, *The American Spectator*, *The Weekly Standard*, *The National Interest*, and *The New Criterion*, as well as through more time-honored conservative publications like *Commentary* and *The National Review*. Following the collapse of the Federal Communications Commission's Fairness Doctrine, which had long required ideological balance on public radio stations, Rush Limbaugh and Laura Schlessinger took advantage of the newly deregulated environment and became the leading voices of conservative talk radio.

One of the biggest developments in the conservative ideology machine was Rupert Murdoch's acquisition of 20th Century Fox and the subsequent creation of the Fox News Channel. Murdoch hired Roger Ailes, media advisor for Republican presidents Richard Nixon and Ronald Reagan. Ailes in turn launched *The O'Reilly Factor* and *Hannity & Colmes*, two militantly anti-intellectual programs that provided conservatism with a populist voice. O'Reilly and Hannity perfected an uncanny ability to whip up reactionary conservative hysteria against imaginary evils, such as the "war on Christmas" and the Islamic takeover of America, while completely shielding capitalism from the slightest criticism.[6] Lastly, following the rise of the internet in the 1990s, conservatives launched a slew of websites, including Drudge Report, World Net Daily, FrontPage Magazine, Newsmax Media, and Townhall.com.[7]

Yet, for all the power and success of its ideology machine, conservatism appeared to be on the losing side of history. It appeared to be a movement restricted to an angry, aging, and increasingly irrelevant rural white population, fated to be left behind by a progressive future represented by women, minorities, immigrants, and LGBTQ people. When Bill Bennett, Secretary of Education under President Reagan and longtime conservative author and pundit, appeared on *The Daily Show with Jon Stewart* in 2006, he conceded that conservatism had lost the key battles of the culture wars. Bennett's case for conservatism amounted to a pathetic plea to Stewart's progressive audience to believe in America once again. Stewart handily and authoritatively asserted that his own side had won.[8]

Bennett's concession of defeat was a testament to what conservatives had long perceived as the cultural dominance of the liberal enemy. Everywhere they looked, from Hollywood to television to the music industry to college campuses, conservatives saw the advancement of women, people of color, and LGBTQ people, as well as the hegemony of secularism and the erosion of Christian values. To conservative eyes, Western culture had de facto become liberal. Conservatives believed the rot of liberal culture was all around them, permeating the ether, polluting the very air they breathed. Hence, the reactionary belief in institutional fictions like "the liberal media," the idea that mainstream newspapers, film, and television were pursuing some sort of radical progressive agenda. But contrary to conservative perceptions, the counterculture movement of the 1960s lost its radical and subversive edge. Corporate America was perfectly happy to promote diversity, so long as it did not threaten—or, rather, precisely because it did not threaten—its economic interests.

By the 1990s, much of the feminist movement had been co-opted by the universal acid of capital. As Nancy Fraser put it, feminism had become capitalism's "handmaiden." It began as a critique of capitalist exploitation but had "ended up contributing key ideas" to capitalism's latest phase.[9] The consummate symbol of corporate feminism was of course Hillary Clinton. During her presidential candidacy in 2016, Clinton rejected all criticisms of her record, including her close relationship with Wall Street, her racist push for mass incarceration, and her long history of warmongering, as nothing more than rabid misogyny. The capitalist class had similarly co-opted the LGBTQ movement.[10] Major corporations began sponsoring pride parades, imposing their rainbow-inflected logos at almost every major march, while masquerading as champions of equality. The stunning popularity of Ellen DeGeneres, friend and hugger of George W. Bush, is an index of the sheer eagerness of the entertainment industry to embrace an apolitical LGBTQ movement, effectively cutting the movement off from its radical, anti-capitalist roots.[11]

The cooptation of the progressive movement reached its zenith with the 2008 election of Barack Obama. Obama's brand of politics ignored economic inequality in favor of a politics of identity and representation. Rather than address the material conditions that had devastated millions of American lives and exacerbated the scourge of income inequality, Obama chose to implement business-friendly policies, while singing the praises of America as a nation of diversity, where even "a skinny kid with a funny name" like himself could feel at home.[12] Writing in 2008, Adolph Reed described Obama as "a vacuous opportunist, a good performer with an ear for how to make white liberals like him."[13] Reed noted that Obama's "fundamental political center of gravity, beneath an empty rhetoric of hope and change and new directions," was unapologetically neoliberal.[14] Obama represented the triumph of identity politics, of capitalism with a multicultural face. To the reactionary conservative mind, however, he represented the triumph of political correctness—affirmative action for the highest levels of political office. For American conservatives, the very image of a black man in the White House was the very last straw.

The birth of the new right

In her book *Kill All Normies*, Angela Nagle observes how the social media revolution deepened the rift between conservatives and liberals, effectively sealing each side off within its own moral universe online.[15] The liberal generation that came of age during the Obama presidency assumed that America had made a radical leap forward and that there was no going back. Young liberals fell into a sense of complacency, indulging their bottomless appetite for irony, meta-jokes, cat memes, netspeak, and filtered pictures of chai lattes on wildly popular websites like Buzzfeed, which unapologetically pushed a liberal hipster worldview that celebrated diversity in all its dizzying minutiae. Meanwhile, this online culture ignored the deeper economic problems that were slowly dismantling the very foundations of American society. The celebration of diversity proved to be a highly successful business model for *Salon, Upworthy, Vox, Vice, HuffPo*, and the now-defunct *Gawker*—liberal websites that specialize in the recognition and celebration of evermore obscure forms of marginality. According to their business model, marginality is a coveted treasure, a new market on which to build moral capital.[16] The online liberal cult of diversity became an all-consuming obsession, ironically leaving its adherents all but clueless about developments in the outside world.

At the same time, a monster was quietly growing in the darker corners of the digital universe. On 4Chan, 8Chan, YouTube, Twitter, and Reddit, a growing impatience and exasperation toward the liberal cult of diversity had devolved into a morbid bitterness and hatred. The story of 4Chan, still the most notorious platform online, remains something of an obscurity to the general public. 4Chan began as a rather innocent and harmless image board, modeled after popular Japanese image boards for anime fans. Like discussion boards, 4Chan users can select boards on which to post images, anything from high-resolution photographs to meaningless doodles created with Microsoft Paint. 4Chan users are almost completely anonymous, which offers a certain license to experiment with forbidden desires and impulses.

4Chan places very few restrictions on what can be posted. Some boards cater to mundane themes and topics, such as travel, music, literature, and sports. Others, like the multiple channels for pornography, are invitations to explore the depths and limits of human perversity. Built into 4Chan is a certain spirit of freedom, irreverence, boundary-pushing, and rebellion against authority. 4Chan thus quickly developed into a space for shock humor, shock porn, and gore. It also became a breeding ground for online pranks and digital vandalism. What we today know as memes originated on 4Chan. Anonymous, the anarchist-hacktivist collective known for its DDoS attacks on government websites, also originated on 4Chan.[17] But the same spirit of rebellion that gave birth to Anonymous also gave birth to the Alt-Right, the neofascist movement determined to drag the entire Western world into a full-blown race war.

As Nagle observes, the new right began, not as a racist movement, but rather as a revolt against feminism. The new right came into being during one of the darkest episodes in internet history, the notorious Gamergate controversy. Reacting to feminist gaming critics, who had critiqued the hyper-masculine themes of popular videogames and called for more female characters and female-centered games, underground legions of young, insecure, hormonal male gamers flew into a white-hot rage. Few had predicted that young male gamers would be so fiercely protective of their beloved videogames.

The popular image of gamers was of weak, passive, timid, and quiet young men—social losers too shy and introverted ever to leave their parents' basements and walk in the antiseptic light of day. But the feminist critique of gamer culture awoke a sleeping monster: the toxic sewer of male anxiety and insecurity. It turned out that the cultural advancement of women, however limited, did not result in a corresponding diminishment in the male desire for power and domination. Rather, that desire had been sublimated into underground channels. In the case of young men addicted to screens, it had been sublimated into pornography and videogames, fantasy worlds in which men still retained a sense of power, authority, and superiority. The feminist critique of videogames thus threatened the only world in which these young men achieved any sense of self. Put simply, feminism posed an existential threat. It therefore had to be fought—with all the viciousness, ugliness, and violence that had been building up in the fragile and insecure male psyche for years.

Gamergate began after videogame developer Zoe Quinn received positive reviews for her game Depression Quest, a story-based, interactive videogame whose protagonist suffers from depression and seeks to get better.[18] Depression Quest was obviously a dramatic departure from more traditional, testosterone-driven videogames. Surprisingly, Depression Quest received positive reviews from gaming critics, who praised its originality, its sophisticated storyline, and the accuracy of its depiction of depression. Outraged by these positive reviews, male gamers plotted on 4Chan, Internet Relay Chat (IRC), and Reddit to manufacture a controversy about Quinn. They decided to spread the malicious rumor that Quinn had slept with gaming critics to secure positive reviews.

Gamers began creating countless sockpuppet accounts on Twitter and started the hashtag #gamergate in an effort to get the rumor to go viral. This backlash quickly and predictably took a turn for the violent. Quinn began receiving ghastly and horrifying rape threats and death threats. Trolls sent her photoshopped images of her face and body bloodied and bruised. They sent her dark and twisted fantasies about beating her nearly to death, but not to the point of brain damage, because they wanted her to be conscious of her agony. They found photos of her, old and new, which they printed out, covered in semen, and sent to her family and friends. Eventually, Quinn was "doxed." Someone had tweeted her home address to her, forcing her to go into hiding.[19]

Gamergate had difficulty taking off at first. The controversy didn't receive the coverage or the viral sharing its orchestrators so desperately desired. But that changed when Milo Yiannapolous, the internet provocateur, self-professing troll, and former "journalist" for Breitbart, began providing just the sort of favorable coverage they had hoped for. Milo validated all of the anxiety and the rage of male gamers. He gave them a mainstream voice. He empowered and emboldened them in their war against feminist gaming critics and feminism generally. In doing so, Milo became the spokesperson and the hero of the Gamergate movement.[20]

It is difficult to exaggerate the importance of Milo in the new online culture wars. He created a new paradigm for conservatism in the digital age. Milo rose to fame as a younger, hipper, digitally savvier, and more fabulous version of Ann Coulter, the noxious conservative polemicist who built a successful career out of attacking "liberals," a category in which she includes everyone from billionaire George Soros to Hillary and Bill Clinton to Bernie Sanders to Karl Marx to Joseph Stalin.[21] Milo drew upon Coulter's contempt for political correctness but replaced her sanctimony and cantankerousness with the irony, cynicism, nihilism, and meta-humor of millennial digital culture. Milo was no traditional conservative. He circumvented the cultural and intellectual refinement of William F. Buckley and the unlettered and vulgar boorishness of Rush Limbaugh. With his dyed blonde hair, his ostentatious manner of dress, and his flamboyantly gay personality, Milo defied every popular stereotype about conservatives.

Here was a gay man telling gay people to get back in the closet, not because he believed homosexuality was wrong, but because being gay was more fun, more "dangerous," when it was prohibited. He trolled the Black Lives Matter movement, dressing up as the policeman from the Village People, and taunting them with a baton. He trolled black actress and comedian Leslie Jones, instigating his 350,000 Twitter followers to harass and bully her. They compared her to a gorilla, resulting in Milo getting banned from Twitter. He also attacked feminists, making them out to be neurotic and deranged control freaks, and treated them as objects of merciless humor and endless laughter. He denied *all* of the injustices to which the LGBTQ movement, the Black Lives Matter movement, and the feminist movement called attention. In short, Milo fought against most of the traditional enemies of conservatism, but through transgression, rebellion, irony, and savage meta-humor. Whereas Coulter specialized in unmasking liberals, Milo specialized in trolling them. He seized upon their fears and actively sought to become their worst nightmare. He embarked upon his "Dangerous Faggot" tour, branding himself a subversive, bringing his provocations straight to their doorstep. Milo shrewdly capitalized on the theme of danger, going so far as to purchase the domain name Dangerous.com and write a book simply titled, *Dangerous*.[22]

In some sense, Milo represented a deal with the devil. If only conservatives would welcome him, an openly gay man, into their fold, he would give them what they wanted: the upper hand in the culture wars. Some conservatives cautiously welcomed him. Others enthusiastically embraced him. Steve Bannon, who would later become Chief Strategist for President Trump, made Milo the technology editor at Breitbart.com. In return, Milo delivered. He wrote pieces with such titles as, "The Solution to Online 'Harassment' is Simple: Women Should Log Off," "Trannies Whine About Hilarious Bruce Jenner Billboard," "Birth Control Makes Women Unattractive and Crazy," "Hoist it High and Proud: The Confederate Flag Proclaims a Glorious Heritage," "Would You Rather Your Child Had Feminism or Cancer?," "Science Proves It: Fat Shaming Works," "There's No Hiring Bias Against Women in Tech: They Just Suck at Interviews," and "Gay Rights Have Made Us Dumber: It's Time to Get Back in the Closet." Milo's penchant for dolling out offense left liberals speechless, fascinated, and terrified all at once. By playing to liberal fears, he succeeded in becoming larger than life. As one headline from Bloomberg put it, "Milo is the Pretty, Monstrous Face of the Alt-Right."[23] It was exactly the kind of headline that Milo himself would have written.

Through his polemical "journalism," his trolling on Twitter, his events on college campuses, and his numerous, shrewdly executed attention-grabbing antics, Milo was among a small, but influential group of young conservatives online who succeeded in changing the popular narrative of the culture wars. Richard Spencer, who coined the label "Alt-Right," has become the most vocal and prominent voice of American white nationalism. Spencer has openly, unapologetically, and defiantly called for the ethnic cleansing of America. Educated at the University of Virginia, the University of Chicago, and Duke University, Spencer is fluent in the language of postmodern cultural theory, which he employs to appeal to college-educated millennials. Spencer achieved international infamy after giving a speech in Washington, DC in 2016, in which he declared, "Hail Trump, hail our people, hail victory!"[24] Upon hearing this brazen declaration, his audience erupted with wild applause and Nazi-style salutes.

Another major figure in the new conservative movement is Gavin McInnes, cofounder of Vice, the millennial-oriented, ultra-hipster, nihilism-drenched news organization. McInnes has since left Vice and become a major figurehead of the white nationalist movement, retaining his hipster style—a ringmaster mustache, nerd glasses, slickly combed hair, suspenders, and thin tie. McInnes provides the movement with hipster credibility and appeal. In 2016, he founded Proud Boys, a cross-national fraternal order of white men pushing a white nationalist and neomasculinist agenda. The new conservative movement also includes Ezra Levant, founder of the Rebel Media, a conservative news organization that specializes in attacking liberals, feminism, and Islam.

The emergent movement includes YouTube personality Lauren Southern, the voice of millennial anti-Muslim hatred. It includes Mike Cernovitch, a proponent of the Men's Rights Movement and a rabid conspiracy theorist who pushed the notorious Pizzagate controversy, which falsely linked Hillary Clinton to an imaginary child sex-trafficking ring run beneath a pizza restaurant in Washington, DC.[25] This dangerous conspiracy theory resulted in a gunman, armed with a semiautomatic rifle, firing shots at the restaurant.

Not least, the movement includes Alex Jones, the comically delusional, perpetually outraged host of InfoWars, without question *the* leading source of the most bizarre, wild, and irresponsible conspiracy theories online today. Jones sees conspiracies in literally everything, feeding his massive audience a diet of continuous paranoia. Jones has long claimed that the Sandy Hook Elementary School massacre, in which a mentally ill gunman brutally slaughtered twenty children, was a liberal hoax. He has accused the parents of the victims of being paid actors. The entire affair, Jones maintains, was a liberal plot designed to confiscate guns from the American people.[26] As of this writing, Jones has been banned from Facebook, Twitter, YouTube, and iTunes. His material was deemed so toxic and dangerous that these platforms collectively decided it was best to deprive him of an outlet.[27]

Despite their differences, the leaders of the new conservative movement are united in their militant opposition to liberals, their resolute hostility to immigrants, and their fanatical support of Donald Trump. Most significantly, they have managed to change the popular narrative of the culture wars. Accordingly, conservatives have become the new rebels, and liberals the new mainstream, the guardians of the new morality. In their essay, "An Establishment Conservative's Guide to the Alt-Right," Milo and Breitbart journalist Allum Bokhari provide a useful overview of the philosophical, political, and pop-cultural influences of the new conservative movement, along with an explanation of the movement's primary rhetorical style.[28] The core intellectual roots of the Alt-Right, they point out, lie in the thought of three key twentieth-century thinkers: Oswald Spengler, the German historian and author of *The Decline of the West*; H. L. Mencken, the American essayist and cultural critic, who followed Nietzsche in celebrating the Übermensch and who advocated for a neo-aristocratic society; and Julius Evola, the Italian political philosopher who mixed mysticism with fascism and called for a return to a natural social hierarchy.

More contemporary intellectual influences are American computer scientist Curtis Yarvin and British philosopher Nick Land, the founding fathers of the so-called Dark Enlightenment, also known as NRx, the "neo-reactionary" movement. The Dark Enlightenment opposes the Enlightenment in both spirit and letter. It argues that we need a new world purged of the Enlightenment's political influence, including the complete dismantling of democracy. Land is also the father of Accelerationism, a school of thought that advocates speeding up the process of advanced capitalism and the development of digital technology, on the grounds that technological capitalism is here to stay and that no other alternative is possible.

Politically, the Alt-Right are inspired by the paleo-conservatism of Pat Buchanan, author of *The Death of the West*, and a major voice in the culture wars.[29] Another source of political inspiration is the Nouvelle Droite, or the French Right, led by Alain de Benoist, the prolific French intellectual who strangely synthesizes elements of right-wing and left-wing thought, with ideas from thinkers as diverse as Oswald Spengler, Carl Schmidt, Julius Evola, Ernst Bloch, and Antonio Gramsci.

But it is the rhetorical style of the new right that, for the purposes of this book, is of the greatest significance. Milo and Bokhari assert that in the face of social and cultural pressure to self-censor, "there will always be a young, rebellious contingent who feel a mischievous urge to blaspheme, break all the rules, and say the unsayable." They state the motivation behind this rebellious impulse rather plainly: "Because it's funny!"[30] While many new conservatives are genuinely driven by neo-reactionary ideas, a large segment of the movement has no intellectual commitments at all. Rather, they are to Baby Boomers what Baby Boomers supposedly were to their parents' generation—rebels looking to shatter traditional norms for the sheer sake of it while enjoying a good laugh.

The bell-bottoms, long hair, wild musical styles, and sexual libertinism of the 1960s have been reincarnated in the form of outrageous memes, online pranks, trolling, internet slang, and Pepe the Frog, the latter a favorite symbol of the white nationalist movement.[31] The new prankster rebels respond to sanctimony of any kind with "the weapons of mass trolling that anonymous subcultures are notorious for—and brilliant at."[32] This segment of the new right is deliberately immature, shameless, and brazenly unprincipled. Nothing they do is out of resentment. Everything they do is purely for the "lulz."[33] Had they lived in the 1960s, they would have been experimenting with drugs, sleeping around with each other, and living the unruly lifestyles for which the counterculture became so famous. They profess to be the true heirs to the counterculture movement, the protean force of freedom, creativity, and rebellion. In a word, they live for *transgression*.

In an especially insightful chapter in *Kill All Normies*, Nagle argues that transgression, once regarded as a central virtue of the counterculture movement, has since been tactically and brilliantly appropriated and repurposed for the agenda of the Alt-Right.[34] Following MacIntyre, we can make a different, but related claim: that transgression has become *the* conservative weapon in the moral instrumentalism of the culture wars. As Nagle argues, Milo and the Alt-Right have consciously channeled a long-standing tradition of transgression in modern Western culture. Transgression has been celebrated by a number of prominent continental thinkers, most notably the Marquis de Sade, Friedrich Nietzsche, George Bataille, Maurice Blanchot, and Michel Foucault. Hyperaware of dominant systems of power and control—religious and secular, institutional and cultural, explicit and implicit—these radical thinkers theorized about, and in some cases practiced, transgression. They did so in the spirit of exploring the very limits and possibilities of human thought, creativity, and experience—philosophical, moral, aesthetic, sexual.

The same rebellious spirit has been expressed in numerous schools of art, including Dadaism, surrealism, cubism, and situationism. Marcel Duchamp's *Fountain*, Piero Manzoni's *Merda d'Artista* (Artist's Shit), and Andres Serrano's *Piss Christ*, each in its own way made transgression the primary medium of their artistic expression. In popular music, a long tradition of shock rock has sought to push cultural boundaries. For musical artists like Screamin' Jay Hawkins, Alice Cooper, The Misfits, and Marilyn Manson, the act of transgression is as much their performative medium as the music itself. These artists built their reputations on shocking and provoking the culture around them.

Transgression, Nagle notes, is best understood through Mikhail Bakhtin's idea of the carnivalesque, a literary, artistic, and performative mode in which the audience is entertained both through the comic and the grotesque.[35] The problem with the carnivalesque, however, is that the power of transgression lies in its novelty, which has a very short shelf-life. Contrary to a certain line of left-wing thought, transgression is neither inexhaustible nor inherently left-wing. At some point, transgression will run its course, after which the provocative, the disturbing, the shocking, and the horrifying will have become the familiar, the ordinary, the harmless, the traditional. The rock band KISS was shocking to parents in the 1970s. Today, they are considered harmless, even a part of the pop-cultural heritage of the West. The counterculture movement suffered this very fate.

The radicality of the counterculture movement has been domesticated and neutralized. In this weakened and watered-down state, the counterculture movement has blended into mainstream culture. Confronting the ascendancy and triumph of liberal identity politics, with its code of political correctness, Milo and the Alt-Right have successfully co-opted the one rhetorical weapon that would finally provide conservatism with the upper edge in the culture wars: transgression. After attending one of Milo's events, Richard Spencer realized the full import of Milo's critique of political correctness. "That was a revelation for me," he said. "What we are doing is known to people, it's edgy and dangerous, it's cool and hip. It's that thing our parents don't want us to do. So that was definitely a huge inspiration."[36]

There is, of course, a tension between conservatism and transgression. Conservatism, as Corey Robin has argued, is the preservation of hierarchy and traditional social order.[37] Transgression, by contrast, is the subversion of hierarchy and social order. However strategic and effective for the conservative cause, transgression must necessarily be limited within the project of conservatism. This much became obvious after the Reagan Battalion, an anonymous group of old-guard conservatives on Twitter, unearthed and disseminated footage of Milo defending pederasty on Joe Rogan's podcast, leading to the prankster's resignation from Breitbart, the cancellation of his book contract with Simon and Schuster, the cancellation of a scheduled appearance at the Conservative Political Action Conference, and his humiliating fall from conservative grace.[38] Milo was forced to create his own publishing company, Dangerous Books, and self-publish his own book.[39] For all of their lack of principle and integrity, it appeared that pedophilia was the one red line that conservatives were not willing to cross. As one indication of just how far Milo had fallen from conservative superstardom, in early 2018, he appeared on InfoWars promoting nutritional supplements.[40] The troll had become an infomercial salesman. By August 2018, he began attacking his fans for not giving him enough support.[41] By December 2018, it was reported that Milo was more than $2 million in debt.[42] The lulz have since given way to resentment.

Tumblr liberalism and Left cannibalism

While the Alt-Right solidified its identity, becoming united in its sense of mission and purpose, a rival community was taking shape in another universe online. This community is a mirror version of the Alt-Right: comparable in its fanaticism, but oriented in a different ideological direction. The fanatical nature of this second community can be illustrated through the story of Keziah Daum. In May 2018, Daum tweeted pictures of herself at her high school prom. What stood out about the pictures was her prom dress. Rather than wearing a conventional dress, Daum instead wore a qipao, a traditional dress worn by women in China. Shortly after her post, Twitter user Jeremy Lam angrily responded to Daum by tweeting, "My culture is NOT your goddamn prom dress," which, as of this writing, has been re-tweeted 40,000 times and liked 176,000 times. Lam proceeded to share the history and meaning of the qipao, asserting that the dress shattered class barriers and was a symbol of Chinese heritage and identity. Lam, whose Twitter bio reads, "almost as intolerant to lactose as i am to your bullshit," further tweeted, "I'm proud of my culture. . . . For it to simply be subject to American consumerism and cater to a white audience, is parallel to colonial ideology." Tens of thousands of Twitter users joined Lam in condemning Daum for the moral offense of cultural appropriation.[43]

When the story reached China, however, it was met with sheer bafflement. Those actually living in Mainland China could not believe that anyone would be outraged over a white American wearing the qipao. Rather, they regarded Daum's choice of dress as the triumphant spread of Chinese culture. "I am very proud to have our culture recognized by people in other countries," one user wrote on the popular Chinese social media app WeChat, a post that has been read 100,000 times. Another WeChat user asked, "So, does that mean when we celebrate Christmas and Halloween, it's also cultural appropriation?" Cultural commentator Zhou Yijun remarked, "It's ridiculous to criticize this as cultural appropriation. From the perspective of a Chinese person, if a foreign woman wears a qipao and thinks she looks pretty, then why shouldn't she wear it?"

Others took issue with Lam's flawed history. The qipao, they pointed out, was introduced by the invading Manchu Qing to the Han people. They also pointed out that the qipao was worn, not by working-class women, but rather by aristocratic women during the 250-year rule of the Qing dynasty, which only ended in 1912. They further pointed out that the qipao was, for the greater part of its history, a baggy dress, and that it only became a body-tight dress following Western influence. They also challenged Lam's contention about the cultural significance of the qipao. As Hung Huang, a fashion blogger based in Beijing, put it, "To Chinese, it's not sacred and it's not that meaningful."[44] Writer and broadcaster Anna Chen lambasted Daum's critics for their skewed sense of priorities. "With President Trump and his acolytes pumping up yellow peril fears around China," she said, "the last thing we need is this trivialised pastiche of serious debate."[45] As *New York Times* reporter Amy Qin wrote, "Asians and Asian-Americans do not always see eye to eye," an obvious and deliberate understatement.[46] Something about social media had created a radically different moral sensibility among Asian-Americans.

Nagle refers to this sensibility as "Tumblr liberalism."[47] While this sensibility can be found on other platforms, such as Facebook, Twitter, and Medium, Nagle takes Tumblr to be the paradigm for an online liberal subculture that functions as the diametrical opposite of 4Chan. Whereas 4Chan users celebrate nihilism and the flagrant violation of all norms and principles, Tumblr liberalism is predicated precisely upon the creation and imposition of new norms and principles. Its ostensible moral core is the fight for radical equality and social justice. It goes far beyond conventional thinking about equality by bringing a spotlight to subtle and invisible patterns of power and domination. It draws attention to various forms of privilege. It condemns those actions said to derive from such privilege. It treats these actions as instances of harm and violence. It challenges offenders, witting and unwitting, by calling them out publicly. To protect the weak and vulnerable from harm and violence, it insists upon trigger warnings and safe spaces. Ultimately, it seeks to dismantle identity-based systems of domination, such as patriarchy, white supremacy, heteronormativity, cisnormativity, and the like.

While the fight for radical equality and social justice is all to the good, Nagle observes a telling feature of Tumblr liberalism: its pattern of disregarding *economic* injustice and inequality, and almost exclusively focusing on diversity, identity, and representation. According to the moral logic of the Tumblr universe, offenses like cultural appropriation are far more severe and far more worthy of sanctimonious outrage than, say, the economic policies that led to the financial crash of 2008 or the energy policies responsible for burning up the planet or the criminal justice policies responsible for the new Jim Crow.[48] Without any consideration of the deep, structural roots of injustice, and without any positive and substantive vision of a good society, Tumblr liberalism turns to diversity as an end in itself.

Tumblr describes itself as "a place to express yourself, discover yourself, and bond over the stuff you love."[49] It offers the opportunity to express one's individuality as far as the imagination can take it. The primary medium for this expression is personal identity, and the most common form of this expression is gender and sexual fluidity. While gender and sexual fluidity are nothing new, Tumblr liberalism develops them into a more general fluidity of identity.[50] Perhaps the most exotic and imaginative form of this fluidity is the Otherkin community, those who identify as nonhuman beings.

Some of the most popular forms of Otherkin include elves, orcs, dragons, werewolves, and vampires.[51] Others identify as gods, angels, aliens, and plants. Others still identify as the weather and abstract ideas.[52] Otherkin call for the recognition of Otherkin rights and equality.[53] They employ the language of social justice to critique power and privilege. As one Tumblr user writes, "trans privilege is having sex reassignment surgery be a real thing, while nowhere offers 'species reassignment surgery' for otherkin [*sic*]." Another writes, "My parents don't understand that I'm not always in control of my body. A toddler and a flying dog CANNOT do work intended for an adult human." Yet another user, identifying as a cat, writes, "i would most certainly be denied a job in most if not all places, especially if i meowed."[54] While these comments read like some sort of practical joke, a parody devised by online pranksters, they represent the moral thinking of the Tumblr universe.

Rather than operating as a structural critique of capital, Tumblr liberalism's focus on diversity, identity, and representation operates in tandem with capital. On Tumblr, identity becomes one more consumer product. Users can choose from a dizzying array of identities, just as they might choose from dozens of brands of cereal, toothpaste, and deodorant at the supermarket. If they wish, they can create new identities, which may very well catch on and proliferate online. The very design of Tumblr actively encourages the creation of new identities and new identity-based communities, which represent new target audiences for advertising, Tumblr's primary source of revenue. Identity fluidity is a good business model for Tumblr. In 2013, Yahoo acquired Tumblr for $1.1 billion.[55]

The fetishizing of diversity and the proliferation of identities online has led to a certain paradox. On the one hand, it feeds a psychology of extreme individual fragility and sensitivity, in which the most trivial words and deeds can trigger a dramatic breakdown. On the other hand, it feeds a psychology of reactionary intolerance, in which those same words and deeds can lead to mob violence, as illustrated by the story of Keziah Daum. This paradox is based on exaggerated, distorted, or even fabricated claims of "harm" and "violence." Innocuous actions are often construed as "erasing" this or that identity, a term that carries the moral gravity of the charge of genocide. One Tumblr user, who describes herself as an "unapologetic fat lady," has accused the entire medical system of working to "erase fat people," merely for classifying obesity as a health problem.[56] In a similar vein, Danish comedian Sofie Hagen launched a Twitter campaign against Cancer Research UK, a prominent cancer awareness charity, for the offense of raising public awareness about the proven link between obesity and cancer. Prompted by Hagen, thousands of Twitter users accused Cancer Research UK of fatshaming, calling for an immediate end to their public awareness campaign.[57]

In his essay, "Exiting the Vampire Castle," the late cultural critic Mark Fisher provides a dark and sobering look at the habit of throwing around wild and irresponsible accusations online and destroying the lives and reputations of others.[58] Fisher uses the "vampire castle" as a metaphor for the noxious phenomenon of online call-out culture. In the vampire castle, says Fisher, "moralism is everywhere . . . solidarity is impossible, but guilt and fear are omnipresent." The central feature of the vampire castle is the propagation of guilt. As Fisher puts it, the vampire castle "is driven by a *priest's desire* to excommunicate and condemn, an *academic-pedant's desire* to be the first to be seen to spot a mistake, and a *hipster's desire* to be one of the in-crowd." Fisher sees liberal identity politics as an apologia for capitalism and the existing class hierarchy. Liberal identity politics protects private wealth and class privilege while masquerading as radical and subversive. Fisher sees the vampire castle as a quasi-religious institution, governed by an elite class of priests who wield manipulative power in the form of "infernal strategies, dark pathologies, and psychological torture instruments," which are designed to crush laypeople into submission. "This priesthood of bad conscience, this nest of pious guilt-mongers," says Fisher, "is exactly what Nietzsche predicted when he said that something worse than Christianity was already on the way."

Nagle sees Tumblr liberalism, not as a quest for equality and social justice, but rather as a liberal competition for social capital. In the moral universe of Tumblr liberalism, social capital is unevenly distributed, in effect creating a hierarchical social world. At the bottom of the hierarchy, by default, are white, straight, cisgender, able-bodied men. Depending upon one's identity, one can hold a higher rank within the hierarchy. Thus, a woman of color automatically holds more social capital than a bottom-rung white man. But a queer and disabled woman of color holds even more social capital. Nagle points out a peculiar feature of the Tumblr universe: the possibility of rising through the ranks, either by becoming marginalized or by calling out the moral infractions of others through public displays of sanctimonious condemnation—in a word, by becoming a vampire.

From its inception, social media have provided the opportunity to build a public reputation and to achieve instant fame by publicly calling out racism, sexism, and homophobia. It was not long until more enterprising and entrepreneurial individuals realized the potential of capitalizing upon unrecognized forms of marginality, inventing new moral offenses, coining new terms for those offenses, and becoming the first to call them out online. This moral entrepreneurialism has proven to be an effective means of establishing social capital in the universe of Tumblr liberalism. Those who put on brazen displays of liberal virtue can build truly massive followings online. With those followings comes real power—the power to affect the lives of others, sometimes for the better, often for the worse.

Nagle points out an obvious problem in this "liberal economy of virtue": there is only so much social capital to go around.[59] If everyone wears the badge of virtuous wokeness, it loses its value. Hence, the fierce competition to be woker than woke, reading into evermore trivial details to extract evermore exaggerated claims of harm and violence, and calling them out through evermore dramatic performances of anger and outrage. This explains the penchant on the part of certain rapacious Tumblr liberals to go after sympathetic and like-minded members of the community, finding fault in their innocuous words and deeds, subjecting them to the ritual of public shaming, tarring, and feathering, forcing them to admit their guilt, and severely demoting them in social rank, while of course promoting themselves. The competition for status has two disastrous effects. First, as Briahna Joy Gray has forcefully argued, it silences Left voices of color who critique popular liberal politicians like Barack Obama and Kamala Harris. It thus ironically becomes a medium of racism.[60] Second, it leads to the sad tendency toward Left cannibalism—when progressives eat their own kind. One of the most noteworthy recent examples of this destructive phenomenon is the infamous *Hypatia* controversy.

In March 2017, Rebecca Tuvel, an untenured assistant professor of philosophy at Rhodes College published her essay, "In Defense of Transracialism" in the feminist philosophy journal *Hypatia*.[61] Tuvel had noticed a discrepancy between the public reactions to Rachel Dolezal, the former head of the Spokane chapter of the NAACP, and Caitlyn Jenner, the American decathlete and reality TV star. After Dolezal's parents outed her as a white woman passing as black, she was forced to resign from her position as NAACP chapter head. By contrast, after coming out as a woman, Jenner graced the cover of *Vanity Fair* and received a standing ovation at the 2015 ESPY awards ceremony. Using the stories of Dolezal and Jenner as a case study, Tuvel argued in favor of a more expansive and fluid understanding of personal identity. Without passing judgment on the Dolezal case, she defended both gender and racial transitions, arguing that the logic of the one applied to the other. She further argued that objections to the very idea of racial transition follow the same essentialist logic as objections to the idea of gender transition. Speaking about the hypothetical case of an individual who decides to change race, Tuvel concludes by saying that society "should accept such an individual's decision to change race the same way it should accept an individual's decision to change sex."[62]

The reaction to Tuvel's article within the scholarly community is one of the strangest moments in modern academic history. Hundreds of faculty members signed an online letter to protest the publication of Tuvel's article. The letter accused Tuvel of causing harm. It called for the article's retraction, stating that its "continued availability" caused "further harm." It insisted that any suggestion about the article's potential to provoke public discussion caused more harm still. It decried "a failure in the review process," which it attributed to an inability on the part of the journal to engage "beyond white and cisgender privilege."[63] The letter identified the article's more serious offenses, such as the use of the term "transgenderism," the deadnaming of Caitlyn Jenner (the act of referring to trans individuals by their former names), and the failure to consult the work of women of color. The letter rapidly circulated through social media, garnering over eight hundred signatures, including from some of the most prominent feminist scholars in the world. Shortly after the letter was posted, a group of associate editors for *Hypatia* expressed regret that the article had been published. They issued a public apology to various marginalized groups. They blamed the review process and agreed that the article should be retracted. In essence, they performed an act of self-flagellation.

The response on social media was even less forgiving. Tuvel's article was called "whack shit," "crap," "offensive," and "violent." Tuvel herself was called "transphobic," "racist," "crazy," and "stupid."[64] Tuvel reports that several of her respected feminist colleagues began referring to her as "Becky," a derogatory term in Black Vernacular English for clueless and sexually promiscuous white women who freely perform fellatio.[65] One popular post on Facebook, which has since been removed, criticized Tuvel for using phrases like "biological sex" and "male genitalia," and charged her with "egregious levels of liberal white ignorance and discursive transmisogynistic violence."[66]

The backlash did not end there. Several of Tuvel's more senior feminist colleagues began pressuring her to retract her article, issuing veiled threats that she would not receive tenure otherwise and that her reputation would be destroyed. Some even hinted that they knew "the right people," those who would ensure that her path to tenure would be blocked.[67] The irony of senior feminist scholars actively threatening to destroy the career of a young and untenured feminist scholar working in the male-dominated discipline of philosophy appears to have been lost upon Tuvel's critics. For her part, Tuvel disclosed that she had endured emotional and psychological torment from being harassed, bullied, threatened, mocked, shamed, and humiliated online.[68]

In an essay titled, "If This is Feminism...," philosopher Kelly Oliver, Tuvel's friend and dissertation supervisor, revealed a glaring tension between the private and public lives of her feminist colleagues.[69] Several of those colleagues privately confessed to Oliver that they sympathized with Tuvel's position, but that they dared not confront her critics online, lest they be subjected to the same wrath. Others wrote to Tuvel privately, reassuring her that her article was *not* guilty of the moral offenses for which she was being shamed on social media.

Even more revealing, some chose to support Tuvel in private while attacking her in public. They sent Tuvel warm and sympathetic emails, even as they joined the angry chorus on social media. "Part of the problem," Oliver wrote, "is that some seem to feel that they are the only ones who have the legitimate right to talk about certain topics." She described the affair as "identity politics run amok" and an "academic turf war." The opportunism exhibited by Tuvel's critics revealed "a kind of academic Selfie culture where all we can do is take pictures of ourselves and never consider the lives of others."[70] She also pointed out the problem of accusing Tuvel of deadnaming, when Jenner herself, a public figure, refers to her former name in her memoir. Worse, some who joined the online condemnation privately admitted that they had no idea what deadnaming was prior to the online condemnation.[71]

But perhaps the most revealing part of the *Hypatia* controversy is the selective outrage of Tuvel's critics. Just two years before the *Hypatia* controversy, University of Pennsylvania political scientist Adolph Reed made more or less the same argument as Tuvel, but with much more direct and acerbic language. Applying a dialectical critique to popular commentary affirming the reality of transgender identities while denying the reality of transracial identities, Reed asserted, "The transrace/transgender comparison makes clear the conceptual emptiness of the essentializing discourses, and the opportunist politics, that undergird identitarian ideologies." He further asserted, "There is no coherent, principled defense of the stance that transgender identity is legitimate but transracial is not, at least not one that would satisfy basic rules of argument."[72] Reed, who is black, was spared the venom directed at Tuvel, despite adopting a harsh tone toward critics of the idea of transracial identities.

It is difficult to imagine something like the *Hypatia* controversy taking place before the age of social media. It is difficult to imagine the accusations, the condemnations, the outrage, the childish name-calling, and the repeated threats to destroy a young scholar's life—all for an argument in favor of identity fluidity—prior to the age of Facebook, Twitter, and Tumblr. The *Hypatia* controversy illustrates the degree to which social media and Tumblr liberalism have colonized even the thought and speech of the academic community. It is also a confirmation of Fisher's and Nagle's observations concerning the sad state of progressive politics today. For while liberal academics were busy bullying a young feminist philosopher committed to social justice, the Alt-Right was busy sowing the seeds for a white nationalist revolt.

In May 2017, Richard Spencer organized a rally to protest plans by the city of Charlottesville, Virginia, to remove the statue of Robert E. Lee from Emancipation Park. One month later, the Ku Klux Klan organized another rally, also in the defense of the statue. On August 11, 2017, the Alt-Right, the Klan, the neo-Confederate League of the South, and several neo-Nazi organizations joined forces to hold the "Unite the Right Rally" in Charlottesville. Hundreds of white nationalists gathered at Emancipation Park holding torches and chanting Nazi slogans like "Blood and soil," "Jew will not replace us," and "Sieg Heil." They shouted their pride in white identity and openly called for the ethnic cleansing of Jews and Muslims.[73] The following day, hundreds of counter-protestors condemned the "Unite the Right Rally" and declared their opposition to white nationalism.[74] Since Gamergate, the Alt-Right had morphed from anti-feminist trolls into militant white nationalists. At Charlottesville, they found the opportunity to become in person what they had been online.[75] They dressed up in battle gear and instigated physical altercations with minorities and counter-protestors, leaving some of them severely injured. By early afternoon, James Alex Fields, a young Nazi sympathizer, drove his car into a crowd of counter-protestors, leaving several of them injured. One of the counter-protestors, Heather Heyer, was rushed to a hospital. She was later pronounced dead.[76]

Conclusion

In the final remarks of *After Virtue*, MacIntyre drew certain parallels between the European Dark Ages and the state of Western democracies today. One of those parallels was the threat posed to civility and to moral community by the reigning political order. MacIntyre warned that, just as civility fell victim to the decline and fall of the Roman Empire, civility today might not survive "the coming ages of barbarism and darkness." But this time, he said, "the barbarians are not waiting beyond the frontiers; they have already been governing us for quite some time."[77] MacIntyre had the acute meta-historical insight to diagnose a general cultural crisis and trace the historical and philosophical roots of that crisis. His prophetic remarks about the "coming ages of barbarism and darkness" have proven to be terrifyingly accurate. When online bullies increasingly shape our public discourse, and when even university professors resort to name-calling, mass shaming, and threats, we are at risk of losing the very possibility of civil discourse.

Kelly Oliver provides a powerful confirmation of MacIntyre's prophetic remarks about the barbarians of the new dark ages. She writes:

> We live in an era of outrage—let's call it the Trump era. That's how Trump got elected, by voicing outrage. His most ardent disciples uncritically and unthinkingly believe everything he says because it is expressed with anger and zest. Civility is suspected of being "political," which has become a dirty word. It's hard to argue with outrage, and that's precisely the problem. *Outrage has become the new truth.* At one extreme, we have Trump and his supporters proudly embracing political incorrectness, and at the other, we have the political correctness police calling for censorship of a scholarly article written by someone working for social justice. On both sides, we have virulent intolerance fueled by hatred. The feminist thought police are the flip side of the alternative facts machine. And both are threats to

the open dialogue that is so vital for critical thought inside and outside the academy.[78]

Oliver brilliantly captures the nature of emotivism in the age of social media: the obliteration of the distinction between truth and outrage. For the Alt-Right, this obliteration takes the form of acts of transgression. For Tumblr liberals, it takes the form of acts of repression. Despite their ideological differences, both sides are cultivating a new type of creature, the troll. A parasite on the culture of democracy, the troll is the antithesis of civility. In the age of social media, the troll has become something even more: a new character in the social drama of our age.[79]

Notes

1 Allan Bloom, *The Closing of the American Mind: How Higher Education Has Failed Democracy and Impoverished the Souls of Today's Students*. New York, NY: Simon & Schuster, 1987.

2 Roger Kimball, *Tenured Radicals: How Politics Has Corrupted Our Higher Education*. Chicago, IL: Ivan R. Dee, 1990.

3 Dinesh D'Souza, *Illiberal Education: The Politics of Race and Sex on Campus*. New York, NY: The Free Press. 1991.

4 Richard J. Herrnstein and Charles Murray. *The Bell Curve: Intelligence and Class Structure in American Life*. New York, NY: The Free Press, 1994. In recent years, *The Bell Curve* has been undergoing something of a revival. Sam Harris interviewed Murray for his podcast, thereby helping to revive Murray's noxious ideas. Unfortunately, those ideas are informing government policymaking. Congressman Paul Ryan recently cited Murray as an expert on poverty. See Gavin Evans, "The Unwelcome Revival of 'race science,'" *The Guardian*, March 2, 2018. https://www.theguardian.com/news/2018/mar/02/the-unwelcome-revival-of-race-science (accessed January 14, 2019). Somehow, the revival of *The Bell Curve* has managed to circumvent Stephen Jay Gould's classic critique, as if it never existed. Stephen Jay Gould, "Critique of the Bell Curve," in *The Mismeasure of Man*. New York, NY: Norton, 1996, 367–90.

5 On the history of conservative think tanks in America, see Jason Stahl, *Right Moves: The Conservative Think Tank in American Political Culture since 1945*. Raleigh, NC: University of North Carolina Press, 2018. See also Jean Stefancic and Richard Delgado, *No Mercy: How Conservative Think Tanks and Foundations Changed America's Social Agenda*. Philadelphia, PA: Temple University Press, 1996.

6   Liam Stack, "How the 'War on Christmas' Controversy Was Created," *The New York Times*.

7   For good overviews of the influence of conservative rhetoric and media on American society, politics, and democracy, see Yochai Benkler, Robert Faris, and Hal Roberts, *Network Propaganda: Manipulation, Disinformation, and Radicalization in American Politics*. Oxford, UK: Oxford University Press, 2018; David Brock, *The Republican Noise Machine: Right-Wing Media and How It Corrupts Democracy*. New York, NY: Three Rivers Press; Kathleen Hall Jamieson and Joseph N. Capella, *Echo Chamber: Rush Limbaugh and the Conservative Media Establishment*. Oxford, UK: Oxford University Press, 2008; Nichole Hemmer, *Messengers of the Right: Conservative Media and the Transformation of American Politics*. Philadelphia, PA: University of Pennsylvania Press, 2016; Mark A. Smith, *The Right Talk: How Conservatives Transformed the Great Society into the Economic Society*. Princeton, NJ: Princeton University Press, 2007.

8   http://www.cc.com/episodes/nrbd8n/the-daily-show-with-jon-stewart-june-6--2006---bill-bennett-season-11-ep-11069 (accessed January 14, 2019).

9   Nancy Fraser, *Fortunes of Feminism: From State-Managed Capitalism to Neoliberal Crisis*. London, UK: Verso, 2013.

10 Amy Gluckman and Betsy Reed, eds. *Homo Economics: Capitalism, Community, and Lesbian and Gay Life*. New York, NY: Routledge, 1997.

11 Yarma Velásquez Vargas, *A Queer Eye for Capitalism: The Commodification of Sexuality in American Television*. Newcastle Upon Tyne, UK: Cambridge Scholars Press, 2010, 13–14.

12 Gary Younge, "'Skinny kid with a funny name' Reshapes US Politics," *The Guardian*. https://www.theguardian.com/world/2008/jan/05/barackobama.uselections20081 (accessed January 14, 2019).

13 Adolph Reed, "Obama No," *The Progressive*, April 28, 2008. https://progressive.org/magazine/obama/ (accessed January 14, 2019).

14 Ibid.

15 Angela Nagle, *Kill All Normies: Online Culture Wars from 4Chan and Tumblr To Trump and the Alt-Right*. Alresford, UK: Zero Books, 2017.

16 As one deplorable example of the fanatical quest to recognize marginal subjects, *Salon* published an article by a self-professed pedophile, who argued that society had judged him unfairly. *Salon* deleted the article after Milo Yiannapolous became embroiled in controversy for defending sex with minors. See Jesse Singal, "Salon Shouldn't Have Unpublished Its Article by a Pedophile Author," February 22, 2017, https://www.thecut.com/2017/02/salon-shouldnt-have-unpublished-its-pedophilia-article.html (accessed April 7, 2019).

17 Gabriella Coleman, *Hacker, Hoaxer, Whistleblower, Spy: The Many Faces of Anonymous*. London, UK: Verso, 2014.

18 Keith Stuart, "Zoe Quinn: 'All Gamergate has done is ruin people's lives,'" *The Guardian*, December 3, 2014. https://www.theguardian.com/technology/2014/dec/03/zoe-quinn-gamergate-interview (accessed January 14, 2019).

19 Zoe Quinn, *Crash Override: How Gamergate (Nearly) Destroyed My Life, and How We Can Win the Fight against Online Hate*. New York, NY: PublicAffairs, 2017.

20 Zaid Jilani, "Gamergate's Fickle Hero: The Dark Opportunism of Breitbart's Milo Yiannopoulos," *Salon*, October 29, 2019. https://www.salon.com/2014/10/28/gamergates_fickle_hero_the_dark_opportunism_of_breitbarts_milo_yiannopoulos/ (accessed January 14, 2019).

21 Ann Coulter, *Treason: Liberal Treachery from the Cold War to the War on Terrorism*. New York, NY: Three Rivers Press, 2003.

22 Milo Yiannapolous, *Dangerous*. Boca Raton, FL: Dangerous Books, 2017.

23 Joel Stein, "Milo Yiannapolous Is the Pretty, Monstrous Face of the Alt-Right: A Few Force in Electoral Politics," *Bloomberg*, September 15, 2016. https://www.bloomberg.com/features/2016-america-divided/milo-yiannopoulos/ (accessed January 14, 2019).

24 Eric Bradner, "Alt-Right Leader: 'Hail Trump! Hail Our People! Hail Victory!'" *CNN*, November 22, 2016. https://www.cnn.com/2016/11/21/politics/alt-right-gathering-donald-trump/index.html (accessed January 14, 2019).

25 Liam Stack, "Who Is Mike Cernovich? A Guide," *The New York Times*, April 5, 2017. https://www.nytimes.com/2017/04/05/us/politics/mike-cernovich-bio-who.html (accessed January 14, 2019). As of this writing, Cernovich has reportedly converted to Islam: https://twitter.com/Cernovich/status/1111797298038595584 (accessed April 7, 2019).

26 Daniel Kreps, "Sandy Hook Shooting Victims' Families Win Legal Victory against Alex Jones, InfoWars," *Rolling Stone*, January 11, 2019. https://www.rollingstone.com/culture/culture-news/sandy-hook-shooting-victims-families-legal-victory-alex-jones-infowars-778032/ (accessed January 14, 2019).

27 Alex Hern, "Facebook, Apple, YouTube and Spotify Ban Infowars' Alex Jones," *The Guardian*, August 6, 2018. https://www.theguardian.com/technology/2018/aug/06/apple-removes-podcasts-infowars-alex-jones (accessed January 14, 2019).

28 Allum Bokhari and Milo Yiannapolous, "An Establishment Conservative's Guide to the Alt-Right," *Breitbart*, March 29, 2016. https://www.breitbart.com/tech/2016/03/29/an-establishment-conservatives-guide-to-the-alt-right/ (accessed January 14, 2019).

29 Patrick J. Buchanan, *The Death of the West: How Dying Populations and Immigrant Invasions Imperil Our Country and Our Civilization*. New York, NY: Thomas Dunn Books, 2002.

30 Bokhari and Yiannapolous, "An Establishment Conservative's Guide to the Alt-Right."

31 Jessica Roy, "How 'Pepe the Frog' Went from Harmless to Hate Symbol," *LA Times*, October 11, 2016. https://www.latimes.com/politics/la-na-pol-pepe-the-frog-hate-symbol-20161011-snap-htmlstory.html (accessed April 7, 2019).

32 Ibid.

33 On the idiosyncratic meaning of the "lulz," see Coleman, *Hacker, Hoaxer, Whistleblower, Spy*, 31–33.

34 Nagle, *Kill All Normies*, 28–39.

35 Ibid., 36. See also Mikhail Bakhtin, *Rabelais and His World*, translated by Hélène Iswolsky. Bloomington, IN: Indiana University Press, 1984, 15, 104, 219, 257.

36 Dan Lieberman, "Milo Yiannopoulos Is Trying to Convince Colleges That Hate Speech Is Cool," *CNN*, February 2, 2017.

37 Corey Robin, *The Reactionary Mind: Conservatism from Edmund Burke to Donald Trump*, 2nd edn. Oxford, UK: Oxford University Press, 2017.

38 Oliver Darcy, "Behind the Anonymous Twitter Account That Took Down Milo Yiannopoulos," *Business Insider*, February 23, 2017. https://www.businessinsider.com/milo-yiannopoulos-reagan-battalion-anonymous-twitter-2017-2 (accessed January 14, 2019).

39 Danuta Kean, "Milo Yiannopoulos to Self-Publish Memoir and Sue Simon & Schuster," *The Guardian*, May 8, 2017. https://www.theguardian.com/books/2017/may/08/milo-yiannopoulos-to-self-publish-memoir-and-sue-simon-schuster (accessed January 14, 2019).

40 Charlie May, "The Fall of Milo: Breitbart's Former Star Is Now Hawking Supplements on Infowars," *Salon*, February 21, 2018. https://www.salon.com/2018/02/21/the-fall-of-milo-breitbarts-former-star-is-now-hawking-supplements-on-infowars/ (accessed January 14, 2019).

41 Taylor Link, "Milo Yiannopoulos Attacks His Fans for Failing to Support Him Emotionally and Financially," *Salon*, August 26, 2018. https://www.salon.com/2018/08/26/milo-yiannopoulos-attacks-his-fans-for-failing-to-support-him-emotionally-and-financially/ (accessed January 14, 2019).

42 Jason Wilson, "Milo Yiannopoulos 'more than $2m in debt', Australian Promoters' Documents Show," *The Guardian*, December 3, 2018. https://www.theguardian.com/australia-news/2018/dec/03/milo-yiannopoulos-more-than-2m-in-debt-australian-promoters-documents-show (accessed January 14, 2019).

43 Chris Bell, "Prom Dress Prompts 'cultural appropriation' Row," *BBC*, May 1, 2018. https://www.bbc.com/news/blogs-trending-43947959 (accessed January 14, 2019).

44 Amy Qin, "Teenager's Prom Dress Stirs Furor in U.S.—But Not in China," *The New York Times*, May 2, 2018. https://www.nytimes.com/2018/05/02/world/asia/chinese-prom-dress.html (accessed January 14, 2019).

45 Anna Chen, "An American Woman Wearing a Chinese Dress Is Not Cultural Appropriation," *The Guardian*, May 4, 2018. https://www.theguardian.com/commentisfree/2018/may/04/american-woman-qipao-china-cultural-appropriation-minorities-usa-dress (accessed January 14, 2019).

46 Amy Qin, "Teenager's Prom Dress Stirs Furor in U.S."

47 Nagle, *Kill All Normies*, 69.

48 Michelle Alexander, *The New Jim Crow: Mass Incarceration in the Age of Colorblindness*. New York, NY: The New Press.

49 www.tumblr.com (accessed January 14, 2019).

50 In *Gender Trouble*, Judith Butler describes the "fluidity of identities." Analyzing the notion of gender parody, she writes, "To be more precise, it is a production which, in effect—that is, in its effect—postures as an imitation. This perpetual displacement constitutes a fluidity of identities that suggests an openness to resignfication and recontextualization."

51 "Why Be Human When You Can Be Otherkin?" *Cambridge University*, https://www.cam.ac.uk/research/features/why-be-human-when-you-can-be-otherkin (accessed January 14, 2019).

52 Callie Beausman, "'I Look at a Cloud and I See It as Me': The People Who Identify as Objects," *Vice*, August 3, 2016. https://broadly.vice.com/en_us/article/zmbeae/i-look-at-a-cloud-and-i-see-it-as-me-the-people-who-identify-as-objects (accessed January 14, 2019).

53 Amber Roberts, "Otherkin Are People Too; They Just Identify as Nonhuman," *Vice*, July 16, 2015. https://www.vice.com/en_ca/article/mvxgwa/from-dragons-to-foxes-the-otherkin-community-believes-you-can-be-whatever-you-want-to-be (accessed January 14, 2019).

54 Max Read, "From Otherkin to Transethnicity: Your Field Guide to the Weird World of Tumblr Identity Politics," *Gawker*, September 6, 2012. https://gawker.com/5940947/from-otherkin-to-transethnicity-your-field-guide-to-the-weird-world-of-tumblr-identity-politics (accessed January 14, 2019).

55 Michael J. de la Merced, Nick Bilton, and Nicole Perlroth, "Yahoo to Buy Tumblr for $1.1 Billion," *The New York Times*, May 19, 2003. https://www.nytimes.com/2013/05/20/technology/yahoo-to-buy-tumblr-for-1-1-billion.html (accessed January 14, 2019).

56 Kelley Calkins, "Amanda Levitt: Fat Activist, Researcher," *Ravishly*, December 3, 2014. https://ravishly.com/ladies-we-love/amanda-levitt-fat-activist-researcher (accessed January 14, 2019).

57 Helena Horton, "Award-Winning Comedian Accuses Cancer Research of 'fat-shaming' for Launching Campaign against Obesity," *The Telegraph*, March 1, 2008. https://www.telegraph.co.uk/news/2018/03/01/award-winning-comedian-accuses-cancer-research-fat-shaming-launching/ (accessed January 14, 2019).

58 Mark Fisher, "Exiting the Vampire Castle," *OpenDemocracyUK*, November 24, 2013. https://www.opendemocracy.net/ourkingdom/mark-fisher/exiting-vampire-castle (accessed January 14, 2019).

59 Nagle, *Kill All Normies*, 68.

60 Briahna Joy Gray, "How Identity Became a Weapon against the Left," *Current Affairs*, September 2017. https://www.currentaffairs.org/2017/09/how-identity-became-a-weapon-against-the-left (accessed January 14, 2019).

61 Rebecca Tuvel, "In Defense of Transracialism," *Hypatia* 32.2 (2017): 263–78.

62 Ibid., 275.

63 Jennifer Schuessler, "A Defense of 'Transracial' Identity Roils Philosophy World," *The New York Times*, May 19, 2017. https://www.nytimes.com/2017/05/19/arts/a-defense-of-transracial-identity-roils-philosophy-world.html (accessed January 14, 2019).

64 Kelly Oliver, "If This Is Feminism…," *The Philosophical Salon*, May 8, 2017. https://thephilosophicalsalon.com/if-this-is-feminism-its-been-hijacked-by-the-thought-police/ (accessed January 14, 2019).

65 Rebecca Tuvel, "Racial Transitions and Controversial Positions: Reply to Taylor, Gordon, Sealey, Hom, and Botts," *Philosophy Today* 62.1 (Winter 2018): 74.

66 Scheussler, "A Defense of 'Transracial' Identity Roils Philosophy World."

67 Oliver, "If This Is Feminism…"

68 Tuvel, "Racial Transitions and Controversial Positions," 74.

69 Oliver, "If This Is Feminism…"

70 Ibid.

71 Ibid.

72 Adolph Reed Jr. "From Jenner to Dolezal: One Trans Good, the Other Not So Much," *Common Dreams*, June 15, 2015. https://www.commondreams.org/views/2015/06/15/jenner-dolezal-one-trans-good-other-not-so-much (accessed January 14, 2019).

73 Hawes Spencer and Sheryl Gay Stolberg, "White Nationalists March on University of Virginia," *The New York Times*, August 11, 2017. https://www.nytimes.com/2017/08/11/us/white-nationalists-rally-charlottesville-virginia.html (accessed January 14, 2019).

74 Farah Stockman, "Who Were the Counterprotesters in Charlottesville?" *The New York Times*, August 14, 2017. https://www.nytimes.com/2017/08/14/us/who-were-the-counterprotesters-in-charlottesville.html (accessed January 14, 2019).

75 On this phenomenon, see Richard Raber and Francesco Fanti Rovetta, "Global Connectivity and Personal Disconnect: Filter Bubbles and the Collapse of Public Discourse," *Open Democracy*, May 24, 2017. https://www.opendemocracy.net/en/richard-raber-francesco-fanti-rovetta/ (accessed April 4, 2019).

76 Lois Beckett, "Charlottesville Suspect Goes on Trial for Murder," *The Guardian*, November 26, 2018. https://www.theguardian.com/us-news/2018/nov/26/charlottesville-car-attacker-trial-murder-kames-alex-fields-heather-heyer (accessed January 14, 2019).

77 MacIntyre, *After Virtue*, 263.

78 Oliver, "If This Is Feminism…" (emphasis added).

79 Hannan, "Trolling Ourselves to Death."

4

Why Not Deliberative Democracy?

This chapter explores the merits of deliberative democracy as a possible answer to the culture wars. It concentrates on the two most prominent theorists of deliberative democracy: John Rawls and Jürgen Habermas.[1] While there is much to respect and admire in their thought, there is also much to critique. Like MacIntyre, Rawls and Habermas uphold a rationalist politics. Unlike MacIntyre, they both propose formal and universal procedures for deliberation. In this chapter, I argue that deliberative democracy as formulated by Rawls and Habermas risks becoming a form of unjustified power and domination. In what follows, I first provide a brief overview of the idea of deliberative democracy. I then review the deliberative theories of Rawls and Habermas respectively. Next, I consider a case study: the Māori argument for the personhood of the Whanganui River. In the light of this case study, I draw from MacIntyre to show that Rawls and Habermas, far from providing a neutral basis for rational arbitration, betray a Eurocentric bias.

The idea of deliberative democracy

Democracy is a fraught idea. Rule by the demos comes in many forms. The two most familiar to us are the liberal and republican models of democracy.[2]

The liberal model, with roots in John Locke, conceives of democracy in market terms. On the liberal view, democracy lacks a substantive moral core. The aim of government is merely to cater to the most powerful voting blocks, each composed of private individuals pursuing their idiosyncratic interests. Liberal democracy moves and sways, sometimes smoothly, often turbulently, with the whims of majority opinion. Conflicts of public opinion are decided by the power of the vote. Political legitimacy is not a matter of right or wrong, better or worse, but rather of sheer numbers. As in the marketplace, liberal democracy is a numbers game.

By contrast, the republican model, with roots in Aristotle, Machiavelli, and Rousseau, posits a substantive moral core. On the republican model, national identity and unity are based on shared traditions and values. Conflicts of public opinion are decided through public reasoning, but with shared traditions and values serving as the neutral court of appeal. Republicanism conceives of freedom through norms.[3] Political legitimacy is determined, not by numbers, but rather by reasoned appeals to an established conception of the common good. It therefore avoids the oscillations and vacillations of public opinion, maintaining a fundamental stability and continuity.

The liberal and republican models provoke a familiar set of criticisms. The liberal model, by basing legitimacy on numbers, is liable to regress into the tyranny of the majority. While this concern has often been expressed by elites about the unruly and unwashed masses, it is also the concern of oppressed minorities about intolerant majorities. On the other hand, the republican model, by basing legitimacy on shared traditions and values, excludes those who do not share those traditions and values, who even object to those traditions and values on principled grounds. Both the liberal and republican models run the risk of devolving into unjustified power and domination. How to avoid this risk?

In recent decades, deliberative democracy has emerged as a promising alternative to the liberal and republican models.[4] At its core, deliberative democracy rests on the idea that political legitimacy is based on rational deliberation between citizens. If liberal democracy locates political legitimacy in numbers, and if republican democracy locates it in shared traditions and values, then deliberative democracy locates political legitimacy in communication. On this view, communication takes priority. Legitimate laws and policies are something to be talked out, not imposed from on high, and they must be talked out on fair terms, terms that do not arbitrarily privilege some political actors over others. The deliberative model can be understood as a fundamental advancement upon Kant's conception of public reason by moving from monological to dialogical deliberation.[5] Both Rawls and Habermas propose deliberative procedures for rational arbitration in a diverse society.

Rawls: Justice as fairness

Rawls is, without question, the most influential political philosopher of the postwar era. Beginning with his initial essay, "Justice as Fairness" (1958), and then with his landmark book, *A Theory of Justice* (1971), Rawls revolutionized moral and political philosophy, in effect making the academic study of justice what it is today.[6] He inspired a generation of political theorists who have either built on his theory or who have sought to revise its weaker components. Rawls also inspired numerous critics—some sympathetic, others hostile—from various schools of thought: libertarianism,[7] communitarianism,[8] feminism,[9] and Marxism.[10] Indeed, Rawls' critics define their own political theory against his. It is therefore a testament to the power of his thinking that more than half a century after first introducing his theory of justice, John Rawls remains *the* political philosopher to be reckoned with.

Rawls begins *A Theory of Justice* with a general description of what he takes to be our most basic moral instincts. "Justice," he says, "is the first virtue of social institutions."[11] At its most basic, justice concerns the political structure of society. If this structure is sound, then society is just. Rawls then says, "Each person possesses an inviolability founded on justice that even the welfare of society cannot override."[12] The structure of society, then, is not an end in itself, but rather the means through which we exercise basic rights, liberties, and freedoms. While many things might in everyday language be said to be *just* or *unjust*, Rawls is explicit that "the primary subject of justice is the basic structure of society, or more exactly, the way in which the major social institutions distribute the fundamental rights and duties and determine the division of advantages from social cooperation."[13]

This raises two key questions. The first concerns these "major social institutions." Rawls divides these institutions into "the political constitution and the principal economic and social arrangements."[14] These arrangements include "the legal protection of freedom of thought and liberty of conscience, competitive markets, private property in the means of production, and the monogamous family."[15] Because these institutions determine an individual's basic rights—the kind of life one may live, and whether one succeeds or fails in pursuing one's goals and dreams—they are a potential source of "deep inequalities."[16] Taken together, they form a large-scale social structure whose specific distribution of rights, duties, and opportunities determine the degree of justice or injustice of a political society.

A second question concerns the core criterion of justice that would enable us to determine whether a political society is just or unjust. Situating himself in the social contract tradition of Locke, Rousseau, and Kant, Rawls states that the principles underlying a political society of "free and rational persons"—the principles that would regulate social relationships and determine what type of government they could create together—can best be understood by the idea of justice as fairness.[17] What, then, does fairness denote?

Rawls asks us to imagine a hypothetical founding moment in the birth of an ideal political society, in which these "free and rational persons" collectively decide from the beginning a set of basic principles by which to govern themselves. Through a process of rational deliberation, the participants in this hypothetical founding moment would converge upon those principles by which all later generations could handily differentiate the just from the unjust. Rawls refers to this imaginary moment as "the original position of equality."[18] The idea is that fairness from the beginning will ensure fairness to the end. The original position would guide the future course of the new political society. But how do we really know that these founding figures would select genuine principles of fairness? How do we know they would not select principles out of a selfish desire for personal gain?

The second part of this imaginary scenario is what Rawls terms "the veil of ignorance."[19] We are to imagine that the founding figures have no knowledge of such personal details as class position, social status, natural strengths and abilities, IQ, life plans, and individual psychology or personality. They also lack knowledge of the state of the economy and of political history. They have no idea if they belong to an older or younger generation. They have no information about the condition of the environment and what forms of conservation are needed to protect it. In short, they know nothing about anything that might set them at odds with each other. They have been so thoroughly stripped, not only of body but also of personality, that all that is left is pure intentionality. Through the veil of ignorance, these disembodied and depersonalized beings find themselves forced to select principles they could live with regardless of what their individual lives might look like once the veil of ignorance is lifted.

We therefore have a better idea of what Rawls intends by the concept of fairness: an equality of rights and opportunities. But which rights? What kind of equality? Rawls is explicit about the exclusive nature of his conception of equality. "Obviously," he says, "the purpose of these conditions is to represent equality between human beings as moral persons, as creatures having a conception of their good and capable of a sense of justice."[20] Only those who possess the cognitive capacity to think about justice, and therefore the moral capacity to feel indignant in the face of injustice, can be said to be subjects of justice. This much becomes even more explicit in the two core principles that supposedly derive from the original position:

> First: each person is to have an equal right to the most extensive scheme of equal basic liberties compatible with a similar scheme of liberties for others.

Second: social and economic inequalities are to be arranged so that they are both (a) reasonably expected to be to everyone's advantage, and (b) attached to positions and offices open to all.[21]

It is on the basis of these two principles that the institutions of society would be selected. Rawls's ordering of the two principles is deliberate, denoting the priority of individual liberties over all else. It is also clear that the focus of justice is the basic structure of society. Justice is essentially about institutions. If the institutions are chosen fairly, and if they uphold fairness after the fact, then a society may be said to be just. In the light of this conception of justice, we would then be able to identify specific instances of injustice in a given society.

It is worth mentioning the nature of the conceptual tools Rawls uses to ensure fairness. Contracts are agreements reached through discourse and communication. The very idea of a social contract is meaningless if it is the product of unilateral declaration. For this reason, Rawls likens the original position to a neutral referee arbitrating between different parties engaged in communication:

> We can view the choice in the original position from the standpoint of one person selected at random. If anyone after due reflection prefers a conception of justice to another, then they all do, and a unanimous agreement can be reached. We can, to make the circumstances more vivid, *imagine that the parties are required to communicate with each other through a referee as intermediary*, and that he is to announce which alternatives have been suggested and the reasons offered in their support. He forbids the attempt to form coalitions, and he informs the parties when they have come to an understanding. *But such a referee is actually superfluous, assuming that the deliberations of the parties must be similar.*[22]

The superfluity of an actual referee denotes the superfluity of communication itself. The original position does not require communication for deciding the foundations of justice. Reasoning in the original position is a monological activity through and through. What, then, about ethical and political disagreements that arise *after* the founding of an ideal political society?

In his essay, "The Idea of an Overlapping Consensus," Rawls acknowledges what he calls "the fact of pluralism," the inescapable diversity of ethical and political belief systems. In a democracy based on individual freedoms and liberties, such a diversity of belief systems is unavoidable.[23] The fact of pluralism raises a certain challenge for modern democracies. If democracy is rule by the people, then what happens when the people disagree about ethics and politics? To answer this question, Rawls draws a distinction between "comprehensive doctrines" and the "political conception of justice."[24]

Comprehensive doctrines include religious belief systems, such as Judaism, Christianity, and Islam. They also include nonreligious theoretical and philosophical systems, such as utilitarianism and Marxism. A comprehensive doctrine can be understood as a substantive conception of right and wrong, and a substantive conception of the good, or "the meaning, value, and purpose of human life."[25] In a modern democracy, there will be a diversity of comprehensive doctrines.

The political conception is different. It is not based on revelation or moral philosophy. Rather, it is based on the institutions of democracy itself. To live in a democracy, to participate in the democratic process, is to endorse the very idea of democracy. It means supporting individual rights, freedoms, and liberties. While the political conception is moral in nature, it differs from comprehensive doctrines by being grounded in democracy. The political conception establishes a moral foundation for deliberation. Whatever we might personally think about truth, ethics, and the good, we nonetheless have a minimum of shared ground. The political conception goes beyond the shared traditions and values of the republican model by appealing to something more basic and universal. Rawls calls this moral foundation the overlapping consensus. It provides political stability and continuity.

In "The Idea of Public Reason," Rawls elaborates upon the terms of public deliberation. He begins by stating that reason is the medium of a democratic society. Reason, he says, is an "intellectual and moral power, rooted in the capacities of its human members."[26] Reason can be either public or private. Public reason has three characteristics that make it distinctively public. First, public reason is the reason of the public, the reason of democratic citizens. Second, public reason is devoted to deliberation about the public good. Third, public reason is free and open by nature. Concerning the subject matter of public reason, Rawls states that it is limited to questions of "constitutional essentials" and "basic justice."[27] This includes the rights of citizenship, institutional equality, the right to private property, and the freedom and limits of religion.

Concerning the forums of public reason, Rawls states that all citizens, whether or not they occupy political office, must abide by the terms of public reason "when they engage in political advocacy in the public forum."[28] By "public forum," he means both official and unofficial public spaces. The former group includes the legislature and the judiciary. The latter group includes any public space in which we might debate politics.

Concerning the content of public reason, Rawls reiterates that public reason is devoted to a liberal political conception of justice, that it prioritizes individual rights and liberties, and that it upholds a basic equality of both rights and opportunities for all citizens. Rawls further insists upon reasonableness and civility as fundamental to public deliberation. The upshot of all of this is that, when discussing matters of justice in the public forum, "we are not to appeal to comprehensive religious and philosophical doctrines," or what we individually regard as "the whole truth."[29] Rawls thus places strict limits on the terms of public deliberation. As will be discussed below, this conception of deliberation is arbitrarily exclusive.

Habermas: Justice as consensus

Habermas is arguably the world's most influential living philosopher. During his teenage years, Habermas was an active member of the Hitler Youth. After watching the Nuremberg trials, he was shocked into political sobriety. Shaken and unsettled, he turned to philosophy for answers and grounding. When he was twenty-four years old, he wrote to Martin Heidegger, then Germany's greatest philosopher, questioning the traces of lingering sympathy for National Socialism in his writings. Disappointed by his conspicuous silence, Habermas abandoned Heidegger's thought and soon joined the Frankfurt School, the neo-Marxist school of social theory led by Theodor Adorno and Max Horkheimer. Habermas identified with the Frankfurt School's resolute opposition to fascism and their determination to prevent another Auschwitz. But Adorno and Horkheimer were pessimistic about a collective political awakening in the era of mass society. Against their sense of cynicism and pessimism, Habermas developed a more optimistic philosophy based on the idea of communication.[30]

Today, Habermas is best known for his theory of communicative action—a grand and complex social theory that conceives of an ideal political society on the basis of rational communication.[31] At its most basic, the theory of communicative action posits an intrinsic logic to linguistic communication that naturally orients speakers toward rational consensus.[32] Habermas contends that speaking a language entails implicit commitments to truth and rationality. To make an assertion (e.g., "The earth is round") is to make a formal claim to validity. In so doing, a speaker makes a move within a discursive space governed by the force of reasons. Such a move implicitly places others in a position to either accept or reject a validity claim. They may either tacitly or overtly accept that claim, or they may put the claim in question by asking for reasons to endorse it. If they are persuaded by the reasons, or if they lack reasons to doubt that claim to begin with, the result is agreement or consensus. In the case of a proposed course of action, the result is socially coordinated action or "communicative action."[33]

In the event that such ordinary communication breaks down, that is, when the movement toward communicative action is obstructed by a challenge to the speaker's validity claim, those involved may choose to engage in what

Habermas calls "discourse."[34] Discourse in this sense rises above the scope of ordinary communication. According to Habermas, there are different types of validity claims, each belonging to a particular type of discourse. Scientific claims belong to scientific discourse, aesthetic claims to aesthetic discourse, moral claims to moral discourse, and so on. Habermas defines moral discourse as "the medium in which we can hypothetically test whether a norm of action, be it actually recognized or not, can be impartially justified."[35]

Moral claims may be tested through a process of rational argumentation, what Habermas calls "discourse ethics."[36] Moral claims vindicated through rational argumentation are valid. Those that fail to be vindicated are invalid. Discourse ethics ultimately seeks to provide explicit principles for moral disagreement, principles to which we could appeal to settle our differences and return to the path to communicative action.

Two principles of moral validity

Habermas offers two principles by which moral disagreements might be resolved. The first is the Discourse Principle (D), which he defines as follows: "Only those norms can claim to be valid that meet (or could meet) with the approval of all affected in their capacity as *participants in a practical discourse*."[37] As William Rehg points out, (D) has four important characteristics that give discourse ethics a decidedly Kantian orientation.[38]

First, (D) is deontological in that it seeks to provide a rational basis for rights. Second (D) conceptualizes moral validity, not in *a priori* terms, but rather in procedural terms. Third, (D) evaluates moral claims in terms of truth and falsity. Fourth, (D) is universalist. That is, it applies to all moral disagreements. It also does not betray a bias. Yet, it is sufficiently general that it does not reflect the particularities of any local culture. Yet, it is not so abstract as to be irrelevant to actual disagreements. As Habermas puts it, (D) is "dependent upon contingent content being fed into it from the outside."[39]

The second principle of discourse ethics is the better-known Principle of Universalization (U). According to this principle, a proposed norm is valid if "*all* affected can accept the consequences and the side effects its *general* observance can be anticipated to have for the satisfaction of *everyone's* interests (and these consequences are preferred to those of known alternative possibilities)."[40] Although (U) might appear to say very much the same thing as (D), the substance is different. Whereas (D) functions negatively by determining which norms *are not* valid, (U) works positively by determining which norms *are* valid. The power and scope of (U) derive from its specific inclusion of interests. The concept of interests is the key to Habermas's theory of impartiality.

On what basis can we determine whether a proposed norm serves the interests of all affected parties? Habermas answers this question by incorporating George Herbert Mead's social psychological concept of reciprocal role-taking. In his classic study, *Mind, Self, and Society*, Mead argues that we can discover the expectations of others by seeing the world through their eyes and anticipating their responses to future actions.[41] Reciprocal role-taking is part of the birth and development of the self. The self comes into being and maintains its stability only through other selves. The process of reciprocal role-taking continues through adulthood and remains a fundamental feature of human relationships. In Mead's view, reciprocal role-taking is an essential part of our humanity.

However, whereas Mead describes a process fundamental to selfhood and therefore to everyday life, Habermas incorporates reciprocal role-taking into discourse ethics. As Thomas McCarthy puts it in his commentary on discourse ethics, Habermas

> builds the moment of empathy *into* the procedure of coming to a reasoned agreement: each must put himself or herself into the place of everyone else in discussing whether a proposed norm is fair to all. And this must be done publicly; arguments played out in the individual consciousness or in the theoretician's mind are no substitute for real discourse.[42]

Habermas therefore takes a feature of everyday experience and develops it into a component of a formal process. The procedural aspect lies in the obligation of each participant to "take an interest in each other's interests, insofar as *all* have to accept the norm in view of its consequences for *each*."[43] In adopting each other's perspectives, the participants will, in theory, arrive at a generalized perspective from which to choose between each other's claims.

The concept of a generalized perspective requires some elaboration. As stated earlier, a moral claim is true and valid if all affected participants agree to it. That agreement may require compromise. If the participants run into an impasse because of conflicting interests, they need to separate mutual from mutually exclusive interests. A generalizable interest is simply the area of mutual interests that affects all participants. When moral claims clash, a generalizable interest holds the power to decide between them. Despite this apparent neutrality, I argue that discourse ethics is fundamentally biased.

Case Study: "I am the River, The River is Me"

The Ngāti Hau is a Māori community located in Te Ika-a-Māui, a land commonly known in the Western world as the North Island of New Zealand. Each of the five Ngāti Hau groups lives along the Whanganui, a long, majestic, and breathtakingly beautiful river. The five communities trace their ancestry to a few Polynesian explorers who discovered the Whanganui in the thirteenth century: Kupe, Turi, Ngā Paerangi, Tamatea, Tamakehu, and Ruaka. Though their ancestral lines are distinct, the Ngāti Hau are nonetheless united by their historical relationship to the Whanganui.[44]

The Ngāti Hau have been living off of the Whanganui for centuries. They derive their culture and heritage from it. Their beliefs and traditions, hopes and dreams, fears and nightmares are intimately bound up with it. Because of its life-giving power, because of the central place it occupies in their belief system, the Ngāti Hau identify with Whanganui in a very literal sort of way. As Gerrard Albert, one of the chief Māori negotiators for the Whanganui, puts it,

> We can trace our genealogy to the origins of the universe. And therefore rather than us being masters of the natural world, we are part of it. We want to live like that as our starting point. And that is not an anti-development, or anti-economic use of the river but to begin with the view that it is a living being, and then consider its future from that central belief.[45]

A traditional Māori proverb says, "I am the river, the river is me." According to the Ngāti Hau, the Whanganui is not just a river. It's a person.

The declaration of the personhood of the Whanganui is a response to almost two centuries of European colonialism that has treated the Whanganui as a mere resource for exploitation. Europeans first invaded Ta Ika-a-Māui in the early nineteenth century. While European encounters with other Māori tribes were often violent and deadly, contact with the Ngāti Hau was infrequent and nonviolent. For this reason, Europeans began settling along the Whanganui. As the settler population expanded, and as Europeans made formal claims to the land, tensions with the Ngāti Hau soon turned violent. Between 1845 and 1872, European settlers battled with numerous Māori tribes in what is today known as the New Zealand Wars.

This series of battles established European legal and political hegemony over the traditional homeland of the Māori. Over the next century, the Ngāti Hau fought for the recognition of the Whanganui as a person under the new colonial legal system. On a few occasions, this involved occupying government buildings and public spaces to raise awareness about their political struggle.[46]

On March 16, 2017, the Ngāti Hau finally succeeded in securing legal recognition for the Whanganui as a person. The ruling brought tears of joy. Gerard Albert explained the rationale behind their historic struggle:

> The reason we have taken this approach is because we consider the river an ancestor and always have. We have fought to find an approximation in

law so that all others can understand that from our perspective treating the river as a living entity is the correct way to approach it, as in indivisible whole, instead of the traditional model for the last 100 years of treating it from a perspective of ownership and management.[47]

Under its new legal status, the Whanganui is entitled to all of the rights and protections typically accorded to human beings. The landmark ruling notably resulted in a financial settlement of NZ $80 million for the Ngāti Hau. Another NZ $1 million was allocated for a legal framework for managing claims concerning the Whanganui. For the Ngāti Hau, it was a major historical victory. Inspired by their example, other Māori tribes are now hoping to secure similar recognition for other natural landmarks in their traditional homeland.

Analysis

The newly secured legal status of the Whanganui was the outcome of over a century of conflict between the worldview of the Māori, which recognizes the personhood of rivers and mountains, and the New Zealand settler state, which limits the concept of personhood to human beings only. How might this conflict be decided through a Rawlsian framework?

In "The Idea of Public Reason," Rawls states that a democratic society is governed by reason, and that reason, being a distinctly human capacity, serves the "human members" of that society.[48] Rawls further states that public reason is devoted solely to what he calls "constitutional essentials" and "questions of basic justice."[49] Most "political questions" do not fall under this domain. That is, most political questions lie outside the scope of justice. This includes calls for "preserving wilderness areas and animal and plant species."[50] Thus, even before elaborating systematically upon the nature of public reason, Rawls makes it abundantly clear that moral arguments for nature have no place in his model of public deliberation. This is not to say that a political society cannot decide upon some law to protect a nonhuman entity such as a river. They can, provided everyone agrees upon it. But in the event of a political disagreement, such as the one between the Māori and the European New Zealanders, only those arguments concerning human rights and liberties would be taken into consideration. All arguments for nature, whether moral, spiritual, or ecological, would be completely excluded. In a Rawlsian democracy, arguments for the personhood of the Whanganui would never get off the ground.

How might this conflict be decided in a Habermasian democracy? The wording of Habermas's (D) and (U) principles makes it abundantly clear that the ability to participate in a discourse and to express consent to a proposed law or policy is a decisive criterion for inclusion in the sphere of morality. Again, (D) states: "Only those norms can claim to be valid that meet (or could meet) with the approval of all affected in their capacity as *participants in a practical discourse.*" (U) holds that a proposed norm is valid if "*all* affected can accept the consequences and the side effects its *general* observance can be anticipated to have for the satisfaction of *everyone's* interests (and these consequences are preferred to those of known alternative possibilities)." Nondiscursive beings and entities, those who cannot participate in this discourse, are ineligible even for moral consideration. As with Rawls, Habermas makes cognitive capacity the relevant criterion for consideration. Humans are thus included; nature, excluded. Lest Habermas be given a more charitable interpretation, he explicitly conceives of morality in anthropological terms. As he puts it,

> From this *anthropological* viewpoint, morality can be conceived as the protective institution that compensates for a constitutional precariousness implicit in the sociocultural form of life itself. Moral institutions tell us how we should behave toward one another to counteract the extreme vulnerability of the individual through protection and considerateness. Nobody can preserve this integrity by himself alone. The integrity of individual persons requires the stabilization of a network of symmetrical relations of recognition in which nonreplaceable individuals can secure their

fragile identities in a reciprocal fashion only as members of a community. *Morality is aimed at the chronic susceptibility of personal integrity implicit in the structure of linguistically mediated interactions, which is more deep-seated than the tangible vulnerability of bodily integrity, though connected with it.*[51]

By linking "personal integrity" to the "structure of linguistically mediated interactions," Habermas categorically excludes nature from the sphere of morality. Rivers can neither act as "participants in a practical discourse" nor "accept the consequences and the side effects" of a proposed norm. It is for this reason that Habermas, speaking about nature more broadly, says, "Human responsibility for plants and for the preservation of whole species *cannot be derived from duties of interaction, and thus cannot be morally justified*"[52]. On this view, arguments for nature inherently lack moral substance. Environmental ethics, for Habermas, is a contradiction in terms.

It might be argued that, while rivers cannot participate in moral discourse, it is still possible for human participants to speak on their behalf and therefore to represent their interests. But this strategy abandons the very point of Habermas's philosophy and reverts to the type of monological and paternalistic reasoning that his discourse ethics is explicitly designed to overcome. In her critique of Habermas, Angelika Krebs writes,

> For discourse ethics, the horror of paternalism is so great that even Kant's monological reflection about what everybody could freely accept is rejected as still too paternalistic, and replaced by the actual discursive consensus of all. Moral thoughts about what is (directly) good or bad for others have no constitutive role to play in the deontological Kantian framework of discourse ethics.[53]

Because of the explicitly anthropological terms on which it rests, Krebs asserts that discourse ethics is "a thoroughly anthropocentric moral theory."[54]

Ethics as consensus makes sense only to the extent that we consider human interests and human consequences. On Habermas's view of ethics, the very idea that rivers could have genuine interests is a nonstarter. This would be a point of fundamental tension between the Ngāti Hau and Habermas. They would object to the anthropocentric terms of discourse ethics. Tellingly, (D) and (U) each lack a clear, noncircular defense against arguments for nature. Discourse ethics, that is, lacks a deeper, more basic justification of (D) and (U), whose universal validity cannot be salvaged once they are rejected on principle. In a case such as this, discourse ethics is at best practically useless and at worst a form of moral authoritarianism.

The illusion of consensus

In the penultimate chapter of *After Virtue*, MacIntyre argues that Rawls, despite including a social component to his political theory, nonetheless reproduces the liberal individualism of the prevailing market economy.[55] The key lesson that MacIntyre draws is that society in the liberal imagination is a mere collection of isolated and disconnected individuals. Individuals come first; society comes second. Hence, individual interests are more basic than social interests.

For Rawls, this priority is so fundamental that he excludes any conception of the common good even from consideration. MacIntyre describes this kind of thinking through the metaphor of a shipwreck, in which a group of strangers find themselves stranded on a desert island. With no shared past, these strangers are forced to devise principles by which to govern themselves. On MacIntyre's reading, what Rawls proposes is a more sophisticated version of the desert island scenario. Since the fictive participants in the original position lack any shared history, they have no conception of community or the social good. In this, the original position reproduces the logic of the marketplace. Just as commodities in a market economy are abstracted out of their histories and fetishized, individuals in the original position are abstracted out of their histories and similarly fetishized.

Although Habermas explicitly avoids the overt individualism of Rawls and the liberal tradition, the primary focus of his discourse ethics is still the individual. Recall that Habermas is concerned with how moral institutions "counteract the extreme vulnerability of *the individual* through protection and considerateness." His interest in "a network of symmetrical relations" reflects his primary concern for "the integrity of *the individual*." Habermas does not go beyond mere reciprocity. That is, he lacks a substantive and material conception of social flourishing. In attempting to strike a balance between the vulgar individualism of the liberal tradition and a substantive and material conception of a healthy and flourishing society, Habermas's political philosophy concludes in a mere abstraction: the dream of a rational society grounded in communicative action. This abstraction offers an impoverished idea of the human subject and fails as a medium of arbitration in a culturally diverse society.

But I would like to go further and argue that just as Rawls and Habermas lack any conception of social flourishing, so too do they lack any conception of *ecological* flourishing, without which we can have no social flourishing at all. Both Rawls and Habermas abstract the individual out of all ecological context, thereby producing a mythical creature—the individual—who stands so far apart from nature that he can survive without any consideration of it, and increasingly in spite of it. The fetishism of the individual reproduces the classical Western hierarchy of humanity over nature.[56] It treats this hierarchy as natural, as just the way things are. This assumption is problematic not just from an ecological standpoint, but also from the standpoints of many non-Western cultures and traditions that revere nature, even to the point of regarding it as sacred.

Rawls and Habermas both hold a hierarchical worldview that would reject as false any conception of kinship between humanity and nature. In this, their deliberative procedures are not just liberal, but Eurocentric. Their procedures would only serve as a tool for perpetuating colonial power and domination.

Deliberative democracy: A straitjacket upon communication

Superficially, the idea of deliberative democracy is appealing. A democracy of dialogue seems more democratic than a democracy of the majority or a democracy of the common good. Superficially, deliberative democracy would seem to prevent the exercise of unjustified power and domination. But despite the pride of place it gives to dialogue, deliberative democracy has a rather skewed and idiosyncratic idea of dialogue. In what follows, I wish to highlight three ways in which Rawls and Habermas, far from eliminating unjustified power and domination, merely reproduce one more version of it.

First, they both impose arbitrary terms upon deliberation. Rawls treats the two liberal principles of the original position as unquestionable, even timeless and ahistorical. Similarly, Habermas treats the (D) and (U) principles as unquestionable. From a certain perspective, these terms are understandable. They express a basic human desire for freedom and liberty. We can appreciate them when compared to authoritarian or majoritarian forms of power and coercion.

But from another perspective, such as that of certain Indigenous traditions or of environmental sustainability, these terms are not only questionable but also just plain wrong. From a Māori standpoint, one could challenge the validity of the two liberal principles of Rawls's original position and Habermas's (D) and (U) principles. At that point, there is no further or deeper standard to which either Rawls or Habermas can appeal. We cannot dig beneath the foundations of the deliberative procedure. In which case, then, each of their models of deliberation effectively breaks down.

Second, deliberative democracy fails to live up to the ideals of fairness and equality. In a diverse society, with so many moralities, deliberative democracy promises a fair and neutral procedure for arbitrating between rival and competing moral claims. This promise is admirable. Fairness and equality are democratic ideals. They stand against arbitrary privilege and unjustified hierarchy. But as with the commitment to freedom and liberty, the commitment to fairness and equality is betrayed by the nature of the deliberative procedure and by zero historical engagement.

The principles undergirding the deliberative project do not treat rival standpoints equally. They do not arbitrate between them fairly. Rather, the supposedly neutral and impartial procedures favor certain outcomes over others. In the case of Rawls, his procedure would favor bourgeois property rights over the collective ownership of the means of production. For both Rawls and Habermas, their procedures would favor a European worldview over a Māori one. The pretension to neutrality and impartiality notwithstanding, deliberative democracy is decidedly partial and biased.

Lastly, deliberative democracy excludes certain voices from dialogue. Numerous critics have taken Rawls to task for his rather militant secularism. His version of secular democracy is so extreme that it excludes religious speech from the public sphere. This, his critics point out, places people of faith at a certain disadvantage. People of faith would speak one way in private but would be forced to speak another way in public. For people of faith, this type of extreme secularism thus results in a rupture of the self. But religious voices are not the only voices that get excluded from the public sphere. Any voice representing what Rawls labels a comprehensive doctrine, be it a formal religion, a philosophical ethics, or Marxism, would also get excluded insofar as it rejects his terms of deliberation. This would include the tradition of the Māori.

Habermas has sought to resolve the problem of religious speech in the public sphere by introducing an option for translation.[57] A religious argument could, in principle, be translated into secular terms, and therefore be included in the public sphere. Habermas thus goes further than Rawls in being more accommodating toward people of faith. Yet, certain moral arguments, whether religious or secular, by virtue of their content alone, would nonetheless get excluded. For Rawls and Habermas, arguments for animals and nature have no place in public deliberation. Thus, the Māori, as well as environmental conservationists, animal rights activists, and other groups that speak for nonhuman animals, would be deprived of a voice. Deliberative democracy as conceived by Rawls and Habermas, far from being open and free, is categorically closed and exclusive.

Notes

1. For other notable works on deliberative democracy, see John Elster, ed. *Deliberative Democracy*. Cambridge, UK: Cambridge University Press, 1998; Amy Gutman and Dennis Thompson, *Why Deliberative Democracy?* Princeton, NJ: Princeton University Press; John Dryzek, *Deliberative Democracy and Beyond: Liberals, Critics, Contestations*. Oxford, UK: Oxford University Press, 2000; James Fishkin, *When the People Speak: Deliberative Democracy and Public Consultation*. Oxford, UK: Oxford University Press, 2009.

2. For a useful overview of the distinctions between the liberal and republican models, see Jürgen Habermas, "Three Normative Models of Democracy," *Constellations* 1.1 (1994): 1–10.

3. Philip Pettit, *Republicanism: A Theory of Freedom and Government*, Oxford, UK: Oxford University Press, 1997, 241, 271.

4. For an overview of deliberative democracy, see James Bohman and William Rehg, eds. *Deliberative Democracy: Essays on Reason and Politics*. Cambridge, MA: MIT Press, 1997.

5. Kant's classic statement on public reason is expressed in his essay "An Answer to the Question: What Is Enlightenment?" See Immanuel Kant, "An Answer to the Question: What Is Enlightenment?" *Practical Philosophy*, Mary J. Gregor, eds. Cambridge, UK: Cambridge University Press, 1996, 11–22.

6. John Rawls, "Justice as Fairness," *The Philosophical Review* 67.2 (1958): 164–94; Rawls, *A Theory of Justice*. Cambridge, MA: Harvard University Press, 2009.

7. Robert Nozick, *Anarchy, State, and Utopia*. New York, NY: Basic Books, 1974.

8. Michael Sandel, *Liberalism and the Limits of Justice*. Cambridge, UK: Cambridge University Press; Michael Walzer, *Spheres of Justice*. Oxford, UK: Blackwell, 1983.

9. Iris Marion Young, *Justice and the Politics of Difference*. Princeton, NJ: Princeton University Press, 1990.

10. G. A. Cohen, *Rescuing Justice and Equality*. Cambridge, MA: Harvard University Press, 2008.

11. Rawls, *A Theory of Justice*, 3.

12 Ibid.

13 Ibid., 7.

14 Ibid.

15 Ibid.

16 Ibid.

17 Ibid., 11.

18 Ibid.

19 Ibid., 136.

20 Ibid., 19.

21 Ibid., 60.

22 Ibid., 139.

23 John Rawls, "The Idea of an Overlapping Consensus," *Oxford Journal of Legal Studies* 7.1 (Spring 1987): 1–25.

24 Ibid., 4.

25 Ibid., 1–2.

26 John Rawls, "The Idea of Public Reason," in James Bohman and William Rehg, eds. *Deliberative Democracy: Essays on Reason and Politics*. Cambridge, MA: MIT Press, 1997, 93.

27 Ibid., 94.

28 Ibid., 123.

29 Ibid., 103.

30 For an excellent intellectual biography of Habermas, see Stefan Müller-Doohm, *Habermas: A Biography*. Cambridge, UK: Polity Press, 2016.

31 Jürgen Habermas, *The Theory of Communicative Action*. Volume I: *Reason and the Rationalization of Society*, translated by Thomas McCarthy. Boston, MA: Beacon Press, 1984; Habermas, *The Theory of Communicative Action*. Volume II: *Lifeworld and System*, translated by Thomas McCarthy. Boston, MA: Beacon Press, 1987.

32 Habermas, *The Theory of Communicative Action*, Vol. I, 99–101, 286–88.

33 Ibid., 101.

34 Ibid., 42.

35 Ibid., 19.

36 Ibid.

37 Jürgen Habermas, *Moral Consciousness and Communicative Action*. Cambridge, MA: MIT Press, 1990, 66 (emphasis in the original).

38 William Rehg, *Insight and Solidarity: A Study in the Discourse Ethics of Jürgen Habermas*. Berkeley, CA: University of California Press, 1994, 31.

39 Habermas, *Moral Consciousness and Communicative Action*, 103.

40 Ibid., 65 (emphasis in the original).

41 George Herbert Mead, *Mind, Self, and Society from the Standpoint of a Social Behaviorist*. Chicago, IL: University of Chicago Press, 1934.

42 Thomas McCarthy, "Introduction," in Jürgen Habermas, eds. *Moral Consciousness and Communicative Action*. Cambridge, MA: MIT Press, 1990, viii–ix.

43 Rehg, *Insight and Solidarity*, 39.

44 David Young, *Woven by Water: Histories of the Whanganui River*. Wellington, NZ: Huia, 1998.

45 Eleanor Ainge Roy, "New Zealand River Granted Same Legal Rights as Human Being," *The Guardian*, March 16, 2017. https://www.theguardian.com/world/2017/mar/16/new-zealand-river-granted-same-legal-rights-as-human-being (accessed January 16, 2019).

46 Young, *Woven by Water*, 286.

47 Roy, "New Zealand River Granted Same Legal Rights as Human Being."

48 Rawls, "The Idea of Public Reason," 93.

49 Ibid., 94.

50 Ibid.

51 Habermas quoted in Angelika Krebs, "Discourse Ethics and Nature," *Environmental Values* 6.3 (1997): 273; emphasis added.

52 Jürgen Habermas, *Justification and Application: Remarks on Discourse Ethics*. Cambridge, MA: MIT Press, 1993, 111.

53 Krebs, "Discourse Ethics and Nature," 275.

54 Ibid.

55 MacIntyre, *After Virtue*, 250.

56 There have, of course, been attempts to defend both Rawls and Habermas on this front. See, for example, Ruth Abbey, "Rawlsian Resources for Animal Ethics," *Ethics and the Environment* 12 (2007): 1–22; Derek Bell, "Political Liberalism and Ecological Justice," *Analyse & Kritik* 28 (2006): 206–22; and Robert J. Brulle, "Habermas and Green Political Thought: Two Roads Converging," *Environmental Politics* 11.4 (2010): 1–20. Given the explicit anthropocentrism of both Rawls and Habermas, however, these attempts remain unconvincing.

57 Jürgen Habermas, "Religion in the Public Sphere," *European Journal of Philosophy* 14.1 (2006): 1–25.

5

Why Not Agonistic Pluralism?

This chapter explores the political thought of Chantal Mouffe as a possible answer to the culture wars. Along with her partner and collaborator Ernesto Laclau, Mouffe has become a major figure in the world of radical thought. Mouffe and Laclau are best known for their book, *Hegemony and Socialist Strategy*, a now-classic work of post-Marxist political theory.[1] Since the publication of this landmark book, Mouffe has become a proponent of agonistic pluralism, a form of democracy that shuns political consensus in favor of an ongoing contest for political power.[2] The similarities between Mouffe and MacIntyre are numerous. Hence, it is necessary to examine her thought in some detail.

Superficially, Mouffe's agonistic pluralism seems like a plausible alternative to deliberative democracy and an answer to the culture wars. Yet, it suffers from certain critical weaknesses. The primary flaws of agonistic pluralism are its rejection of rational argumentation and the norm of truth in the public sphere. Mouffe's anti-rationalism is fundamentally at odds with MacIntyre's rationalist conception of politics. In this chapter, I argue that by disavowing rational argumentation and rejecting the norm of truth in the public sphere, Mouffe's agonistic pluralism only feeds the toxic chaos of the culture wars.

Between the modern and the postmodern

Chantal Mouffe and Ernesto Laclau occupy a unique place in contemporary social and political theory. On the one hand, they are highly critical of modern epistemology and ontology. They take issue with modernist pretensions to universality and strong claims about the objective nature of the social world. On the other hand, they remain firmly committed to the modern project of representative democracy and to modern democratic institutions. In this, Laclau and Mouffe are markedly different in their critique of modernity from that of Friedrich Nietzsche and Michel Foucault. Their political project is closer to that of Jacques Derrida, who proposes the idea of "democracy to come."[3]

The main foil against which Mouffe and Laclau formulate their political theory is classical Marxism. Mouffe and Laclau see Marxism as the failed project of viewing human history through the reductive lens of class struggle. On their reading of Marxism, every form of oppression and violence, including racism, sexism, homophobia, and environmental degradation, can be explained in terms of the eternal conflict between capital and labor. Race, gender, and sexuality are merely epiphenomenal. Class is primary. Hence, the only meaningful form of politics is class struggle. Once the capitalist order has been dismantled and the working class is emancipated, every form of systemic oppression and violence will cease to exist. Thus, to fight racism or sexism or homophobia and environmental degradation, the most practical course of action is to join the class struggle, the only true form of social solidarity.

For Laclau and Mouffe, this worldview is no longer tenable. While it might have made sense during the late nineteenth and early twentieth centuries, the social and political world has since changed so dramatically that Marxism no longer holds much explanatory or practical value. The nature, structure, and scope of capital have markedly changed since the nineteenth century. The factory is no longer the most useful model for understanding the dynamics of capitalism. Capital is now more fluid and mobile. The capitalist mode of production is now more diverse. Labor is now more fragmented and dispersed. Resistance at the point of production makes little sense in an era of globalized finance, data, and information capitalism. The rise of the welfare state, which preserves the capitalist political and economic order through a social compromise with labor, further complicates the traditional conception of class struggle. Moreover, since the 1960s, we have seen the rise of social movements based on identity, not class, a development that further challenges the Marxist worldview. The civil rights movement, the women's movement, and the LGBTQ movement are not instances of class struggle. Rather, these movements cut across class lines. Other movements, such as the anti-war movement and the environmental movement, while not based on identity, are still not based on class. Yet another major development is the rise of the mass media, which have changed the cultural and political terrain considerably, and which have opened up new possibilities for social and political struggle.

In the opening chapter of *Hegemony and Socialist Strategy*, Mouffe and Laclau critique the Marxist discourse concerning the transition from a capitalist to a socialist political and economic order. The primary target of their criticism is the Marxist view of historical change. They take issue with the idea that history is driven by the internal contradictions of capitalism. They reject the thesis that a unified working class will develop a singular revolutionary will and that capitalism will be overthrown in a decisive and inevitable revolutionary moment. Such a conception of historical change, they believe, obviates the messy, but indispensable role of politics. The Marxist view of history ignores the diversity and heterogeneity of social and political struggles. Worse, it leads to authoritarian and totalitarian thinking, what Laclau and Mouffe call "the Stalinist imaginary."[4]

The diversity of social and political struggles creates a certain crisis for Marxism: How do we explain the gap between the *ideal* of a united and revolutionary working class and the *reality* of a divided and nonrevolutionary working class? Mouffe and Laclau explore the ways that influential Marxist theorists have grappled with this problem, including Rosa Luxemburg, Georgi Plekhanov, George Sorel, and Karl Kautsky. Mouffe and Laclau critique their contortions and strained explanations, which they treat as evidence of a severe theoretical defect in Marxism. But they nonetheless find value in this exercise, for it reveals the emergence of the idea of hegemony, which they contend holds lasting explanatory and political value.

Mouffe and Laclau extract their conception of hegemony through a comparison between Lenin and Gramsci. In Lenin, they uncover a conception of hegemony as "political leadership within a class alliance."[5] Relations of production divide people by class. Each class—the bourgeoisie, the petit bourgeoisie, the middle class, the peasantry, the proletariat, the lumpenproletariat—is unified by class-specific interests. Thus, different classes with overlapping interests can potentially unite in a war against a common enemy. Because class alliances do not form naturally, they require political leadership. This is the point at which, as Mouffe and Laclau note, Leninism begins to display its authoritarian impulse. Leninism imposes ideological unity and attacks internal division and disagreement. It treats class struggle as primary and universal. It insists that a unified working class is the sole historical vehicle of revolutionary change. Leninism posits a hierarchy of vanguard party leaders over the working class. The former possess a scientific understanding of society and history. The latter hold the potential to achieve such an understanding but require the guidance and tutelage of the former.

By contrast, Mouffe and Laclau find in Antonio Gramsci a more democratic and grassroots conception of hegemony. In *Prison Notebooks*, Gramsci retains the idea of hegemony as a strategic alliance but locates the glue that holds this alliance together in grassroots organizing and the power of common sense.[6] Rather than a revolution from above, Gramsci frames the challenge to capitalism as emerging from below. By nature, this revolution is fundamentally democratic. It acknowledges the facts of difference and pluralism. It synthesizes these differences, as opposed to suppressing them through authoritarian violence, to create a counter-hegemonic historic bloc capable of a war of position against the capitalist class. On Gramsci's view, the struggle against capitalism is not a matter of historical inevitability. Rather, it is contingent upon the democratic energies and organizational will of the common people.

Mouffe and Laclau see in Gramsci's democratic conception of hegemony a powerful explanatory and political tool that leaves behind the outmoded reductionism and essentialism of the Marxist-Leninist worldview. This democratic conception is compatible with a poststructuralist understanding of language, subjectivity, society, and history. Following the anti-foundationalism of Jacques Derrida and Michel Foucault, they see the social world as a complex and contingent system of disparate elements always in a state of flux. They see identity, not as given and fixed, but rather as the ever-evolving product of discursive negotiation. Mouffe and Laclau take the contingency and fluidity of the social world and of social identities, not as chaos and meaninglessness, but rather as an open field of possibilities for restructuring the world along evermore egalitarian lines.

Social identities, Mouffe and Laclau contend, come into being as "nodal points," temporary formations that enable human subjects to possess purpose and intelligibility.[7] Despite the lack of a permanent structure, despite the ongoing play of disparate elements, the social world nonetheless exhibits recurring patterns, what Laclau and Mouffe, following Foucault, call "regularity in dispersion."[8] These patterns provide practical grounds for making critical distinctions and for political strategizing. The loss of foundations is therefore by no means a reason for political impotence and aimlessness.

For Mouffe and Laclau, the hegemonic fight against inequality necessarily takes a democratic and pluralist form. It acknowledges and respects the integrity of different social identities and historical struggles, refusing to subsume them all under one overarching and universal struggle. The basis for the strategic alliance, or counter-hegemony, between disparate social groups, is a revised conception of socialism. Unlike the Marxist conception of socialism, which centers upon workers' control over production, Mouffe and Laclau reconceive socialism as the elusive ideal of radical equality, an ideal toward which we will always be striving, but which we will never fully achieve. The process of challenging existing hierarchies and articulating new forms of social relationships is the ongoing point of politics. While *Hegemony and Socialist Strategy* is unquestionably

Mouffe and Laclau's philosophical masterpiece, Mouffe subsequently developed the idea of radical democracy further in her subsequent work.

Radical democracy

In a series of books, Mouffe presents a powerful and sustained critique of certain dominant schools of political theory.[9] She proposes a radical conception of democracy that builds upon certain themes that she had earlier developed with Laclau in *Hegemony and Socialist Strategy*. Writing in the 1990s, Mouffe initially framed her project in the historical context of the fall of communism, the end of the Cold War, and the rise of the Third Way, the neoliberal politics of resolute centrism formulated by Anthony Giddens and exemplified by Bill Clinton, Tony Blair, and Gerhard Schroeder.

The new orthodoxy of centrist politics, in which center-left politicians compete with center-right politicians, was thought to have brought about an end to the traditional divide between Left and Right. One inadvertent effect of the new centrist politics was to fuel the rise of reactionary right-wing movements in the Western world. Deprived of a voice in mainstream politics, large numbers of agitated citizens flocked to nationalist movements, zeroing in on minorities as the enemy. For Mouffe, this indicates the ineradicable dimension of antagonism in modern democracies.

Mouffe takes the growth of nationalist movements as a sign of a serious crisis that necessitates a fundamental rethinking of democracy. According to Mouffe, this crisis reflects a failure to grapple with two phenomena: *the political* and *the democratic paradox*. The political is a concept taken from the thought of Carl Schmitt, the German legal theorist, critic of liberalism, and "crown jurist" of the Third Reich. The political denotes the antagonistic dimension of liberal democracy. According to Schmitt, liberal democracy is predicated upon a distinction between friends and enemies, between "us" and "them." Democracy, in a word, is conflict.

Mouffe rejects Schmitt's politics but nonetheless finds truth and value in his concept of the political. Contemporary democracy and democratic theory either ignore the political or suppress it altogether through the imposition of a rational center from which antagonism has been purged. The democratic paradox, by contrast, refers to a certain tension inherent in liberal democracy. On the one hand, liberalism is the institution of individual rights and the rule of law. On the other hand, democracy is popular sovereignty, the rule of the people. Mouffe observes that liberalism and democracy stand in a contradictory relationship. They operate according to distinct aims and logics. Hence, the dominance of the one entails the negation of the other.

Mouffe sees the liberal and republican traditions, and their latter-day deliberative and communitarian rivals, as different attempts to grapple with the democratic paradox. In her view, the paradox is irresolvable. There are only better and worse ways of managing the tension between liberalism and democracy. The dominant models of democratic theory have failed to grapple with the democratic paradox. They lean too far one way, thereby compromising the other, and vice versa. Mouffe therefore undertakes a critical rethinking of the democratic tradition. She engages with the dominant schools of democratic thought, offering trenchant critiques of the liberal, deliberative, and communitarian schools. Against these schools, she advocates radical democracy, which makes the political the heart of democratic practice. The "task" of radical democracy, Mouffe says in *The Return of the Political*, is to "deepen the democratic revolution and to link diverse democratic struggles."[10] This link is the counter-hegemonic solidarity between different struggles.

Radical democracy is an explicit rejection of Third Way politics. By restoring the political, it encourages both Left and Right to reenter democratic politics and pursue their respective political projects to bring the political back to life. According to Mouffe, restoring the political simultaneously reactivates the Left while sublimating the frenetic and reactionary passions of the Right. The active and practical heart of radical democracy is agonistic rivalry: the contest between various social movements for political power and hegemony. Mouffe describes radical democracy as a form of liberal socialism which synthesizes the ideals of freedom and liberty found in the liberal tradition with the goal of equality found in the socialist tradition.

Mouffe draws from a diverse range of theoretical sources to guide her conception of radical democracy. From Claude Lefort, one of the founding members of Socialisme ou Barbarie, Mouffe conceives of modern democracies as resting, not on absolute certainty, but rather on a fundamental indeterminacy. From Hans Blumenberg, the theorist of metaphor, she adopts a distinction between modernity as a "political project" and modernity as an "epistemological project," enabling her to pursue the former and reject the latter.[11] Radical democracy thus has both, a modern and postmodern orientation.

Mouffe's critique of the epistemological project of modernity is heavily influenced by Jacques Derrida, Hans-Georg Gadamer, and Ludwig Wittgenstein. From Derrida, she takes the rejection of essentialism and foundationalism, and the embrace of contingency, fluidity, and irreducible plurality. From Gadamer, she takes the concept of tradition, which, she says, enables us to understand ourselves as historical subjects. Mouffe acknowledges traditions as the condition of possibility for political action. From Wittgenstein, Mouffe takes the concepts of language games and forms of life. Through these concepts, she challenges the universalist pretensions of deliberative democracy.

Ultimately, she locates radical democracy within a branch of the civic republican tradition whose principal forefather is Machiavelli. Following Quentin Skinner, Mouffe finds in Machiavelli a form of civic virtue and political life whose primary focus is the pursuit of individual liberty, not the common good.

Critique of deliberative democracy

As stated above, Mouffe defines radical democracy in part against deliberative democracy. Her two primary targets of criticism are John Rawls and Jürgen

Habermas. Mouffe acknowledges critical differences between them. However, she finds considerable overlap, especially in their neo-Kantian orientation. The problem with this orientation, she contends, is its pretension to universality. In aspiring to the universal, they suppress the political, thus producing a distorted idea of democracy that would only feed the problem of reactionary right-wing movements.

Mouffe criticizes Rawls for his distinction between the public and the private. For Rawls, some beliefs, such as articles of religious faith, belong in the private sphere. Only those beliefs on which we can reasonably agree belong in the public sphere. Mouffe sees this crafty move as a way of suppressing pluralism. Rawls's overlapping consensus is a way of rigging public deliberation so as to avoid having to deal with conflicting beliefs.

Similarly, she takes Habermas to task for his distinction between ethics and morality. Habermas defines ethics as the local and particular idea of the good. Morality, by contrast, consists of context-transcending principles. But this distinction, Mouffe contends, is illusory. It is one more way of excluding certain beliefs from public deliberation while permitting only those likely to secure agreement on Habermas's idiosyncratic terms. Neither Rawls nor Habermas, she maintains, are able to deal with the political and the challenge of pluralism. Their logic lends itself to imposition rather than mediation.

Mouffe sees deliberative democracy as the misguided attempt to secure allegiance to democratic practices and institutions through the purely cerebral medium of rational argumentation. The problem with this approach, she believes, is that rational argumentation cannot secure allegiance. Allegiance is not the outcome of syllogistic reasoning, from the premise of abstract principles to the conclusion of practical action. Rather, allegiance to democracy can only be cultivated through practice. We cannot sell the idea of democracy in the abstract. We need to foster a democratic ethos through civic participation. Taking her cue from Wittgenstein, Mouffe conceives of democracy as a form of life. This way of conceiving of democracy forms the basis for her critique of rationalism.

Drawing from Wittgenstein, Mouffe holds that meaning and belief are rooted in forms of life. The fallacy of Rawls and Habermas is to presume that we can meet each other on common ground. According to Mouffe, there is no such common ground. There is only this or that form of life. What Rawls and Habermas each present as common ground, a universal meeting place, is but one specific and local form of life. For this reason, Mouffe dismisses their rationalism as an outdated relic of the epistemological project of modernity. Mouffe quotes Wittgenstein, who says:

> Where two principles really do meet which cannot be reconciled with one another, then each man declares the other a fool and heretic. . . . I said I would "combat" the other man,—but wouldn't I give him *reasons*? Certainly; but how far do they go? At the end of reasons comes *persuasion*. (Think what happens when missionaries convert natives.)[12]

Deliberative democracy, then, is the false hope that we can arbitrate between different forms of life through the medium of reason. In the idiom of the philosophy of science, forms of life are incommensurable. That is, they lack common ground. As such, there is no way of either transcending or bridging forms of life through reason.

Agonistic pluralism

Unlike Rawls and Habermas, who treat rational argumentation as the heart of democratic practice, Mouffe regards political passions as "the driving force" of democracy.[13] Passions are a powerful phenomenon. Left untamed, they can quickly boil over into violent and reckless impulses. Mouffe sees this risk as one of the principal problems of deliberative democracy. Its ideal of cold and impersonal reason makes no room for political pathos.

From the deliberative point of view, passions are irrational. Mouffe strongly disagrees with this view. The passions are not external to democracy. Rather, passions are the stuff of democracy. Only when the passions are excluded from democratic practice do they risk becoming irrational and therefore a danger to democracy. The main challenge of democratic politics, as Mouffe sees it, is to "sublimate the passions by mobilizing them towards democratic designs."[14]

According to Mouffe, the key to sublimating the passions is to redefine the political in competitive, as opposed to militaristic, terms. Instead of an antagonistic relationship, conceived as an ultimate war between enemies, Mouffe advocates an agonistic relationship, conceived as an ongoing struggle between adversaries. Enemies seek to destroy each other. Destruction is permanent. Adversaries, by contrast, seek only to defeat each other. Defeat is temporary.

An ongoing competition between political adversaries, she says, is "the very condition of a vibrant democracy."[15] By providing antagonists with a democratic outlet for their political passions, their rivalry will be transformed into an agonistic contest. Though they will not achieve a rational consensus about the good, the right, and the just, they *will* achieve a practical consensus about the legitimacy of democratic politics and institutions.

What, then, is the nature of agonistic conflict? What is its aim? According to Mouffe, each political movement has an agenda. That agenda is hegemonic by nature. The point of participating in democratic politics is to establish a hegemonic order. Mouffe dismisses as naïve and fanciful the deliberative democratic fantasy of a political order felicitously free of asymmetrical power relations. Every society, democratic or otherwise, is by necessity composed of asymmetrical power relations. Democratic politics is the unapologetic contest for political power, the quest to establish those asymmetrical power relations according to a particular hegemonic agenda.

But by what means does one political adversary defeat another? If not by rational argumentation, then what? The answer lies in the construction of strategic alliances. The most powerful strategic alliances prevail in parliament and at the ballot box. As Mouffe puts it, "This will create a new hegemony, which will be the outcome of the articulation of the greatest possible number of democratic struggles."[16] For Mouffe, then, democracy is in the end a numbers game. Mouffe is quick to point out, however, that the diversity and heterogeneity of moral standpoints do not preclude the possibility of agreement.

Adversaries can switch sides. To embrace the other side is to "undergo a radical change in political identity."[17] Rather than "a process of rational persuasion," however, such a change of identity is "more a sort of conversion."[18] By "conversion," Mouffe makes it clear that she means the type of nonrational conversion alluded to by Wittgenstein above and by Thomas Kuhn in *The Structure of Scientific Revolutions*. By invoking "conversion," as opposed to rational persuasion, the implications for truth in democratic politics also become clear. As Mouffe puts it, "To defend political liberalism and pluralism within a perspective which is not rationalist, we have to see parliament not as the place where one accedes to truth."[19]

Left populism: Agonistic pluralism in action

Most recently, Mouffe has given more substance to the idea of radical democracy and agonistic pluralism. In light of the recent waves of populist movements in the West, Mouffe presents populism as agonistic pluralism in action. Her book, *For a Left Populism*, is a complement to Laclau's *On Populist Reason*, which challenges the long-standing view of populist movements as the irrational energies of a volatile and unruly mob.[20] Against this condescending view of populism, Laclau argues that mass movements are governed by their own distinct and sophisticated rationality, one that does not conform to traditional views of rational thought and action. Mouffe builds upon Laclau's work to frame populism as a form of civic republican virtue: enacting democratic citizenship by taking it to the streets.

Mouffe sees the present historical conjuncture as a populist moment. After thirty years of neoliberal policies, which have disempowered democratic citizens and driven them to the margins, the centrist political establishment now faces its reckoning. This reckoning takes two forms. On the one hand, it takes the form of reactionary right-wing nationalism, which appeals to "freedom" and "liberty" to attack immigrants and minorities. On the other hand, it takes the form of left-wing movements that challenge deeply entrenched power structures in the name of equality and social justice. According to Mouffe, this intensified rivalry between Left and Right will be the defining conflict of our time. As she puts it in *For a Left Populism*, "In the next few years ... the central axis of the political conflict will be between right-wing populism and left-wing populism."[21]

For Mouffe, the challenge for radical democracy is to conceive of populism in neither essentialist nor totalizing terms. She calls the project of building a left populism the "construction of a people."[22] This project entails identifying different movements struggling against the neoliberal order. It further entails respecting the specificity and integrity of each movement. The "people" are the sum total, the chains of equivalence, that unite different struggles to form a historic bloc. Mouffe affirms a role for a charismatic leader to guide the people. This leader, far from being an authoritarian strongman, is from the people and remains on par with the people. In short, a Gramscian organic intellectual.

Critique: Beyond objectivism and relativism?

In *The Return of the Political*, Mouffe invokes the post-foundationalist turn in the philosophy of science to mark a similar turn in political theory. She points to the importance of Thomas Kuhn and Mary Hesse for her conception of radical democracy. This conception rejects the idea of rationality as singular and universal in favor of "multiple forms of rationality."[23]

According to Mouffe, the idea of rationality as multiple and varied is crucial for rejecting the false dichotomy between universal standards and arbitrary choice. Mouffe suggests that we can indeed make rational choices in the absence of universal standards. Following Hannah Arendt in *Between Past and Future*, Mouffe contends that the political sphere, while not being the sphere of truth, nonetheless allows for valid and legitimate judgments. How exactly validity and legitimacy without truth are possible or even coherent she does not say. To those who dismiss Mouffe's position as relativist, she contends that they "remain in the thrall of a traditional problematic which offers no alternative between objectivism and relativism."[24]

Mouffe's use of the phrase "between objectivism and relativism" is an allusion to the work of Richard J. Bernstein. In *Beyond Objectivism and Relativism*, Bernstein argues that much of modern intellectual life has become strained by the tension between the two diametrically opposing tendencies of objectivism and relativism.[25] For Bernstein, these are not so much technical terms as they are general labels that designate broad intellectual currents and attitudes in the realm of both formal philosophical inquiry and everyday life. These twin tendencies are also known by other readily familiar oppositional terms: objectivism and subjectivism, realism and anti-realism, universalism and relativism, foundationalism and relativism, and so on.

According to Bernstein, objectivism can best be described as "the basic conviction that there is or must be some permanent, ahistorical matrix or framework to which we can ultimately appeal in determining the nature of rationality, knowledge, truth, reality, goodness, or rightness."[26] Relativism, by contrast, is the rival conviction that these central philosophical categories are, in the end, "relative to a specific conceptual scheme, theoretical framework, paradigm, form of life, society, or culture."[27]

On Bernstein's reading of our current intellectual zeitgeist, certain schools of thought such as hermeneutics and pragmatism, are systematic attempts to move beyond the twin extremes of objectivism and relativism. This movement entails the negotiation of conflicting viewpoints on contingent and open-ended grounds. As Bernstein indicates in his careful analysis, the movement beyond objectivism and relativism entails the possibility of rational choice between competing traditions, paradigms, forms of life, and the like. Yet, this possibility is precisely what Mouffe denies. As she puts it,

> It is always possible to distinguish between the just and the unjust, the legitimate and the illegitimate, *but this can only be done from within a given tradition, with the help of standards that this tradition provides*; in fact, there is no point of view external to all tradition from which one can offer a universal judgment.[28]

Thus, despite her claim of traversing a middle ground between objectivism and relativism, Mouffe remains firmly trapped within this tragic dichotomy. Mouffe takes the lack of an external point of view to preclude the possibility of rational choice. It makes little sense to deny rational choice, yet also deny being a relativist.

By applying this flawed logic to political theory, Mouffe arrives at a model of democracy that fails to address the very real concerns about power that motivate Rawls and Habermas. Mouffe's vision of democratic politics resembles something like a tennis tournament, in which different groups vie with each other for political power. But in this game of victory and defeat, Mouffe supplies no rules for fair competition. Without such rules, it is impossible to see how any victory can be achieved except through some decidedly unfair means. Remarkably, Mouffe appears to ignore the material inequalities that confer some groups with a decided political advantage over others. In a society of extreme economic and social inequality, those with greater economic and social power will hold an unfair advantage over others, rendering any political victory an effect of that unequal power.

Mouffe's agonistic democracy is thus tragically structured by the material conditions of inequality created by the very neoliberal order to which her "socialist" strategy is ostensibly opposed. The very point of the deliberative model of democracy is to mediate social conflict through fair and neutral standards, thus undercutting, at least in principle, the unfair advantages that some groups hold over others. But if Mouffe's issue with deliberative democracy is its intrinsic bias and unfairness, it is difficult to see how an unmediated contest for power is any less biased and unfair. Mouffe's agonistic democracy merely replaces the biases of the deliberative procedure with the structural inequalities of the economic order.

Despite professing not to be a relativist, Mouffe has not sufficiently considered the implications of relativism for democratic politics. There appears to be no awareness that her politics are, in a critical sense, relativist. In his essay, "Relativism, Power, and Philosophy," MacIntyre spells out the consequences of relativism for social and political life.[29] As he observes, human relationships devoid of shared standards of truth and justice are necessarily mediated by arbitrary will and power. Without shared standards of truth and justice, MacIntyre argues, we have no hope of "unmasking and dethroning arbitrary exercises of power." In which case, we would be unable to critique "tyrannical power within communities and imperialist power between communities."[30]

By way of example, MacIntyre considers the cases of Spanish and English imperialism. The Spanish imposed an alien concept of private property upon the Indigenous cultures of the Americas. The English similarly imposed an alien concept of individual property rights upon the Irish. In both cases, the concepts of private property and individual property rights had no place in the local languages. Thus, those cultures looked upon these alien concepts, not in benign terms, but rather in terms of theft and seizure. As MacIntyre puts it,

> What is from the one point of view a just act of war will be from the other theft; what is from the one point of view an original act of acquisition, of what had so far belonged to nobody and therefore of what had remained available to become only now someone's private property, will be from the other point of view the illegitimate seizure of what had so far belonged to nobody because it is what *cannot* ever be made into private property—for example, common land. The Spaniards brought alien concepts of ownership deriving from Roman, feudal, and canon law to their transactions with the Indians; the English brought concepts of individual property rights

recognized by English common-law decisions to Ireland at a time when there was certainly a translation for the Latin "jus" in Irish, but none for the expression "a right" (understood as something that attaches not to status, role, or function, but to individuals as such).[31]

If we follow Mouffe's logic, we give up on rational choice between competing frameworks, in which case we necessarily deprive ourselves of any impartial basis for condemning Spanish and English imperialism as categorical forms of injustice. The Spanish and English imperial conquests would be no more or less legitimate than the resistance against them. And the historical legacies of these conquests, which continue to shape the material lives of Indigenous communities of the Americas to this day, would have no bearing in Mouffe's conception of agonistic democracy. Rather tellingly, Mouffe's agonistic democracy ignores the material histories and legacies of colonialism that continue to shape Western democracies. In the agonistic contest for power, history appears not to matter at all, thus reproducing capitalist logics of time and history. Rather, the only decisive criterion is "the greatest possible number of democratic struggles."[32]

Politics without truth?

Throughout *The Return of the Political*, Mouffe invokes numerous thinkers—Arendt, Foucault, Wittgenstein, Rorty—to argue that truth is relative and that democratic politics should not aim for truth. As Mouffe would have it, truth is always limited to a specific tradition. Hence, the pursuit of tradition-independent truth is the pursuit of a chimera. This line of reasoning has material consequences for democratic politics. As Mouffe puts it,

> We have to see parliament *not as the place where one accedes to truth*, but as the place where it ought to be possible to reach agreement on a reasonable solution through argument and persuasion, while being aware that such

an agreement can never be definitive and that it should always be open to challenge.[33]

According to Mouffe's anti-rationalist conception of politics, we can at best aim for mere agreement, but not truth. But this conception of politics is incoherent. Without the ideal of truth, we would be unable to either agree or disagree at all. Without truth, political discourse—and, indeed, linguistic communication in general—would cease to be possible. Truth is indispensable to speech, an argument that Huw Price makes rather convincingly.[34]

Price devises an elaborate thought experiment involving a hypothetical speech community lacking the norm of truth. When the members of this speech community speak to each other, they do not aim for truth, because truth as a category does not exist for them. As Price observes, these hypothetical speakers would at best be able to convey personal feelings, desires, and preferences. They would be able to say, "I like this dish" and "I want to order that dessert," or "I believe this" and "I demand that." They could at best take each other to task for speaking inconsistently or insincerely.

What they could not do, however, is to hold each other accountable for speaking *incorrectly*. They could not *disagree* with each other, for correctness and incorrectness would have no place in their fictional linguistic universe. The inhabitants of this universe may clash in their desires and preferences. They may align those desires and preferences into a common will. But they could not in any meaningful sense agree or disagree with each other since there could be no assertions about impersonal truth about which to agree or disagree in the first place. As Price rightly puts it, "Without truth, the wheels of argument do not engage; disagreements slide past one another."[35]

Agreement and disagreement alike thus require a linguistic framework premised on the very idea of truth. If we abandon the idea of truth, then we necessarily abandon the bulk of linguistic communication as we know it. Without truth, we could not have political discourse at all. Mouffe's anti-rationalist idea of agreement without truth is incoherent. It would make no sense in practice. Just as Price's hypothetical speech community could never exist in real life, neither could Mouffe's idea of parliament.

Aside from the incoherence of pursuing agreement without truth, there is a second concern about Mouffe's proposal for a politics without truth. In *Hegemony and Socialist Strategy*, Mouffe and Laclau stress the compatibility between democracy and totalitarianism. As they put it,

> The discursive compass of the democratic revolution opens the way for political logics as diverse as right-wing populism and totalitarianism on the one hand, and a radical democracy on the other. Therefore, if we wish to construct the hegemonic articulations which allow us to set ourselves in the direction of the latter, we must understand in all their radical heterogeneity the range of possibilities which are opened in the terrain of democracy itself.[36]

Mouffe and Laclau recognize that the dissolution of hierarchy opens up the possibility of either reconceiving society along more egalitarian lines or creating new hierarchies. The deconstruction of hierarchy is the singular task of radical democracy. By contrast, the construction of hierarchy is the logic of totalitarianism. Radical democracy opens up "an unending process of questioning," in which no laws are fixed or immune to being contested.[37] Totalitarianism, by contrast, denies social diversity and heterogeneity by manufacturing an artificial unity. It achieves this unity through the declaration of false universals—foundational principles presented as above critique and contestation. By purging the norm of truth from democratic politics, radical democracy supposedly becomes a bulwark against totalitarianism.

But if Mouffe is concerned about totalitarianism, then it can be argued that a political sphere purged of the norm of truth would only fuel the possibility of totalitarianism. George Orwell, one of our most valuable guides for understanding the nature of totalitarianism, makes the following observation in his essay, "Literature and Totalitarianism," written after his participation in the Spanish Civil War:

> Totalitarianism has abolished freedom of thought to an extent unheard of in any previous age. And it is important to realize that its control of thought is not only negative, but positive. It not only forbids you to express—even to think—certain thoughts, but it dictates what you shall think, it creates an ideology for you, it tries to govern your emotional life as well as setting up a code of conduct. And as far as possible it isolates you from the outside world, it shuts you up in an artificial universe in which you have no standards of comparison.[38]

Orwell is, of course, best known for his haunting depiction of totalitarianism in *1984*. This depiction draws from his personal observations of the nature of General Franco's totalitarian regime. As James Conant observes in his reading of *1984*, the aim of totalitarianism is more than mere totalizing logic.[39] Rather, it is the creation and imposition of a false social universe in which political subjects become imprisoned and from which there is no escape. Totalitarianism denies impartial standards of thought and judgment. It tells us what to think and how to think. It destroys our capacity for critical thought. It dismantles the very ideas of truth and objectivity. It thrives on falsehood, fantasy, myth, and delusion. It rests on beliefs about the world formed *in spite* of what actually happens in the world.

In a totalitarian society, a society purged of the ideal of truth, we lose the possibility of resistance. We could at most protest our lack of freedom. We could protest physical violence to our bodies. But what we could not do, because we would lack the necessary conceptual tools, is judge the official dogma of a totalitarian state to be false. The strength of totalitarianism rests on the dissolution of the very idea of objective reality.

Resistance to totalitarian power lies in more than a mere independence of the will. It also lies in the capacity for independent thought. Resistance, that is, entails the possibility of questioning totalitarian ideas by making judgments of truth and falsity—categories that Mouffe abandons in her anti-rationalist conception of politics. Far from enabling a radical democracy, a political sphere purged of the ideal of truth would only establish the conditions for totalitarianism to take root.[40]

Notes

1 Ernesto Laclau and Chantal Mouffe, *Hegemony and Socialist Strategy: Towards a Radical Democratic Politics*, 2nd edn. London, UK: Verso.

2 Mouffe is by no means the sole theorist of agonistic democracy. Other prominent theorists include Hannah Arendt, Bonnie Honig, William Connolly, and James Tully. See Hannah Arendt, *Between Past and Future*. New York, NY: Penguin, 1977; Bonnie Honnig, *Political Theory and the Displacement of Politics*. Ithaca, NY: Cornell University Press, 1993; William E. Connolly, *Identity/Difference: Democratic Negotiations of Political Paradox*, Ithaca, NY: Cornell University Press, 1991; William E. Connolly, *The Ethos of Pluralization*. Minneapolis, MN: University of Minnesota Press, 2004; William E. Connolly, *Pluralism*. Durham, NC: Duke University Press, 2005; James Tully, *Strange Multiplicity: Constitutionalism in an Age of Diversity*. Cambridge, UK: Cambridge University Press, 2007; James Tully, *Public Philosophy in a New Key. Volume I: Democracy and Civic Freedom*. Cambridge: Cambridge University Press, 2008; James Tully, *On Global Citizenship: James Tully in Dialogue*. London, UK: Bloomsbury, 2014. For a useful overview of agonistic democracy, see Mark Wenman, *Agonistic Democracy: Constituent Power in the Era of Globalization*. Cambridge, UK: Cambridge University Press.

3 Jaques Derrida, *Specters of Marx*, translated by Peggy Kamuf. New York, NY: Routledge, 1994.

4 Ibid., 4.

5 Ibid., 55.

6 Antonio Gramsci, *Selections from the Prison Notebooks*, edited and translated by Quintin Hoare and Geoffrey Nowell Smith. New York, NY: International Publishers, 1971, 419–25.

7 Laclau and Mouffd, *Hegemony and Socialist Strategy*, 112.

8 Ibid., 105.

9 Mouffe, *The Return of the Political*. London, UK: Verso, 1993; *The Democratic Paradox*. London, UK: Verso, 2000; *On the Political*. London, UK: Routledge, 2005; *Agonistics: Thinking the World Politically*. London, UK: Verso, 2013; *For a Left Populism*. London, UK: Verso, 2018.

10   Mouffe, *The Return of the Political*, 18.

11   Ibid., 10, 41.

12   Ludwig Wittgenstein, *On Certainty*, edited by G. E. M. Anscombe and G. H. Von Wright. New York, NY: Basil Blackwell, 160; emphasis in the original.

13   Mouffe, *Agonistics*, 6.

14   Ibid., 9.

15   Mouffe, *For a Left Populism*, 56–57.

16   Mouffe, *The Return of the Political*, 18.

17   Mouffe, *The Democratic Paradox*, 102.

18   Ibid.

19   Mouffe, *The Return of the Political*, 103.

20   Ernesto Laclau, *On Populist Reason*. London, UK: Verso, 2005.

21   Chantal Mouffe, *For a Left Populism*, 6.

22   Ibid., 63.

23   Mouffe, *The Return of the Political*, 14.

24   Ibid.

25   Richard J. Bernstein, *Beyond Objectivism and Relativism: Science, Hermeneutics, and Praxis*. Philadelphia, PA: University of Pennsylvania Press, 1983.

26   Ibid., 8.

27   Ibid.

28   Mouffe, *On the Political*, 15; emphasis added.

29   MacIntyre, "Relativism, Power, and Philosophy," 5–22.

30   Ibid., 12.

31   Ibid., 8.

32   Mouffe, *The Return of the Political*, 18.

33   Ibid., 130.

34   Huw Price, "Truth as Convenient Friction," *The Journal of Philosophy* 100.4 (2003): 167–90.

35   Ibid., 185.

36   Laclau and Mouffe, *Hegemony and Socialist Strategy*, 168.

37   Ibid., 186.

38 George Orwell, "Literature and Totalitarianism," in *Essays*, New York, NY: Alfred A. Knopft, 2002, 362.

39 James Conant, "Rorty and Orwell on Truth," in Abotton Gleason, Jack Goldsmith, and Martha Nussbaum, eds. *On Nineteen Eighty-Four: Orwell and Our Future*. Princeton, NJ: Princeton University Press, 2005, 86–111; Conant, "Freedom, Cruelty, and Truth: Rorty versus Orwell," in Robert Brandom, ed. *Rorty and His Critics*. Malden, MA: Blackwell, 2000, 268–341.

40 Jason Hannan, "Truth as First Casualty in American Politics," xi–xxxvi.

6

Ground of Fire

This chapter explores the philosophical basis for MacIntyre's rationalist approach to politics. This approach sets him apart from the universalism of Rawls and Habermas, and from the anti-rationalism of Mouffe. It consists of viewing of society as based in conflict, accompanied by a conception of practices, traditions, and narratives as the fundamental building blocks of human communities. To view human societies as fundamentally composed of conflict might seem to suggest that the culture wars are unavoidable. In what follows, I will show why this view is mistaken.

Justice as strife

MacIntyre begins the second chapter of *Whose Justice? Which Rationality?* by invoking Heraclitus's doctrine of strife.[1] In one of his surviving fragments, Heraclitus says, "One must realize that war is common, that justice is strife, and that all things come to pass through strife and are so ordained." In a related fragment, Heraclitus says, "War is the father of all, and king of all."[2] If these aphorisms strike us as paradoxical, counterintuitive, or even offensive, that's because they represent a cosmic, not a local, perspective. If we step back from the immediate, the local, and the mundane, then what we perceive as war and strife can be perceived instead as mere parts of a much larger and more complex system. War and strife, from a Heraclitean point of view, are *constitutive* of order.

To better appreciate what Heraclitus intends by justice as strife, it helps to consider another of his fragments, this one expressing his doctrine of fire. As Heraclitus says,

> This world, which is the same for all, no one of gods or man has made; but it was ever, is now, and ever shall be an ever-living Fire, with measures of it kindling and measures of it going out.[3]

In his commentary on this passage, the Australian philosopher John Anderson draws a contrast between two different conceptions of stability.[4] According to the first, stability can be conceived as non-movement. A house of cards, a frozen lake, the ruins of a city no longer alive and bustling with people—these are all stable insofar as they lack movement.

However, stability can also be conceived in opposite terms, that is, as movement, flow, dynamism, and exchange. Fire in the passage above is at once an example of, and a metaphor for, this second conception of stability. A candle flame appears static to the untutored eye. In reality, it burns fuel to stay alive. Beneath the superficial appearance of static light is a complex process of combustion. When that process comes to an end, the flame disappears. The flame thus thrives on change. Fire is harmony through transformation. In contrast to stability as non-movement, fire represents Heraclitus's view of stability as change.

The doctrine of fire helps us understand better the doctrine of strife. War, conflict, tension, strife—these are the underlying conditions of all things. As Anderson puts it, "But for the general phenomenon of change and opposition, things would never persist and exhibit their distinctive character."[5] Everything, then, achieves its being through strife. All things burn like a flame. Fire is the ground upon which we walk, the fabric of the universe, the core of our very being.

While Heraclitus is not referring explicitly here to the social world, but rather to reality in general, the basic idea expressed above nonetheless applies to the human condition aptly, perhaps even quintessentially. Without some minimal tension and conflict, human societies as we know them would cease to exist. From this point of view, the pursuit of political consensus, the attempt to ground a rational society in some foundational singularity, is the pursuit of folly, a misguided attempt to achieve stability by unwittingly short-circuiting the underlying tensions, contradictions, and dynamism that fuel human societies.

Both Heraclitus and Anderson were major influences on MacIntyre's basic understanding of our social universe.[6] Inspired by their metaphysical view of reality, MacIntyre contends that conflict is "the key to understanding the nature of social institutions and social orders."[7] Human societies, he says, are "milieus of conflict, arenas within which opposing modes of belief, understanding, and action engage in argument, debate, and, at extremes, war."[8] Conflict can, if mismanaged and left unchecked, lead to chaos and violence. However, this need not be the only outcome of conflict, for conflict can also be a source of stability.

If we incorporate conflict into our social and cultural life, if we integrate it into our politics and institutions, then it need not be chaotic and violent. On the contrary, conflict can be positive, creative, and generative. Conflict, then, is not an obstacle to be overcome through the pursuit of consensus and unity, but rather something to be cultivated, managed, charted, even protected. How then should we engage with conflict? How do we cultivate constructive, as opposed to destructive, conflict? Answering this perennial riddle is one of the key themes of MacIntyre's philosophical project.

To view conflict as basic to human societies, of course, bears a strong resemblance to the political thought of Chantal Mouffe. But the resemblance ends there. Mouffe's politics, as I have endeavored to show, are fundamentally anti-rationalist. MacIntyre's, as I will show in this chapter and the next, are fundamentally rationalist. Mouffe abandons the ideals of truth and reason. MacIntyre vigorously upholds them both. Mouffe denies the possibility of rational choice between traditions. MacIntyre takes active steps to show

how it's possible. Mouffe sees politics as a competition of strategic alliances, to be decided by the power of sheer numbers. MacIntyre sees politics as a competition of arguments, to be decided by the power of reason.

To make better sense of what separates MacIntyre from Mouffe—and from Rawls and Habermas—it is necessary to understand what MacIntyre takes to be the contingent bases of human societies, the ground of fire that generates social tension and conflict in the first place.

The DNA of human communities

Recall that the starting point for Rawls's theory of justice is the so-called original position, a neutral meeting place in which all who come to the table have been stripped of class position, social identity, and personal history. The participants in the original position are disembodied beings, vessels of pure intentionality. Again, MacIntyre aptly describes the original position through the metaphor of a shipwreck, a sort of philosopher's edition of *Gilligan's Island* or *Lost*, where a group of strangers build a social order from scratch, without any shared social history.[9] From this abstract exercise, Rawls formulates a theory of justice with truly wide-ranging implications for law, public policy, and the public sphere. Again, for MacIntyre, the original position is a nonstarter. It divorces judgment from desire and history, and from the local and the particular. Its pretension to timelessness and universality masks its arbitrary foundations, as well as the tenacious power of bourgeois ideology.

Against the false abstraction of the original position, MacIntyre's starting points for a rational ethics and politics are the social and historical circumstances of everyday life, the practical bases that furnish us with the very identities that Rawls extinguishes from the outset. These starting points include three distinct, but closely related, concepts: *practices, traditions,* and *narratives.* For MacIntyre, these are the building blocks of social life, the DNA of human communities. Without them, we could not have human communities in any meaningful sense at all. Practices, traditions, and narratives are among the most recognizable concepts in MacIntyre's thought. They are central for his case for reviving the Aristotelian tradition of the virtues. Yet, these concepts are also a potential source of misunderstanding, since each of them has become a sort of vacuous buzzword in the humanities in recent years. It is therefore necessary, whenever one writes about MacIntyre, to define what he means by these concepts so as to not confuse them with their counterparts in the writings of others.

Practices

By *practice*, MacIntyre means a distinct kind of social activity with several key features.[10] Practices are, first and foremost, complex activities. That is, they involve more than simple and mindless repetitions. Rather, practices are elaborate in design and structure. They require skill and judgment. They have rules and norms, standards and criteria, ends and goals. One doesn't just participate in a practice. One does so either well or poorly. Performance in a practice is judged by its internal standards and criteria. Most importantly, practices offer certain internal goods or rewards. Examples of practices include sports, music, teaching, scholarship, activism, and politics.

The reasons for participating in a practice can vary. There's a difference, for example, between playing baseball for the sheer love of the sport and playing baseball for money and fame. Those who genuinely love the sport, who enjoy the thrill of competing against another team, will take the integrity of the game seriously. They would not be content being handed a victory they didn't actually earn. But those who are in it solely for the money and the fame will have an incentive to cheat. Hence, the plague of rampant steroid use in Major League Baseball, which has led to dozens of suspensions over the last two decades. The problem with playing solely for money and fame is that it feeds the corruption of the sport.

To take the game seriously, to play it for its own sake, is to respect the rules of the game, rules that bind all players together and hold everyone accountable. These rules allow for the possibility of fair victory and defeat. Playing baseball means accepting the outcomes of the game, outcomes you cannot decide by an emotivist declaration of will or preference. Hence, the victories and defeats in baseball are decisive. The losing team acknowledges its loss. A baseball game does not typically conclude in a disagreement over the outcome. There are, of course, fights from time to time, but these are obvious anomalies. Fights are not intrinsic to the game. Rather, they are the outcomes of bad character.

Baseball also involves certain relationships and attitudes between the players, both between the members of a team and between competing teams. To play on a team is to cooperate with your team members, to understand the purpose and responsibilities of each position, and to work together in a concerted effort to win the game. Although the object is to win, the game still demands a certain positive relationship with the other team. It means giving the other team its due, acknowledging when it wins. It also means treating the other team with a minimum of respect. Hence, the ritual of shaking hands after a game, a way of demonstrating that love of the sport exceeds the desire to win.

Thus, intrinsic to baseball is a self-contained universe of ethics. The rules and norms, the ends and goals, the roles and relationships, and the internal goods and rewards of the game, provide baseball with a normative structure. Those who take the game seriously, who play the game for its own sake and not for external rewards like money or fame, will have a natural incentive to play baseball with integrity, to abide by a certain code of conduct, to exercise certain traits of character like truthfulness, courage, and patience. The difference between a practice and a simple and repetitive activity like hammering nails is that practices have an ethics. We can speak of a code of conduct for baseball, not for hammering nails. It would not matter very much if you took steroids to hammer nails more effectively.

For MacIntyre, practices are small-scale arenas for the social embodiment and realization of the virtues. Practices characteristically have a *telos*, a goal that provides meaning, point, and purpose. To participate in a practice is to know what you're doing and why you're doing it. To achieve that *telos* requires the exercise of certain types of *aretê*, of virtue or excellence. Thus, practices foster character and entail judgments of that character. Practices are also notably not algorithms. You can't participate in a practice by following a step-by-step set of procedures. Rather, practices require the exercise of *phronêsis*, of practical wisdom and judgment. Also, to participate in a practice for the internal rewards is to participate out of desire, as opposed to abstract duty or obligation.

Unlike a Kantian ethics, the rules and norms, the standards and criteria, the roles and responsibilities, and the virtues and vices that make up a practice are socially constructed, socially embodied, and, hence, socially specific. Their authority rests on social recognition, not on objective and impersonal foundations. Moreover, to participate in a practice is to acknowledge the role of *desert* and therefore to treat each other justly according to what each deserves.

Lastly, taking part in a practice over the long term, knowing it well, learning from trial and error what works and what doesn't, gives us an idea of what it means for the practice to thrive and flourish, to achieve what Aristotle calls *eudemonia*. But while practices are small-scale arenas of ethics, their complexity means they cannot survive without some discussion about their purpose and nature. Hence, the need for traditions.

Traditions

By *tradition*, MacIntyre means the historical continuum of knowledge, beliefs, and debates about a practice.[11] A tradition is a repository of collective understanding that helps guide a practice over successive generations. Baseball, for example, did not suddenly appear one day in a historical vacuum. Although no one knows exactly where and when the first baseball game was played, baseball appears to have emerged in nineteenth-century America as an offshoot of a much older British bat-and-ball game known as rounders. Baseball was played in different variations in different parts of the United States. The baseball played in Massachusetts, for example, was different from the baseball played in New York. What we today know as baseball is the New York variety.

At first, baseball was just a kid's game. The general public took little notice of it. It wasn't until gamblers began placing bets on baseball games that the public began taking a more active interest in the sport. And it was not until gambling began corrupting the sport itself, through what was called "game-fixing," that a tradition was born devoted to preserving the integrity of the sport from the corrupting influence of money. It is through this tradition that the rules of baseball and a code of ethics eventually became codified. This tradition, which preserved the game in the face of adversity, is what gave baseball its current form and what enabled baseball to become the de facto national sport of America.[12]

If we play baseball today, we thus play a game whose structure and design, and whose rules and norms bear the stamp of anonymous forebears who lived over a century ago. In some sense, to play the game is to defer to the authority of those anonymous forebears, even though we will never know them and even if we are not aware of their authority at all. The game exercises an implicit authority over everyone who plays it. Thus, we not only have an explicit relationship with our teammates and with the other teams but also have an implicit relationship with those who came before us. The baseball community, as it were, extends over time.

Like baseball, every practice is shaped, guided, and maintained through a tradition. A tradition is a reflective conversation by a practice-based community over the nature, meaning, purpose, and goods of the practice. This conversation becomes crucial in the face of new obstacles that potentially compromise the integrity of a practice. For example, although professional baseball players have long used performance-enhancing drugs, it was not until 1991 that Major League Baseball formally banned the use of steroids. Up until then, there was no consensus about how steroid use affected the game.

Similarly, following the rapid growth of the #MeToo movement in 2017, several universities have recently moved to ban professor-student relationships on the grounds that such relationships jeopardize the practices of teaching and learning by compromising the well-being of the student.[13] While there is no consensus at present over the ethics of professor-student relationships, the debate about such relationships is part of an ongoing conversation in the academic community about teaching as a practice and the university as an institution. In short, it's a debate within a tradition.

Narratives

A practice can become a big part of our lives. It can define who we are, shape how we think, and foster traits of character that leave their stamp well beyond the confines of the practice. But what if we take part in more than one practice simultaneously? What if two different practices both become a big part of our lives—each defining who we are, each shaping how we think, each fostering distinct traits of character? What if the imprint of these two practices creates a division within the self and possibly a loss of personal meaning and coherence? For the millennial generation today, this question is not a luxury or an abstract question for the armchair of a philosophy seminar, but rather an urgent and practical question with severe implications for mental health and personal well-being.

A 2017 *Harvard Business Review* article entitled "The Hardest Thing About Working in the Gig Economy? Forging a Cohesive Sense of Self" illustrates one of the personal consequences of working in a precarious economy in which short-term work with negligible benefits has become the new normal.[14] The three authors, all business school faculty, interviewed forty-eight workers who held anywhere from two to an astounding six jobs simultaneously over a period of five years. The authors report that, among the many struggles the workers faced, was "how to feel and be seen as authentic when they wear more than one occupational hat." The authors acknowledge that "one's occupation is such a core part of one's identity" that workers with more than one job "may find themselves plagued with issues of authenticity: who am 'I' really, if I'm all these things at once?" The article functions as a kind of self-help piece for those who want to "diversify their careers," but who "don't want to lose their sense of self while doing so."[15]

The advice itself is rather revealing. On the one hand, the authors suggest "searching for a common thread across your portfolio" to identify "a unifying purpose." This "common thread" can help "create a sense of synergy" between multiple jobs. They even suggest looking at each job "as part of a larger whole." Yet, on the other hand, they say, "Embrace yourself as being composed of multiple (sometimes distinct) identities."[16] The authors insist that "authenticity" can still be achieved across these multiple and distinct identities. As they put it, in words that cannot fail to raise eyebrows,

> the bottom line is that, for plural careerists, being authentic does not mean being the same across time and context. People often assume consistency is a marker of authenticity. But, in fact, attempting to be consistent to a single self can actually become a barrier to authenticity. We are, as humans, many things. And working multiple jobs can help people to activate and enact the multiple dimensions of their true nature.[17]

The authors quote one informant who says, "It's not like there's this 'me' there and all you have to do is find 'the right job' that maps onto the static image of 'me,' like a tracing." The authors advise those who hold "one job or five" to focus on "the process of authentication as opposed to the state of authenticity"—whatever that is supposed to mean.[18]

Whether anyone working in the gig economy would actually join in on this bizarre celebration of multiple personality disorder is doubtful. The authors have recognized a very real and serious problem among young workers, namely, the loss of personal meaning and a sense of coherence to their lives. But as apologists for the gig economy, a cruel and sadistic system of exploitation, the authors offer a callous rationalization for that system, albeit a half-hearted and meaningless one, to rebrand exploitation as a form of self-discovery.

The gig economy represents the latest mutation of capitalism, which constantly seeks out ever-inventive ways to exploit labor. Capitalism thrives on a society composed of isolated, atomized, and disconnected individuals, who better suit the interests of capital than those integrated into strong and closely knit communities. The atomized individual under capital is already a distorted being, a creature specially molded by and for labor exploitation. But the gig economy takes things further. It demands more than the submission and degradation of an already atomized individual. It demands that the individual be broken down into isolated and disconnected pieces, multiple and partial selves, that may each be subjected to new methods of exploitation still. It is in the light of liberal capitalism's fetishism of the individual and its division of the self into disparate fragments that MacIntyre's concept of *narrative* can best be understood.

Millennial workers, who find themselves caught between multiple jobs, whose lives feel increasingly incoherent and meaningless, might understandably begin to wonder, "What am I doing? Who am I? What's the point of my life?" These questions, far from unusual, are the start of a personal quest for meaning and purpose, a search for some way to make sense of their lives from one job to the next, from one day to the next, from one moment to the next. Anyone who asks these questions is seeking to connect the dots between the data of practical experience. The hope is to arrive at some clear picture of their lives. In a sense, they are beginning a philosophical investigation. As MacIntyre points out, there are two depressing ways to answer these questions.

The first is provided by behaviorism, the school of psychology that teaches that human behavior is the effect of systematic conditioning through repeated patterns of stimulus and response.[19] According to this view, human behavior is no different from that of Ivan Pavlov's dogs, who were conditioned to salivate at the ringing of a bell. From a behaviorist standpoint, humans are no different from animals, because humans *are* animals. If you are waiting tables at a restaurant, for example, then that is because you've been conditioned to wait tables. Properly speaking, there is no "you" there. And there is no point to your life. Behaviorism would thus provide a depressing answer to the personal quest for meaning and purpose.

The second way to answer these questions is provided by Jean-Paul Sartre and the German sociologist Ralf Dahrendorf.[20] According to Sartre and Dahrendorf, what you happen to be doing and who you are depends on whatever role you occupy at a given moment. If, in one moment, you happen to be teaching, then you're a teacher in that moment. If, in another moment, you happen to be driving a cab, then you're a cab driver in that moment. But for Sartre and Dahrendorf, there is no overarching identity or frame by which to connect these specific roles in any meaningful or coherent way. For Sartre and Dahrendorf, too, there is no point to your life.

On the one hand, this offers a certain freedom. It means you can give whatever meaning you wish to your local and immediate experiences. On the other hand, it means giving up the quest for any larger meaning and purpose, because life is ultimately meaningless, pointless, and, frankly, absurd—the signature themes of the existentialist worldview. Existentialism, then, would also provide a depressing answer. But are the answers provided by behaviorism and existentialism the only ones?

MacIntyre explains that a positive answer to the quest for personal meaning and purpose hinges on whether we can render human actions, from the simple to the complex, intelligible. We can appreciate MacIntyre's conception of intelligibility through contrasts, such as the human versus the nonhuman, and the rational versus the irrational. There's a difference, for example, between a toaster and a person making toast, between Pavlov's dogs and Pavlov himself, and between Caligula and Marcus Aurelius. We can explain the toaster in terms of its mechanical design, Pavlov's dogs in terms of their systematic conditioning, and the mad emperor in terms of his madness. But for the other side of these contrasts, for those we take to be rational people, we explain their behavior in terms of their *intentionality*, of their goal-oriented or object-oriented state of mind. And intentions, as MacIntyre observes, presuppose contexts of purpose.

In an essay for the *Chronicle Vitae* entitled, "Summer Survival Strategies for Adjuncts," Josh Boldt provides an example of the importance of contexts of purpose for interpreting human behavior.[21] He describes the challenges that adjunct college instructors face during the summer months, when course offerings are slim, when adjunct contracts are slimmer, and when adjunct pay typically dries up by August. Boldt runs through the list of odd jobs he has taken in the past to make ends meet. These include working as a mover, a wedding photographer, a landscaper, and a ditch digger. Boldt reports having resorted at one point to delivering pizzas. He says he avoided delivering pizzas in towns where he taught because, as he puts it, "the thought of ringing the doorbell of a current student was too much to bear."[22] A student who orders a pizza and then opens the door to find their professor making the delivery would very likely wonder, "What on earth is *he* doing here?" What might seem baffling and unintelligible, and likely amusing and scandalous, from the student's perspective would be perfectly intelligible from the perspective of the professor and those who know him well: he's delivering pizzas to help make ends meet because he lacks a permanent teaching position and adjunct pay is horribly insufficient. The action would thus be intelligible in the light of a larger context of purpose.

For countless adjunct instructors who are forced to work odd jobs, just to make ends meet, from delivering pizza to performing sex work, taking such jobs can be explained in light of the broader goal and dream of eventually becoming a full-time professor.[23] Making sense of a specific action like delivering a pizza in the absence of a larger context of purpose would be like tearing a random page out of a novel and attempting to make sense of what was going on.

The comparison to a novel is very much to the point, for it is MacIntyre's key to understanding the nature of rational and intelligible behavior. In what is arguably the most memorable chapter he has ever written, MacIntyre advances the provocative thesis that our lives take the form of a dramatic narrative.[24] Each of us, according to this view, is a character, the protagonist of our very own story. We move through time, from one episode to the next, not randomly and aimlessly, but in the light of an unfolding story, one that is still being written. We don't have absolute power over the story of our lives, but neither are we completely powerless.

However we write that story, under the constraints of the social and natural world, we write with an eye toward some goal, some *telos*. That *telos* may be short term or long term. It may be hazy or clear. It may change or remain fixed. But without a *telos*, without an object-oriented state of mind, we could not be the subject of intelligible behavior at all. Without a *telos* of some kind, nothing we say or do would be intelligible, either to others or to ourselves. In which case, we would not be living through a meaningful story, but a meaningless and pointless one.

Young workers caught between multiple jobs, who have yet to figure out what story they wish to write because they have never been given the chance to discover what their purpose might be, and young workers who know what that purpose is, but who have no hope of ever achieving it in the gig economy, will be plagued by the sense of meaninglessness, pointlessness, and incoherence. For the *Harvard Business Review* to tell these young workers to embrace multiple and distinct identities is to tell them to give up the quest for narrative unity and coherence. Their advice for cultivating "authenticity" is, in short, a recipe for madness.[25]

But if our lives are stories, then those stories surely do not start or end with us. Rather, it means there's a prequel to the story of our lives and that other stories intersect with our own. Our friends and family, our neighbors and co-workers, each have their own story, in which they are the protagonist and we are but secondary characters. Tracing this complex web of stories, without which we could have no story of our own, brings to light our social and historical embeddedness. There is a reason why biographies typically begin by discussing the subject's parents and grandparents, and the history of the town in which the subject was born, for no one is born into a vacuum. Rather, each of us is born into a social history. The languages we are raised to speak, the beliefs and values, the habits and customs, the entire cultural framework through which we are socialized into the world provide us with the initial ground of our social existence, the beginning of our moral identity.

The virtues in three stages

From his observations about practices, traditions, and narratives, MacIntyre draws a powerful lesson about the virtues. That lesson comes in three stages.[26] The first stage, as discussed above, concerns the place of the virtues within practices. Practices are the most basic ground for the point, place, and exercise of the virtues. But practices are not the only ground. The realization that a meaningful life is best understood as a dramatic narrative, one oriented toward a goal or purpose, calls for the exercise of the virtues in the context of our personal lives, beyond the mere confines of a practice.

Insofar as we search for meaning and purpose, itself a goal-oriented pursuit, the virtues are those habits of character and forms of excellence that facilitate our search for meaning and purpose. And if each of us pursues meaning and purpose, without which there could be no unity or coherence to our lives, then we are apt to realize that none of us is alone in this search. The search for meaning and purpose is not limited to a desperate few. Rather, it is a defining part of what it means to be human, of what it means to be a creature of intentionality. And if everyone, at some point in their lives, takes up the quest for meaning and purpose, then in the context of a broader political community, the virtues are those habits of character and forms of excellence that guide our public institutions in enabling and facilitating the general search for meaning and purpose. The second stage is thus the extension of the virtues from the context of practices to that of personal life and the greater political community.

The third stage concerns what we inherit by virtue of our history and social context. If we are born into a social history, if we are defined by our past, and if we inherit the legacies of our forebears, then we are the heirs, whether we realize it or not, to traditions—moral, social, political, spiritual. These traditions are different from those that guide practices like baseball or teaching. Moral, social, political, and spiritual traditions provide the contexts of purpose in which we live out our lives, the larger frames of collective meaning that bring communities together. And if traditions are defined by goals, and by the search for meaning and purpose, then the achievement of those goals and the pursuit of that meaning and purpose is best facilitated by certain traits of character. Traditions are therefore large-scale arenas for the social embodiment and exercise of the virtues. They provide a shared normative framework for their adherents, a nonarbitrary basis for deciding between moral claims.

To take a recent example, First Nations in Canada and the United States have had to confront the aggressive push by the energy industry and their representatives in government to construct oil pipelines on Indigenous lands. The energy industry has been all too happy to offer large financial rewards to First Nations as an incentive to allow for oil development. These financial rewards can bring badly needed revenue to reserves, many of which suffer from crushing poverty and misery. Yet, in the cases of the Dakota Access Pipeline in North Dakota and the Kinder Morgan Pipeline in British Columbia, a number of First Nations have vigorously resisted the push for the construction and expansion of pipelines.

This resistance is guided by Indigenous traditions, which teach that land and water are sacred. There is thus both an ecological and a spiritual basis for the opposition to the energy industry. Within these traditions, the ecological and the spiritual far outweigh the financial and the economic. Hence, the Standing Rock Nation in North Dakota and over 150 First Nations in Canada have united in their resistance to the energy industry, not out of an emotivist declaration of will and preference, but on the basis of tradition.

MacIntyre describes traditions in organic terms. He distinguishes living from decaying, disintegrating, and dead traditions. Just as we are immersed in a personal quest for meaning and purpose, living traditions are similarly immersed in a collective quest for their own meaning and purpose. A living tradition thrives on a rich and vibrant internal debate. To use the metaphor of fire, a living tradition is kept alight through vigorous, but constructive disagreement. It further thrives on the virtues of justice, truthfulness, and courage. By implication, a decaying and disintegrating tradition abandons the quest for meaning and purpose. It stifles internal debate. It imposes a uniformity of opinion, stamping out dissent. It fails to embody the virtues of justice, truthfulness, and courage. Rather, it exemplifies their opposites, the vices of injustice, deceit, and cowardice.

Traditions: The stuff of rationality

In our popular political parlance, *tradition* is viewed as a conservative concept. It is taken to be virtually synonymous with authority, dogmatism, and irrationality. In debate handbooks, "appeal to tradition," also known as *argumentum ad antiquitatem*, is classified as a fallacy: the attempt to win an argument by pointing to the way things have always been done.[27] In political philosophy, *traditionalism* has historically been associated with Edmund Burke, who opposed revolutionary movements for social justice and equality in the name of defending the traditional social hierarchy. The Enlightenment further tarnished the idea of tradition by setting it against reason, the latter supposedly being timeless, universal, and free of cultural bias.

In defending traditions, MacIntyre does not defend the above caricature of tradition. Indeed, he does not regard the mindless appeal to authority as rational. Rather, as a historicist—that is, as someone who recognizes that everything has a history, including our conceptions of reason and rationality— MacIntyre holds that the only true form of rationality is that within traditions.

This is not an uncritical celebration of all traditions. It does not mean that all traditions are rational or that all traditions are equal. Again, he distinguishes between the living and the dying. Rather, if we wish to make sense of social conflict, then we need to understand both the nature of that conflict and the nature of rational choice. Hence, MacIntyre provides a thorough analysis of the nature and structure of traditions.

This analysis is provided in *Whose Justice? Which Rationality?* MacIntyre begins by emphasizing the historical contingency of each tradition. This means every tradition undergoes the historical stages of genesis, development, evolution, transformation, and, in certain cases, decline and fall. Contingency implies change and flux. No community can be said to be still and unchanging. Every tradition is sparked into existence by the need to answer challenges to a practice. To the extent a tradition is responsive to challenges, to that extent is it caught up in change and flux. A minimum of this type of responsiveness is a feature of all living traditions.

MacIntyre identifies three stages in the "initial development" of a tradition.[28] The first stage is when an emerging community recognizes certain texts and founding figures as the basic sources of answers. The beliefs set out by these texts and founding figures serve as first principles: the premises by which to guide subsequent thought. The second stage is when the conventional habit of deferring to the foundational texts and human authorities proves to be deficient. The community will discover contradictions and conflicting interpretations, which give rise to disagreements. The discovery of internal contradiction may impair a tradition. Worse, a community may encounter external challenges for which their tradition is insufficient.

The third stage in the life of a tradition is when a community attempts to answer these external challenges. MacIntyre refers to these challenges as "stimuli" and says the responses to such stimuli depend partly upon the existing "stock of reasons" and modes of justification internal to a tradition, and partly upon the exercise of a certain "inventiveness" to overcome and compensate for the limitations of these internal standards.[29] In this third stage, certain beliefs will be reinterpreted, others revised, and still others discarded altogether. New texts and authorities might be added to the existing canon. This process of revision is not a purely formal and abstract process. As MacIntyre puts it,

> Since beliefs are expressed in and through rituals and ritual dramas, masks and modes of dress, the ways in which houses are structured and villages and towns laid out, and of course by actions in general, the reformulations of belief are not to be thought of only in intellectual terms.[30]

It is not just that formal beliefs composed of propositional content undergo revision. Everything that expresses the beliefs of a community even in aesthetic form is also subject to change.

This third stage is not to be confused with those periods of rupture characteristic of what Thomas Kuhn calls revolutions. MacIntyre affirms that the third stage involves nothing like a mass conversion from one worldview to another, although such a conversion may very well serve as the founding moment of a new tradition. Unlike a revolution, the third stage exhibits enough of logical and normative continuity such that it remains one and the same tradition. As MacIntyre puts it, "Some core of shared belief, constitutive of allegiance to the tradition, has to survive every rupture."[31]

What makes the third stage so significant is the need, in practice, to differentiate between the concepts of truth and falsity. The third stage introduces the possibility of distinguishing between prior and present beliefs. Those beliefs that have come to be discarded are taken to be false, while those that are retained and remain operative are taken to be true. MacIntyre insightfully suggests that we come to appreciate the concept of truth by practical attributions of falsity to discarded beliefs. As he puts it, "The original and most elementary version of the correspondence theory of truth is one in which it is applied retrospectively in the form of a correspondence theory of falsity."[32]

By this, MacIntyre intends to say that we do not begin from an explicit concept of truth. We come to appreciate the concept of truth by learning that of falsity first, much like we come to appreciate the concept of order by acquiring first a sense of disorder. Such conceptual distinctions arise in the course of practical experience, that is, prior to any formal act of theorizing. We might initially believe, for example, that capital punishment deters certain crimes. But if we learn that there is no correlation between that punishment and crime rates—or that capital punishment has the opposite effect—then we would be compelled to revise our original beliefs about capital punishment. Our initial belief would have led to a disappointment of expectations. In that case, it would make sense to dismiss that belief as a falsehood. It is this ability, through memory and practical experience, to recall past beliefs that have led to disappointment that we distinguish between the concepts of truth and falsity.

According to MacIntyre, practical distinctions between the concepts of truth and falsity presuppose a theory of mind, of the way the mind works in relation to the natural and social world. The mind, he contends, works actively to acquire a reliable grasp or picture of the world. The mind is not like a camera that takes neutral snapshots. It's not a mirror that offers an unmediated reflection or image of the natural and social world. Rather, the mind is active and responsive, seeking, as the need arises, to secure an evermore reliable grasp of the world, one that will not be disappointed by the test of experience. This conception of mind is therefore not that idealized by the tradition of Cartesian thought, in which the basic or foundational units of knowledge are unmediated representations of the world. What MacIntyre proposes instead is a conception of mind

> as *activity*, of mind as engaging with the natural and social world in such activities as identification, reidentification, collecting, separating, classifying, and naming and all this by touching, grasping, pointing, breaking down, building up, calling to, answering to, and so on.[33]

Reliable knowledge about the world is simply that which survives the test of practical experience and proves resistant to disappointment. The mind, moreover, is purpose-driven, such that the types of experience that impinge upon the pursuit of one or another goal serve as the test of reliability.[34]

None of this is to say that the mind does not produce pictures or representations of the natural and social worlds—it clearly does. It is just that these pictures and representations are, and can only be, works-in-progress, whose accuracy we gauge by their capacity to avoid disappointment in the course of seeking to achieve "some specific purpose of mind."[35] Such working pictures and representations are therefore open to revision in the light of disappointing experience. Although we treat our current pictures and representations as corresponding to the world, there is, strictly speaking, no actual relation of correspondence, no metaphysical link between words and things.

The theory of mind as active and corrective implies a theory of truth, that is, an account of the place of truth in ordinary linguistic practice. This account is not to be confused with a formal, analytical definition of truth. To take a claim or picture to be true is to treat it in practice as though it would forever stand up to the test of practical experience. It is to hold, even if implicitly, that such a claim or picture will never lead to disappointment, "no matter how searching the enquiry, no matter how much evidence is provided, no matter what developments in rational enquiry may occur."[36] Such a claim or representation therefore invites the test of rigorous scrutiny—of questions, objections, challenges, counter-claims, and counter-representations.

To treat a claim or representation as true is, in effect, to nominate it for competition in the arena of "dialectical questioning."[37] What counts as success or failure in this arena is a vital and unavoidable question, but it is a question nonetheless secondary to the commitment to rational accountability implicit in the very act of making a claim to truth. The goal of such accountability is, as MacIntyre puts it, "to discover which is the best answer to be proposed so far."[38] Those claims and representations that have thus far withstood the test of dialectical questioning and the "framing of objections" are the most deserving of the status of truth and therefore of our rational allegiance.[39] This type of allegiance, however, is, at best, provisional, for it leaves open the possibility that, at some future point, the claims that have thus far warranted our assent may, through the very same process that vindicated them, be rationally defeated.

As MacIntyre points out, the account of rationality sketched thus far is incompatible with two readily familiar models of rationality that have historically dominated a good deal of modern philosophical thinking. The first of these is the Cartesian model, which begins the process of inquiry on the basis of what it takes to be self-evident metaphysical first principles immune to the need for revision and rational justification. By contrast, a tradition-constituted model of rationality begins the process of inquiry on the basis of what it fully recognizes as premises generated in the course of history and the status of which is therefore contingent at best. Such premises are treated in practice as first principles, even timeless first principles.

Their justification, however, is specific to historical circumstance; justification is by no means self-evident. According to a tradition-constituted model of rationality, the validity of a tradition's first principles is justified only insofar as it withstands the test of dialectical questioning in the course of a very specific history. Those principles are therefore not immune to the possibility of revision or even of abandonment altogether.

The second model of rationality is the one famously spawned by Hegel. It posits in advance an endpoint to the process of inquiry, a final moment at which the search for answers will have reached its ultimate logical conclusion. The Hegelian model envisions a trans-historical subject that, in the course of time, will achieve the kind of awareness and self-awareness that effectively brings all inquiry to an end. By contrast, the tradition-based model of rationality claims no such finality or endpoint. It rests in the end upon nothing more than pure contingency and provisionality. As MacIntyre puts it, "No one at any stage can ever rule out the future possibility of their present beliefs and judgments being shown to be inadequate in a variety of ways."[40]

Although MacIntyre does not mention it here, the tradition-based conception of rationality is distinct also from the deontological model of rationality exemplified in the thought of Kant. The deontological model produces final and authoritative moral judgments. It is a monological conception of rationality that rules out in advance the need for rational discourse and communication. By contrast, the tradition-based model is open-ended and indeterminate. Although it is admittedly norm-laden and therefore presupposes a minimum of normative commitments, these norms and commitments are epistemic, not moral or political. The open-endedness and indeterminacy of the tradition-based model therefore encourages—requires, in fact—communication and rational deliberation.

Thus, according to a tradition-based model of rationality, neither first principles nor practical judgments are exempted from the demands for rational justification. Between the two, challenges to first principles are more far more serious. Sometimes, traditions face challenges that can't be answered by mere revision and interpretation. In scenarios of this kind, the entire theoretical edifice of a tradition threatens to unravel, thereby plunging its adherents into what MacIntyre calls an epistemological crisis.[41]

These moments of crisis disrupt the search for answers. Aims are questioned, beliefs are found deficient, presuppositions are suspected of being misleading. A tradition racked by an epistemological crisis can no longer rely upon the first principles that carried it up to this point. Where first principles had once provided unity, they now feed doubt and confusion. Doubt grows. Division intensifies. Disagreement proves irresolvable. The standards by which a tradition had so far measured its success now stand to indict that same tradition for ceasing to make progress. In the face of an epistemological crisis, the adherents of a tradition are compelled to undertake nothing short of a full-scale reformation.

According to MacIntyre, a successful reformation would need to exhibit three features. First, the reformed tradition would have to answer the challenge that forced it into a crisis, without falling back upon those principles, methods, and assumptions that failed them in the first place. Second, the reformed tradition would need to possess the explanatory power to account for the weaknesses and deficiencies of those earlier inadequate principles, methods, and assumptions. Third, it would have to provide the kind of perspective from which a tradition's adherents could document its development, evolution, and reformation while making explicit the principles that would need to survive each historical stage to guarantee "fundamental continuity."[42]

Those traditions unable to survive an epistemological crisis face one of three outcomes. Its adherents can fall back upon the dogmatic assertion and reassertion of the very principles, methods, and assumptions that generated an epistemological crisis in the first place. Earlier in the argument, MacIntyre refers to "the appeal to the authority of established belief" as the "weakest form of argument."[43] He notes also that those founding texts and figures whose authority is taken to derive from "their relationship to the divine" will characteristically be "exempt from repudiation."[44] Traditions based upon such authority are therefore prone to falling back upon dogmatic assertion and reassertion.

The second possible outcome for traditions confronting an epistemological crisis is to undergo a revolution from which a new, and substantially different, tradition will emerge. Revolutions characteristically exhibit a fundamental break with the theoretical structure of the earlier tradition. They involve a radical change in perspective. Now, the old tradition appears radically different. The third possible outcome is the dissolution of a tradition altogether, in which there is neither reformation nor revolution, and in which the community ceases to be a community in anything except a historical sense.

Conclusion

Why does MacIntyre bother with all this talk of epistemological crises? The answer is that they afford the kind of second-order perspective by which the members of a tradition can distinguish between truth and justification. This second-order perspective allows them to conclude that what they might believe to be true and just could later be shown, by their own standards, to be false and unjustified. Truth as an ideal is greater than what we take to be justified. This insight is the mark of a certain intellectual maturity, the kind of maturity that allows for rational choice between traditions. In the next chapter, I explore MacIntyre's model of rational choice in detail.

Notes

1   Alasdair MacIntyre, *Whose Justice? Which Rationality?* Notre Dame, IN: University of Notre Dame Press, 1988, 12.

2   Heraclitus, *Fragments*. A Text and Translation with a Commentary by T. M. Robinson. Toronto, ON: University of Toronto Press, 185.

3   Ibid., 184.

4   John Anderson, *Lectures on Greek Philosophy*, edited by Creagh McLean Cole. Sydney, Australia: University of Sydney Press, 68–72.

5   Ibid., 69.

6   MacIntyre refers to the "great Australian philosopher John Anderson," who observes that "it is through conflict and something only through conflict that we learn what our ends and purposes are" (*After Virtue*, 163–64). MacIntyre sees Aristotle as lacking an appreciation of the role of conflict in discovering our ends and purposes.

7   MacIntyre, *Whose Justice? Which Rationality?* 12.

8   Ibid.

9   MacIntyre, *After Virtue*, 250.

10 For an account of MacIntyre's conception of practices, see *After Virtue*, 181–204.

11 On MacIntyre's concept of traditions, see *After Virtue*, 194, 222–23.

12 John Thorn, *Baseball in the Garden of Eden: The Secret History of the Early Game*. New York, NY: Simon & Schuster, 2011.

13 Colleen Flaherty, "Relationship Restrictions: Academe Sees a New Wave of Faculty-Student Dating Bans in the Era of Me Too," *Inside Higher Ed*, May 24, 2018. https://www.insidehighered.com/news/2018/05/24/academe-sees-new-wave-faculty-student-relationship-restrictions-era-me-too (accessed January 16, 2019).

14 Brianna Caza, Heather C. Vough, and Sherry Moss, "The Hardest Thing about Working in the Gig Economy? Forging a Cohesive Sense of Self," *Harvard Business Review*, October 27, 2017. https://hbr.org/2017/10/the-hardest-thing-about-working-in-the-gig-economy-forging-a-cohesive-sense-of-self (accessed January 16, 2019).

15 Ibid.

16 Ibid.

17 Ibid.

18 Ibid.

19 MacIntyre, *After Virtue*, 208.

20 Ibid., 204.

21 Josh Boldt, "Summer Survival Strategies for Adjuncts," *ChronicleVitae*, April 15, 2014. https://chroniclevitae.com/news/444-summer-survival-strategies-for-adjuncts (accessed January 16, 2019).

22 Ibid.

23 Alastair Gee, "Facing Poverty, Academics Turn to Sex Work and Sleeping in Cars," *The Guardian*, September 29, 2017. https://www.theguardian.com/us-news/2017/sep/28/adjunct-professors-homeless-sex-work-academia-poverty (accessed April 4, 2019).

24 MacIntyre, *After Virtue*, 204–25.

25 George Monbiot traces the roots of loneliness and much of contemporary mental illness to our free market society. See his "Neoliberalism Is Creating Loneliness: That's What's Wrenching Society Apart," *The Guardian*, October 12, 2016. https://www.theguardian.com/commentisfree/2016/oct/12/neoliberalism-creating-loneliness-wrenching-society-apart (accessed April 4, 2019).

26 Ibid., 273.

27 Douglas N. Walton, *Informal Fallacies: Towards a Theory of Argument Criticism*. Philadelphia, PA: John Benjamins, 1987, 200.

28 MacIntyre, *Whose Justice? Which Rationality?* 355.

29 Ibid.

30 Ibid.

31 Ibid., 356.

32 Ibid.

33 Ibid., emphasis added.

34 MacIntyre's discussion of the mind and its interactive relationship to the social environment is remarkably similar—virtually indistinguishable, in fact—from the account of the mind developed by such classical pragmatists as John Dewey and George Herbert Mead. See John Dewey, "The Reflex Arc Concept in Psychology," *Psychology Review* 3 (1896): 357–70; and Mead, *Mind, Self, and Society*.

35 MacIntyre, *Whose Justice? Which Rationality?* 357.

36 Ibid., 358. MacIntyre's conception of truth is indistinguishable from Cheryl Misak's account of Charles S. Peirce's theory of truth. On Misak's illuminating reading, the key is indefeasibility. See Cheryl Misak, *Truth and the End of Inquiry: A Peircean Account of Truth*. Oxford, UK: Oxford University Press, 2004.

37 Ibid.

38 Ibid.

39 Ibid.

40 Ibid., 361.

41 Ibid., 361; Alasdair MacIntyre, "Epistemological Crises, Dramatic Narrative and the Philosophy of Science," *The Monist* 60.4 (1977): 453–72.

42 MacIntyre, *Whose Justice? Which Rationality?* 362.

43 Ibid., 359.

44 Ibid., 355.

7

The Ship at Sea

In his book, *Empiricism and Sociology*, Otto Neurath offers the following indelible metaphor for the nature of knowledge in the modern world:

> We are like sailors on the open sea who must reconstruct their ship but are never able to start afresh from the bottom. Where a beam is taken away a new one must at once be put there, and for this the rest of the ship is used as support. In this way, by using old beams and driftwood, the ship can be shaped entirely anew, but only by gradual reconstruction.[1]

Popularized by Willard Van Orman Quine in *Word and Object*, Neurath's metaphor of the boat offers a vivid critique of foundationalism, the dream of a solid bedrock on which to build the edifice of eternal knowledge.[2] As the metaphor indicates, we will never reach the shores of such knowledge. Instead of building on solid land, we must settle for reconstructing a ship already at sea.

Yet, the absence of foundations is not a reason for hopelessness or resignation. We *can* build knowledge about the natural world. We *can* do things with this knowledge. The ship can still sail. But the status of our knowledge is provisional at best, for it can always be improved upon, even superseded, at some later point. This conclusion is disappointing to some, liberating to others.

Though he did not intend it, Neurath's boat is also a useful, if imperfect, metaphor for making sense of moral and political discourse. On the one hand, we lack anything like foundations in morality and politics. We have no fixed ground on which to stand, no basis for objective or universal judgments. On the other hand, neither are we fated to meaninglessness and disorder. We need not suffer from what Richard Bernstein calls the Cartesian anxiety, "the dread of madness and chaos where nothing is fixed, where we can neither touch bottom nor support ourselves on the surface."[3] We *do* have contingent ground on which to stand. We *do* have a ship to keep us afloat. But the substance of this ground, the nature of the ship, is a matter of controversy. As I have argued, Rawls and Habermas get it wrong. They claim a permanent anchor that doesn't exist. Mouffe, I have argued, gets it wrong, too. She would have us toss out the tools that would enable us to navigate the high seas.

Chapter 5 examined Mouffe's agonistic pluralism and radical democracy. This conception of democracy rests on certain key premises. One of those premises is the idea that rational argumentation between different frameworks is impossible. There are material consequences to this premise. It means democratic politics is a nonrational practice. It means there's no place for the norm of truth. Without truth, politics becomes an unmediated battle of wills for political power. Worse, politics without truth is one of the components of totalitarianism.

Yet, if Mouffe's starting premise is correct, if we cannot arbitrate between different frameworks, then we are indeed fated to a nonrational politics, exemplified by the culture wars today. A rational alternative thus hinges on the possibility of arbitrating between different frameworks. One of MacIntyre's most important philosophical achievements is to show how this is possible. Yet, it is one of the least recognized aspects of his political philosophy. In what follows, I wish to make explicit the rationalist component of MacIntyre's project.

"A Heady and Exotic Doctrine"

Mouffe's argument against rational argumentation hinges on the acceptance of what has come to be known as the incommensurability thesis. There is something strangely seductive about the idea of incommensurability, of two different conceptual universes with very little, if anything, in common. Incommensurability, as Donald Davidson describes it, "is a heady and exotic doctrine."[4] It is easy to get carried away with it. There are, of course, different versions of this doctrine.

Wittgenstein provides an elementary version of it in *On Certainty*.[5] But the classic statement on incommensurability comes to us from Thomas Kuhn in *The Structure of Scientific Revolutions*. Reading *Structure* has become a rite of passage in graduate studies in the humanities and social sciences. More than half a century after it was first published, *Structure* still sparks lively debates, heated disagreements, and bitter objections. For many academics, especially those partial to postmodern thought, *Structure* is treated almost as a work of scripture. The challenge that Kuhn poses to the idea of a universal scientific method and to the modern ideal of scientific progress has a delightful subversiveness to it.

But the claim that different frameworks are separated by an unbridgeable chasm and that we cannot rationally arbitrate between them is often taken to be an unquestionable premise. Mouffe relies partly upon Kuhn, though largely upon Wittgenstein, when she writes, "It is generally acknowledged that rational argumentation is only possible when there is a shared framework."[6] Mouffe treats the incommensurability thesis as though it were a given, a premise as basic as the law of gravity. Her project hinges upon this rather weighty bit of logic. Remarkably, she does not actually demonstrate the validity of this logic, but rather treats it as indisputable. In doing so, Mouffe seems to imply that only a fool would think that we could argue across frameworks. To evaluate the merits of this logic, it is necessary to revisit Kuhn's original statement on incommensurability.

Incommensurability: The classic statement

Kuhn conceived of *The Structure of Scientific Revolutions* as a historian of science. During his early years at Harvard, he taught undergraduate courses in the history of science. In this capacity, he covered a wide range of historical ideas: modern, premodern, medieval, ancient. He covered antiquated scientific theories that, to our lights, seem surprising, bizarre, foreign, even amusing. After moving to Berkeley in 1956, Kuhn became acquainted with Stanley Cavell and Paul Feyerabend. Cavell was a devoted student of Wittgenstein's philosophy and very likely introduced Kuhn to his writings. On the influence of Cavell, Feyerabend, and Wittgenstein, Kuhn developed the ideas that would eventually become *Structure*, which was published as a volume in Neurath's series *The International Encyclopedia of Unified Science*.

With the publication of *Structure*, Kuhn effectively launched the field of science studies as we know it today. He came under harsh criticism for some of the ideas contained in it. He took this criticism seriously and subsequently revised his core thesis, eventually settling upon a final version. The effect of *Structure* since then has been profound. The concepts of paradigms, paradigm shifts, and incommensurability have achieved a kind of universal currency within the humanities and social sciences. We now even hear talk of "paradigms" and "paradigm shifts" beyond the arcane discourses of the academic world.

The main task of *Structure* is to challenge the modern myth of rational scientific progress which views the history of science as a linear process of the slow, but steady accretion of scientific truth. Kuhn's reading of the history of scientific theories, however, paints a very different picture. Instead of a linear process of accretion, he finds long periods of relative stability, what he calls "normal science," which are interrupted by dramatic moments of rupture. Kuhn attributes the periods of normal science to what he calls "paradigms," which can roughly be understood as a basic conceptual framework for scientific investigation. The term he gives to moments of rupture is "revolutions."

For Kuhn, the really interesting question is what happens during scientific revolutions. Why does a community of scientists "abandon" an existing paradigm in favor of a new one? What does it take for this community to "convert" to a new worldview?[7] The use of the terms "convert" and "conversion" is telling. It indicates that the switch to a new paradigm is not rational, but rather a leap of faith, much like the conversion experiences of those who embrace a new religion.

To clarify the nature of conversion, Kuhn identifies three distinct, but related features of radical difference that he terms "incommensurability." The first feature of incommensurability is the absence of a "neutral system of language or concepts."[8] The absence of such a system creates a barrier for the rational comparison of scientific theories. Such a comparison requires a common set of criteria for evaluating competing theories. But different paradigms have different criteria. They have different aims and research methods. Any evaluation, therefore, can only be carried out on one set of terms or another. Hence, the members of rival paradigms "are always at least slightly at cross purposes."[9] Each side rests on basic premises and assumptions. There is some degree of overlap, but a larger degree of difference. Differences in basic premises and assumptions mean we have no way of demonstrating the superiority of one side to the satisfaction of the other. As Kuhn puts it, "Though each may hope to convert the other to his way of seeing science and its problems, neither may hope to prove his case."[10]

The second feature of incommensurability concerns semantic differences. Although different paradigms may share numerous terms, the semantic webs in which those terms derive their meaning differ. So, for example, a concept like *motion* will mean one thing in an Aristotelian paradigm, but something else in a Galilean paradigm. These differences in meaning can influence the outcome of scientific experiments and observation. They create different expectations and therefore yields different conclusions. But also, if scientists mean different things despite using the same terms, it can create confusion when they talk to each other. The "inevitable result" of semantic differences are "misunderstanding" and "partial" communication. As Kuhn puts it, the two sides "must fail to make complete contact with each other's viewpoints."[11]

The third feature of incommensurability concerns differences in the way scientists view reality. According to Kuhn, the members of different scientific paradigms "practice their trades in different worlds."[12] They do not just think and speak differently; rather, they see reality through radically different lenses. Thus, if the members of different paradigms investigate one and the same natural phenomenon, one side may see something the other side does not see, maybe even cannot see, owing to a constitutive blind spot. This third feature leads Kuhn to the provocative conclusion that conversion to a new paradigm is a prerequisite to communication with its members. Following this logic, you cannot merely peer into another scientific universe and expect to figure out what's going on. Rather, communication and understanding require nothing short of a full-scale transformation of mind in the form of a "gestalt switch."[13] At first, you see one pattern. After adjusting your vision, you see another pattern. To speak to the Other, we need to change patterns. To speak to a Copernican, we must first become Copernicans.

Because of these three features of incommensurability—theoretical, semantic, and perceptual—Kuhn insists that "neither proof nor error is at issue" in the conversion to a new paradigm.[14] This raises an important question: What guides scientists to adopt a new way of scientific thinking? If not proof, then what? How, exactly, is conversion "induced"? Kuhn's answer to this question is "techniques of persuasion."[15] But it is not just any kind of persuasion. It is decidedly *nonrational* (though not irrational) persuasion.

Despite insisting upon the impossibility of formal proofs, Kuhn concedes that scientific arguments do play some role in conversions. But he denies that they play a decisive role or even an important one. Rather, the primary reasons for which scientists switch their allegiance to a new paradigm are multiple, varied, and very often nonscientific in character. These nonscientific reasons range from the "idiosyncrasies of autobiography and personality," to the nationality and reputation of one's teachers and fellow scientists.[16] Although explanatory power is the main criterion for rational choice during periods of normal science, it takes a back seat during scientific revolutions. According to Kuhn, aesthetic reasons and considerations, such as the beauty or simplicity of a new paradigm, are very often the primary motives for conversion.

To summarize, when a group of scientists convert to a new paradigm, they do so on the basis of a random, and not always connected, cluster of reasons and motives: aesthetic, circumstantial, personal, rational. Because of the vast differences between paradigms, the movement from one to another is necessarily one of fundamental rupture and discontinuity unguided by any overarching logic or rationality. Hence, Kuhn's insistence upon "conversion experiences" and "gestalt switches," in which the transformation "must occur all at once (though not necessarily in an instant) or not at all."[17]

Limits of communication

In the postscript to *Structure*, Kuhn addresses several charges leveled by his critics, two of which he responds to in detail. The first is the charge that he condemns scientists from different paradigms to permanent incommunicability. Kuhn emphatically denies this, drawing a distinction between partial and total incommunicability. He concedes that semantic differences limit communication and understanding between two sides. These differences lead to "communication breakdown."[18] But this breakdown is the beginning of communication, not the end.

If scientists find themselves in the middle of a breakdown, then they should come to see each other as "members of different language communities."[19] Seeing each other in this way is a reason to learn each other's languages. When they do, they can figure out what led to the breakdown in the first place. By learning each other's languages, they can help translate those problematic areas that created a communication barrier. Translation enables each side to "experience vicariously something of the merits and defects of each other's point of view."[20]

The second charge that Kuhn addresses is that of irrationalism. Kuhn equally emphatically denies that conversion to a new paradigm proceeds either on the basis of purely subjective reasons or through "mystical apperception."[21] Instead, he affirms that conversion is guided by "good reasons."[22] More importantly, despite the impossibility of rational arbitration, all scientists regardless of their paradigms share a common goal, namely, problem-solving. Thus, scientists have more in common than we thought. Because they share the goal of problem-solving, they have a mutual incentive to learn each other's languages and see each other's point of view.

Kuhn's answer to the charges of incommunicability and irrationality alike is translation. Curiously, he defines translation as a "technique of persuasion."[23] Through translation, scientists from one side can enter into the universe of the other, see the natural world through its lens, and, without making a conscious decision or reaching a formal conclusion, realize at some point that they have thoroughly internalized that lens and that there is no turning back. To reach this point of no return is to be "persuaded."[24] Persuasion, in short, is conviction without demonstration. Although translation offers no guarantees of resolving conflicts between paradigms, it is nonetheless the medium of persuasion.

MacIntyre on rational choice

In his essay, "Epistemological Crises, Dramatic Narrative, and the Philosophy of Science," MacIntyre offers an original and provocative critique of Kuhn's negative conclusion concerning the possibility of rational choice between incommensurable paradigms. That critique begins with a meditation on the character of epistemological crises in everyday life. As MacIntyre describes it, an epistemological crisis results when some unexpected event or experience throws the meaning of one's life into profound confusion. For example, an honors student who receives a failing grade for the first time, an established politician who loses an election to a little known newcomer, someone who discovers that their spouse is having an affair—these individuals are all liable to experience a crisis of self-understanding and understanding of others.

The immediate difficulty confronting those who experience such moments of acute personal crisis is how to interpret the disorienting experience, for any number of interpretations of that experience may appear equally plausible. Worse, the inability to choose between so many equally plausible interpretations may lead to further confusion and frustration, possibly leaving the subject in a state of agonizing paralysis.

MacIntyre points to Shakespeare's *Hamlet* as a fitting dramaturgical example of the kind of crisis he has in mind. The play begins after the death of King Hamlet, whose brother Claudius has ascended to the throne and married Queen Gertrude. Outside Elsinore Castle, the junior Hamlet encounters a ghost, claiming to be his father. The ghost tells the young Hamlet that Claudius had him poisoned. He urges the young Hamlet to avenge his death. Shaken by the encounter, Hamlet vows to seek justice. To conceal his intentions, he feigns madness. But this outward act of madness obscures a growing inner crisis, for Hamlet is torn between the need to do what is right and the need to know what actually happened—between justice and evidence. Seeking revenge without first confirming what actually happened would not be justice. Yet, searching endlessly for evidence would undermine the cause of justice.

The problem with Hamlet's search for evidence is that he does not know whom to trust. He questions the authenticity of the ghost. He questions everyone around him, including Gertrude, Ophelia, as well as Rosencrantz and Guildenstern. Hamlet faces a tension between evidence and interpretation. On the one hand, what he treats as evidence will determine his interpretive framework. On the other, what he treats as his interpretive framework will determine what he regards as evidence. Hamlet therefore finds himself trapped in "epistemological circularity."[25] His sense of reality begins to crack. He realizes that the original story of his family, on which he had relied for so long, is no longer reliable.

He therefore scrambles desperately to find a new story, a new way to make sense of the reality around him, a story that not only will enable him to restore intelligibility to his life but which will also be *true*. That is, whatever picture of reality he comes up with must strike a balance between evidence and intelligibility. Too strong an emphasis upon evidence at the cost of intelligibility, or too strong an emphasis upon intelligibility at the cost of accurately understanding the world around him, is a recipe for madness. This tension becomes debilitating for Hamlet. Beneath the public act of madness, he privately plunges into actual madness, even reaching the brink of suicide. In the end, Hamlet discovers the true story, but only moments before his death.

MacIntyre therefore wonders: What does it take to emerge from such a crisis? How to avoid the descent into madness? According to MacIntyre, if epistemological crises are the outcome of unreliable narratives, then they are resolved by the discovery of a more powerful narrative, one that enables the subject to see her past in a new and more illuminating light. A more powerful narrative enables the human subject to understand not only the appeal of the old narrative but also why it was unreliable. The old narrative, having been placed under the gaze of the new one, thus becomes an explicit object of reflection.

At this point, we can think about what we used to think. We can also understand why it was wrong. According to MacIntyre, to have recovered from an epistemological crisis is to have learned a practical lesson in philosophy, namely, the distinction between truth and justification, or between "is" and "seems." If we appreciate that our old beliefs were unreliable, we can appreciate that what we believe now or in the future can also turn out to be unreliable. There is no good reason to think that we have arrived at *the* truth. Those who take this lesson to heart would in effect have become what in the idiom of American pragmatism are known as fallibilists.

MacIntyre compares the fictional experience of Hamlet to the actual experiences of Descartes and Hume, two figures whose epistemological crises played a defining role in their philosophical development. In seeking to purge himself of all inherited belief and bias so as to begin from a blank slate and build knowledge on a foundation of absolute certainty, Descartes notoriously claimed to have doubted everything, including his very own existence. But this claim could not have been true. As MacIntyre points out, Descartes could not possibly have purged himself of all belief and bias, for he failed to realize that the very language through which he articulated his radical doubt was itself suffused with belief and bias. Descartes managed to recover from his crisis but through self-delusion. He could not see the implicit background of belief that sustained him through his period of doubt to his eventual recovery.

Hume's crisis, as MacIntyre observes, was very different. Unlike Descartes, Hume really did doubt everything, or at least began to, until he lost his grip on the world and eventually himself, resulting in a devastating mental breakdown. It took Hume years to recover a sense of the world around him and himself. As MacIntyre points out, the difference between Descartes and Hume is that Descartes's skepticism rested on a stable background of implicit belief, while Hume's skepticism was so extreme that he was no longer able to make sense of his own skepticism. Unable to understand the world or himself, Hume descended into a real-world version of Hamlet's madness.

But what do these stories of crisis and madness have to do with the philosophy of science? MacIntyre argues that Kuhn's description of conversion experiences is *Cartesian in nature*: scientists switching from one paradigm to another without acknowledging the continuity of belief that makes such a move possible in the first place. The lesson that we learn from Descartes is that even a radical change of perspective requires some basic continuity of belief, of normative and conceptual commitment, while the lesson we learn from Hume is that even to move toward something like an absolute transformation is to lose the possibility of making sense of that movement, risking a descent into incoherence and madness. The passage from an old paradigm to a new paradigm, then, must be something other than the nonrational "gestalt switch" that Kuhn describes. But how are we to make sense of that passage? What does the adoption of a new paradigm involve, if not a conversion experience and "gestalt switch"?

MacIntyre answers this question by considering one of the most dramatic episodes in the history of science. After being trained in the principles and methods of Aristotelian physics, Galileo discovered a recurring anomaly in the then-prevailing explanations of motion: the inability to account for differences in the velocity of moving objects. Why, for example, does a stone roll down a hill at one speed, but down a steeper hill at a faster speed? Aristotle had theorized that the physical world consisted of four elements: earth, water, air, and fire. All physical objects come from these elements. Every object has a nature. The nature of a rock, being made from earth, is to return to earth, where it reaches its natural resting place. The nature of a flame is to move upward, where it similarly reaches its natural resting place.

Aristotle had further theorized that objects move according to two types of motion: natural and violent. Natural motion is propelled by internal forces. A rock falling to the ground is natural motion propelled by the internal force of the rock. A rock that is pushed or thrown is a case of violent motion brought about by some external force. But this theory of motion, which remarkably went unchallenged for almost 2,000 years, could carry the Aristotelian physicist only so far. When confronted by more complex physical phenomena, such as different rates of velocity, it proved explanatorily powerless. Aristotle's distinction between natural and violent motion could be of no use here since the differences in velocity could not be explained by appeal to internal and external forces. Something was missing.

Galileo's achievement was not to fill in the missing piece while sticking with Aristotelian physics, but rather to propose an altogether different model of physics, one replete with new theoretical principles and empirical assumptions about the physical world. By discarding the idea of essential natures and by redefining the idea of motion, Galileo was able to introduce a new set of variables, such as time, acceleration, and friction. In so doing, Galileo developed a more powerful conceptual system, one that enabled him to answer long-standing, unresolved questions about motion *and* to make sense of the theoretical weaknesses of Aristotelian physics. Galileo's new physics thus not only made a difference to scientific practice but also made a difference to historical understanding. As MacIntyre writes:

> The criterion of a successful theory is that it enables us to understand its predecessors in a newly intelligible way. It, at one and the same time, enables us to understand precisely why its predecessors have to be rejected or modified and also why, without and before its illumination, past theory could have remained credible. It introduces new standards for evaluating the past. It recasts the narrative which constitutes the continuous reconstruction of the scientific tradition.[26]

The appeal of Galileo's physics is not just that it resolved a recurring problem in Aristotelian physics, but that it also explained why Aristotelian physics had consistently failed to solve it. Those who switched to Galileo's physics could now recognize the errors and limitations of their previous understanding.

In the postscript to *Structure*, Kuhn argues, in apparent contradiction to his original remarks in the first edition, that "one need not unravel the details of biography and personality" to understand "why science develops as it does."[27] But for MacIntyre, the details of biography and personality—the role of experience—are very much to the point. They can explain why scientists abandon existing paradigms for new ones, and why the movement between them is one of continuity as opposed to rupture. "What is carried over from one paradigm to another," MacIntyre argues, "are epistemological ideals and a correlative understanding of what constitutes the progress of a single intellectual life."[28] These ideals enabled Galileo to make sense of his attempt at a new physics and enabled countless scientists to make sense of their transition from the old physics to the new. Contrary to Kuhn, MacIntyre reads paradigm shifts as rational transitions from weaker to stronger science, a development intelligible in the light of the epistemological ideals and commitments that survive each transition.[29]

MacIntyre therefore differs from Kuhn on the possibility of rational comparison and choice. Kuhn recognizes that the incommensurability thesis requires a new idea of rationality as historical and multiple. MacIntyre agrees but contends that this new idea must reflect a better understanding of the history of science. "It is more rational," he says,

> to accept one theory or paradigm and to reject its predecessor when the later theory or paradigm provides a standpoint from which the acceptance, the life-story, and the rejection of the previous theory or paradigm can be recounted in a more intelligible historical narrative than previously.[30]

Drawing from Imre Lakatos, MacIntyre links the theoretical power of a paradigm to its historiographical power to account for its relationship to a rival paradigm.[31] That is, he takes theoretical and historiographical power to be one and the same thing. By linking theory and method to narrative and history, MacIntyre thus convincingly shows how rational choice between paradigms is possible.

Comparative reason

MacIntyre thus offers a way out of the objectivist-relativist divide by demonstrating the possibility of rational choice without foundations. The key here lies in the power of the implicit. By focusing on implicit epistemological ideals and commitments, the kind of ideals and commitments we hold by virtue of being subjects of speech and action, it is possible to appeal to standards to which we are bound in practice, if not in theory.

This focus means breaking our objectivist preoccupation with explicit premises by taking into account the implicit practical reasoning of the human subject. It means moving away from what Hilary Putnam calls a "God's Eye View," the pretension to some standpoint outside of time, history, and culture.[32] From a God's Eye View, we would pretend to look at the explicit principles of some paradigm and then pronounce it correct or incorrect—objectively. On MacIntyre's comparative approach, we would focus instead on the passage of the human subject from one paradigm to another, and the difference that passage makes to her practical reasoning.

How would the human subject be affected by adopting a new worldview? How would her practical reasoning change in the light of her ideals and commitments? The answer is that the passage to a new paradigm would result in what Charles Taylor, building upon MacIntyre, calls a "gain" or a "loss"—a positive or a negative change in explanatory power.[33] Gains and losses are measured by the pursuit of ideals and commitments. The relationship between paradigms is such that the passage between them will not be the same in both directions. If, in one direction, the passage to a new paradigm results in a gain in explanatory power, then the passage in the reverse direction will result in a loss.

Explanatory power is of two kinds. First, there's a paradigm's power to explain natural phenomena. Second, there is a paradigm's power to explain another paradigm. It was one thing for Galileo's physics to explain motion. It was another for Galileo's physics to explain why Aristotle's physics could not explain motion. The power to explain theoretical weaknesses and blind spots in a competing paradigm is the mark of rational superiority. This type of comparison cannot be made from a God's Eye View external to all paradigms. Rather, it is made internally, by moving back and forth between paradigms and documenting the differences. Those differences will take the form of a narrative history.

It helps to return to the example of Galileo. We can write a plausible narrative of a scientist who, having been trained in Aristotle's physics, becomes frustrated by the inability to explain the projectile motion of an arrow. This scientist then discovers in Galileo's physics a framework powerful enough not only to answer this puzzle but also to explain why Aristotle's physics had reached an impasse. Because of a firm commitment to truth and understanding, this scientist then abandons Aristotle's physics for his own. By contrast, it would be difficult, if not impossible, to write a plausible narrative of a scientist who, having been trained in Galileo's physics, and being committed to the ideals of truth and understanding, would choose to abandon a framework that explains projectile motion for one that does not *while remaining committed to those same ideals*. To move from Galilean to Aristotelian physics is thus to lose the ability to answer tricky questions about motion. It also means losing the ability to explain the success of Galilean physics. A gain in one direction is a loss in the other.

Frameworks in science and ethics

All of this is to say that Mouffe is wrong when she denies the possibility of rational argumentation between frameworks. Her talk of frameworks betrays a dichotomized, all-or-nothing view: either we have common premises between frameworks or we cannot reason with each other at all. What MacIntyre shows is that we can safely discard the all-or-nothing coin. We have another way of thinking about disagreement, one that takes into account something missing from the talk of frameworks, namely, the human subject who moves between them.

And if scientific frameworks are rationally arbitrable, then there is no good reason not to think that ethical frameworks are not similarly arbitrable. This is the point of *Whose Justice? Which Rationality?* in which MacIntyre applies his insights about scientific paradigms to his analysis of moral traditions. If we look at the passage of the human subject from one scientific paradigm to the next, and examine the difference it makes in practical reasoning, then we should be able to do the same for the transition between traditions.

If we look at our social and political history, say, the fight for equality, we can see that the transition from older, more hierarchical worldviews to newer, more egalitarian ones follows a pattern similar to paradigm shifts in the history of science. The shift, for example, from a homophobic culture to a more tolerant and inclusive one follows this pattern.

Only a few decades ago, it was perfectly legal and morally acceptable to discriminate against queer people. In the homophobic imagination, queer people represented a threat to the order of nature. They were thought to be morally corrupt, perverse, ill, twisted, deviant. They were placed in the same moral category as child molesters. Hence, queer sex was illegal and queer people were criminalized, both justified by the belief that queer people were intrinsically bad and therefore deserved to be punished.

But this worldview has been falling apart all over the Western world within our lifetimes. Decades of activism, beginning with the gay liberation movement of the 1960s, have challenged the homophobic worldview, subjecting it to systematic critique. Activists have challenged the traditional myth of queer people as corrupt, devious, ill, perverted, and the like. They have shown that queer people are no less decent and honorable than any other groups. They have asserted queer people's basic humanity and dignity. They have emphasized their contributions to society. They have appealed to the principles of liberty and equality, pointing out the inconsistency in allowing liberty and equality for some, but not for others.

Perhaps most importantly, activists have challenged the view that same-sex marriage will somehow undermine society, a view still held by reactionary conservatives committed to preserving the old social order. The biggest indicator of a paradigm shift in our culture, of course, has been the legalization of same-sex marriage across the Western world.

In many personal cases, what brought about this change of heart was the news that a loved one—a child, a sibling, a friend—had come out of the closet. This change of heart was the outcome of being unable to square the traditional belief about queer people as corrupt and perverse with a personal relationship with a loved one who had come out as queer. The internal tension between the traditional belief and the living and direct counterexample was so severe that they felt compelled to abandon their old beliefs.

In some cases, we have biographical evidence of this change. For example, Dick Cheney, a stalwart Republican, changed his views about same-sex marriage on the influence of his daughter Mary, who is queer. At a 2004 campaign rally in Iowa, Cheney angered his fellow conservatives by refusing to support George W. Bush's push for a constitutional amendment that would ban same-sex marriage. When confronted about this issue, Cheney said, "Lynne and I have a gay daughter, so it's an issue our family is very familiar with. With the respect to the question of relationships, my general view is freedom means freedom for everyone. . . . People ought to be free to enter into any kind of relationship they want to."[34]

For a prominent conservative politician to abandon such a traditional article of conservative belief is an indication of just how powerful living counterexamples can be. In this case, those living counterexamples provide a rational basis for abandoning the old worldview for a new one. While this example does not by any means capture all the complexities of the cultural shifts in ethics, it does illustrate how such cultural shifts can be understood as rational transitions, as opposed to non-rational conversions.

Speaking across the divide

If we can decide between ethical frameworks rationally, then what would a dialogue between ethical traditions look like? How would we talk to one another? On whose terms? These questions are deceptively simple. Speaking across the divide is not like sitting down with a neighbor to hash things out. At stake are the tricky questions of mutual understanding and speaking on equal terms. To that end, MacIntyre proposes a model of communication and dialogue that serves as a practical blueprint for the encounter between traditions.

This model of communication and dialogue can be understood as a middle ground between two extremes. The first extreme is the postmodern thesis of the impossibility of communication. This view denies that the subject possesses a unitary mind organized by a singular intentionality. On this view, there is no seat of human consciousness. The mind is but a play of forces.

This view further denies that one mind can convey an idea intact to another mind, for messages too are composed of a play of forces. Hence, they lack any stable meaning. The transmission of messages from one mind to another, what we typically call "communication," is therefore an illusion. We are, in some sense, imprisoned within our own bubbles. Understanding each other is therefore mere guesswork, with no way of separating right from wrong, better from worse, interpretations. At best, we can communicate that we cannot communicate. We can speak from within our bubbles, only to hear each other's muffled sounds.[35]

The second extreme view holds that a shared framework is a condition of communication. Donald Davidson, a fierce and brilliant critic of relativism, expresses this view as follows:

> Given enough common ground, we can understand and explain differences; we can criticize, compare, and persuade. The central point is that finding the common ground is not subsequent to understanding, but a condition of it. . . . If we understand their words, a common ground exists, a shared "way of life." A creature that cannot in principle be understood in terms of our own beliefs, values, and mode of communication is not a creature that may have thoughts radically different from our own: it is a creature without what we mean by "thoughts."[36]

This is not mere quirky definition of "common ground." It is a categorical denial of radical difference. For Davidson, the only distinction here is between how we interact with people versus entities like plants. We do not get into disagreements with plants. We do not negotiate differences with plants or question their beliefs, for the simple reason that nothing in the observable behavior of plants demands such an interaction. But it is different with those whom we take to be people.

Even if we do not understand a person's arguments, the sheer fact that we can understand that an argument is being made at all means that we already share sufficient common ground. If we have differences, those differences are intelligible only against a background of shared belief. Put simply, difference implies commonality. To put these two extreme views into visual terms, the postmodernist thesis imagines a vast and unbridgeable gulf, whereas Davidson imagines that we already stand on the same ground. MacIntyre avoids these two extremes. He holds that the divide is very real, but that we can stand on both sides at once.

For MacIntyre, the medium of communication between traditions is translation. This, too, is a deceptively simple idea and therefore requires some elaboration. MacIntyre holds that every tradition lives through time and history in the language of some practice-based community. This language is not like clothing. It cannot be discarded and replaced. A tradition does not exist prior to, or independently of, some practice-specific language. Rather, that practice-specific language is the flesh, blood, bones, and spirit of the tradition. Hence, when MacIntyre speaks of "language," he means something very specific. As he puts it,

> The conception of language presupposed [here] is that of a language as it is used in and by a particular community living at a particular time and place with particular shared beliefs, institutions, and practices. These beliefs, institutions, and practices will be furnished expression and embodiment in a variety of linguistic expressions and idioms; the language will provide standard uses for a necessary range of expressions and idioms, the use of which will presuppose commitment to those same beliefs, institutions, and practices.[37]

This means that English (or French or German or Spanish or Arabic or Latin or Greek or literally any other language) as a neutral, practice-independent language is a myth. Just as there is no ideal form of the human body, but rather only specific human bodies, there is no ideal form of English, but rather specific Englishes. There is the English of seventeenth-century British royalty, the English of the founders of the American republic, the cockney English of the East London working class, the English of Southern Appalachia, contemporary

African-American Vernacular English (AAVE), and so on. There is the English of economics, the English of legal scholars, the English of biomedical science, the English of Lacanian literary and cultural criticism, and the Englishes of other academic disciplines. Academic discourses in particular are notorious for their impenetrability. This does not mean that these traditions are self-enclosed worlds to which outsiders can have no access. Part of what it means to study a discipline is to learn the specialized language of that discipline.

Hence, the encounter, and often the confrontation, between traditions is defined in part by the differences in their languages. A useful way to visualize what MacIntyre calls the "linguistic relationship" between traditions is a Venn diagram with two overlapping circles. The overlapping part can be understood as the translatable areas of each other's languages. The nonoverlapping part can be understood as the untranslatable areas. The relationship between traditions is never one of absolute translatability or untranslatability, but rather of *partial* translatability.

There is no way to know in advance what areas can and cannot be translated, no way to know what the Venn diagram looks like without first doing the hard work of learning each other's languages. This involves a full-scale immersion in each other's worlds. It involves "knowing the culture, so far as is possible, as a native inhabitant knows it, and speaking, hearing, writing, and reading the language as a native inhabitant speaks, hears, writes, and reads it." And it involves learning more than mere words. As MacIntyre puts it, "Gestures, modes of ritual behavior, choices, and silences may all on occasion express utterances."[38]

In learning each other's languages, each side will come to appreciate the limits of translation, of why you can discuss certain things in one language but not in another, and vice versa. In short, each side will acquire an understanding of the blind spots of the other. A lesson therefore emerges: the only way to hold a fair dialogue between traditions is to think and speak in both languages. A dialogue in two languages requires a sufficient grasp of each other's worldviews so as to maintain a perpetual awareness of what each worldview enables and disables. What MacIntyre proposes is a higher order conception of reciprocal role-taking, in which speakers move back and forth between the semantic, aesthetic, and performative complexities of each other's universes—speaking and acting on each other's dramatic stages.

Reciprocal role-taking between traditions entails a certain critical feat of empathy, whereby we place ourselves "imaginatively within the scheme of belief inhabited by those whose allegiance is to the rival tradition."[39] We would speak and reason through concepts that are not our own and which we do not necessarily endorse. We would make provisional use of such concepts

> in the way an actor speaking his or her part may say things which he or she does not in his or her own person believe. We possess such concepts without being able to employ them in the first person, except as dramatic impersonators, speaking in a voice which is not our own.[40]

It is through such acts of "empathetic conceptual imagination" that we may enter into another community of discourse so as to speak and reason in terms set by that discourse. By speaking each other's languages and reasoning through each other's terms, we can see our own tradition from the standpoint of the other.[41]

For MacIntyre, the challenge of this dialogue is understanding. But this understanding is of two kinds. The first kind entails understanding the tradition with which you are at odds. The second kind entails a better understanding of one's own tradition. In what sense might one acquire a better understanding of one's own tradition if it forms the very ground of one's perspective? The answer is *a second-order perspective on one's perspective*: learning another worldview so as to achieve some distance from one's primary worldview and thereby being able to recognize recurring patterns of anomalies, logical contradictions, conceptual limitations, and theoretical weaknesses to which one might hitherto have been oblivious. It is only through this kind of understanding of the Other and heightened understanding of the Self that rational comparison and choice between traditions is possible at all.

Conclusion

It is difficult to overestimate the sheer significance of MacIntyre's conception of rational choice. It is certainly one of the greatest, if least recognized, of his philosophical achievements. MacIntyre in effect charts a route out of two extremes. The first is the false universalism of Rawls and Habermas. The second is the anti-rationalism of Mouffe. It is one thing to talk about moving between objectivism and relativism, as Mouffe does. It is quite another to provide an explicit way out of this difficult dichotomy. MacIntyre pulls off this tricky and complex balancing act. Against the formal proceduralism of deliberative democracy and the quasi-religious conversions of agonistic pluralism, MacIntyre offers a model of rational choice without foundations. As MacIntyre shows, we need not step outside of time and history. We need not attain a God's Eye View to mediate a clash of standpoints.

On the contrary, we can turn to common ideals. This does not necessarily conclude in agreement and consensus, nor does it need to. Rather, it enables the possibility of vindication and defeat. It replaces the search for the *right* answer with a contest for the *best answer so far*. MacIntyre thus shows how we can respect the reality of social conflict without succumbing to the mutual destruction of the culture wars.

Notes

1 Otto Neurath, *Empiricism and Sociology*, edited by Marie Neurath and Robert S. Cohen. Boston, MA: D. Reidel Publishing Company, 1973, 199.

2 Willard Van Orman Quine, *Word and Object*. Cambridge, MA: MIT Press, 2013, 3.

3 Bernstein, *Beyond Objectivism and Relativism*, 18.

4 Donald Davidson, "On the Very Idea of a Conceptual Scheme," *Proceedings and Addresses of the American Philosophical Association* 47 (1973–1974): 5–20.

5 Wittgenstein, *On Certainty*, 160; emphasis in the original.

6 Mouffe, *The Return of the Political*, 144.

7 Thomas Kuhn, *The Structure of Scientific Revolutions*. With an Introductory Essay by Ian Hacking. Chicago, IL: University of Chicago Press, 2012, 144.

8 Ibid., 146.

9 Ibid., 148.

10 Ibid.

11 Ibid., 148–49.

12 Ibid., 150.

13 Ibid.

14 Ibid, 152.

15 Ibid.

16 Ibid.

17 Ibid., 150–51.

18 Ibid., 200.

19 Ibid., 202.

20 Ibid.

21 Ibid., 199.

22 Ibid., 203.

23 Ibid., 151.

24 Ibid., 203.

25 MacIntyre, "Epistemological Crises, Dramatic Narrative, and the Philosophy of Science," 454.

26 Ibid., 460.

27 Kuhn, *The Structure of Scientific Revolutions*, 200.

28 MacIntyre, "Epistemological Crises, Dramatic Narrative, and the Philosophy of Science," 467.

29 For a similar reading of the history of the history of science, see Paul Thagard, *Conceptual Revolutions*. Princeton, NJ: Princeton University Press, 1993. Thagard takes inspiration in part from Hegel's *Science of Logic*, which proposes an organic and evolutionary view of conceptual change.

30 MacIntyre, "Epistemological Crises, Dramatic Narrative, and the Philosophy of Science," 467.

31 For Lakatos's view of historical change in science, see his essay, "History of Science and its Rational Reconstruction," in Imre Lakatos, *The Methodology of Scientific*

Research Programs: Philosophical Papers, Volume I, John Worrall and Gregory Currie, eds. Cambridge, UK: Cambridge University Press, 1978, 102–38. Despite his critical remarks about Hegel, Lakatos's rationalist view of the history of science bears the unmistakable stamp of Hegel. See John Kadvany, *Imre Lakatos and the Guises of Reason*. Durham, NC: Duke University Press, 2001, 301–3, 232–36.

32 Hilary Putnam, *Reason, Truth, and History*. Cambridge, UK: Cambridge University Press, 1981, 74.

33 See his essay, "Explanation and Practical Reason," in *Philosophical Arguments*. Cambridge, MA: Harvard University Press, 1995, 42.

34 Dan Collins, "Cheney Does His Own Thing," *CBS News*, August 26, 2004, https://www.cbsnews.com/news/cheney-does-his-own-thing/ (accessed January 17, 2019).

35 For an example of this sort of thinking, see Briankle Chang, *Deconstructing Communication: Representation, Subject, and Economies of Exchange*. Minneapolis: MN: University of Minnesota Press.

36 Donald Davison, *Problems of Rationality*. Oxford, UK: Oxford University Press, 2004. 37.

37 MacIntyre, *Whose Justice? Which Rationality?* 372–73.

38 Ibid., 374.

39 Ibid., 395.

40 Ibid.

41 MacIntyre's argument bears an uncanny similarity to the idea of reciprocal role-taking developed by George Herbert Mead in *Mind, Self, and Society*.

EPILOGUE: REASON AS RESISTANCE

Toward the end of *After Virtue*, MacIntyre points out one of the many tragic transmutations of ethics under capital.[1] The historical shift from a precapitalist mode of production, in which goods were produced in the home, to a capitalist mode, in which goods were produced in the factory, fundamentally transformed the nature of work. In the precapitalist mode, work had its place within the overall life of a community. In that setting, work was subordinated to the ends of community. But in the new mode, work became divorced from community and subordinated to the ends of private capital.

Now governed by the logic of endless growth, workers became mere cogs in a large and impersonal machine. Alienated from the goods produced by their own labor, alienated from any conceivable rewards internal to work itself, their sole reason for working became the mere acquisition of wages. At the mercy of subsistence wages, they were forced to restructure their entire outlook and orientation in the world.

In doing so, workers internalized the logic of capital, eking out a meager living, thereby making *pleonexia*, or acquisitiveness, which Aristotle regarded as a vice, a virtue. Under capital, greed is virtuous—the worldview of Gordon Gekko. MacIntyre thus traces the corrosive effects of capital upon the ethics, ethical language, and ethical discourse of modernity. One of these effects, he warns, is the loss of civility and "the coming ages of barbarism and darkness."

Drawing from this analysis, we can make a similar observation about the effects of social media upon communication. Just as capital tore work away from the life of the community and forced it into the factory and the office, digital capitalism has torn communication away from the life of communities and forced it online. So much of contemporary life—school, work, community, friendship, romance, religion, activism, democracy—exists on Facebook, Twitter, YouTube, Instagram, Tumblr, and LinkedIn. Total avoidance of these platforms means being in the dark about the goings-on of so much everyday social, cultural, political, and professional life. There is a very real pressure to join these platforms and to never leave them. But participating in social media has its own costs.

The "social" part of social media is misleading. What was supposedly designed to bring people together—to connect one another, to build networks, to meet new people, to make new friends, to discover new communities, to reimagine existing communities—has produced the opposite effect. The reason is that individualism, social atomism, and acquisitiveness are encoded into the design of these platforms. The original and paradigmatic social media platform, of course, is Facebook, which was intended to be a kind of digital high school yearbook, one that you could update as you liked. Facebook sought to reproduce the juvenile culture of high school in a digital platform.

Like high school, Facebook was designed to be a popularity contest—at first, a competition for friends; now, a competition for "Likes," hearts, comments, shares, and followers. In short, Facebook is a competition for social, and increasingly material, capital. This same "social" logic is built into the design of every other social media platform. Reproducing the logic of capital, it sets individuals against each other. It feeds a culture of acquisitiveness, a ravenous and insatiable appetite for popularity, measured rather quantitatively.

There is no point at which acquisitive social media users could ever be satisfied with their numbers of friends, followers, "Likes," or hearts. Instead, the mad drive for social capital breeds a pathological narcissism, exemplified by the popular obsession with selfies. Online, the self is carefully and neurotically curated. The self becomes a brand, one that carries power and therefore requires constant management. Social media further erode human communities and social bonds. These platforms further isolate the already isolated, lonely, and fragmented modern individual. They drive the individual into the sewer of paranoia, suspicion, and hostility. They breed incivility and primitive, atavistic, toxic, and destructive instincts. In short, social media are a breeding ground for the culture wars.

As discussed in Chapter 3, two creatures have emerged from this breeding ground. The first is the alt-right troll. A product of online subcultures and a symptom of extreme cultural rot, the troll has morphed from an irritating, but insignificant online reprobate into a major player in democratic politics. Once confined to the dark underbelly of cyberspace, the troll has emerged from the cave and the shadows of anonymity into the clear light of day. No longer hidden behind an avatar and obnoxious screen name, the troll does not fear being seen or named.

Milo, the paradigmatic troll, rose to fame *as* a troll. He built his reputation harassing and bullying women and people of color online. Milo proudly and defiantly identifies as a "virtuous troll," a kind of cheeky public servant whose mission is to eradicate the pestilence of liberal sanctimony and political correctness.[2] Though now disgraced and no longer relevant, Milo nonetheless gave shape and substance to a new political archetype, one that not just attacks progressives, but also abandons any pretense to civility or basic human decency. Rather, this new archetype deliberately embraces tastelessness, shamelessness, and sheer viciousness as its defining ethos. The troll has become a kind of parasite upon the culture of democracy, latching on to progressives like some sort of leech, feeding on their earnest passions like blood, and seizing upon their solidarity for the weak and the oppressed as points of vulnerability. To allow oneself to become offended before a troll is to expose an open wound, into which the troll rubs so much salt and vinegar.

The second creature is equally vicious but driven by different motives. Hyperaware of the minutest transgressions, driven by a quest for absolute political purity, this second creature has become another source of corrosion to the culture of democracy. It inviglates over the speech and actions of others, prosecuting them for every moral infraction, and consigning the guilty to a realm of the damned, from which redemption is all but impossible. Unlike the right-wing troll, this second creature eats its own kind. It cannibalizes its kin for the crime of imperfection, subjecting them to merciless judgment, actively seeking their downfall, even reveling over their death.³ The Left is thus caught up in a battle not just with the Right, but with itself. It has become ravaged by an internecine war that undermines its own cause and empowers the other side. Together, these two creatures are eating away at what remains of civility, promoting an environment of animosity, paranoia, spitefulness, and raw, insatiable hatred.

Evidently, ethics and communication both suffer under capital. They are both degraded, twisted, and impaired. Just as greed is turned into a virtue, so is incivility. In the closing words of *After Virtue*, MacIntyre writes, "What matters at this point is the construction of local forms of community within which civility and the intellectual and moral life can be sustained through the new dark ages." MacIntyre's contention should surely be updated to include Sherry Turkle's call for "reclaiming conversation" from the antisocial prison of social media.⁴ To that end, there is wisdom in reconceiving conversation, not as some generic "art," but rather as a practice.

That is, conversation should be understood as a social activity composed of *dos* and *don'ts*, roles and responsibilities, and internal goods and rewards. The practice of conversation is another powerful arena for the cultivation and exercise of the virtues, especially those of courage, friendliness, patience, truthfulness, modesty, and magnanimity. If digital capital intentionally breeds political tribalism, if it thrives and profits from the toxicity of the culture wars, then one of the most powerful acts of resistance against capital today is reclaiming conversation. In the spirit of that reclaiming, it is worth considering an example of civility and rational dialogue, one that exhibits many of the features of MacIntyre's model of communication.

Bernie at Liberty

Today, we look back upon the 2016 US presidential election as the fateful event that put Donald Trump into the most powerful office on earth. The dark and ominous cloud that afterward hung over America, and indeed the rest of the world, has obscured from public memory the more positive historical events leading up to that one portentous moment. One of the surprising success stories of the 2016 election cycle was the presidential campaign of Bernie Sanders, which, though unsuccessful, was historic in more ways than one. Sanders was the first Jewish candidate to win a nominating election and also to win major state primaries. He was the first candidate in the 2016 election cycle to secure one million donations. He was the first democratic socialist to win a major party primary. And in 2015, he became the first democratic presidential candidate to accept an invitation to speak at Liberty University.

By accepting the invitation from Liberty, Sanders agreed to something that few non-Republicans since Liberty's founding have dared to do. He entered the lion's den of American conservatism and the epicenter of American Evangelical Christianity. Liberty has hosted numerous prominent Republicans, including Donald Trump, Sarah Palin, Mike Huckabee, Mitt Romney, and Newt Gingrich. Speaking at Liberty has long been considered a way for Republican politicians to establish their conservative bona fides with the American Evangelical community. Ted Cruz, for example, spoke at Liberty the day he announced his presidential candidacy in 2015. Founded by Jerry Falwell in 1971, the mission of Liberty University is to "develop Christ-centered men and women with the values, knowledge, and skills essential to impact the world." As a nonreligious democratic socialist, Sanders entered territory widely regarded as hostile to Democrats and to leftists.

Yet, Sanders was given a surprisingly warm welcome at Liberty. As a politician of principle, who has consistently criticized the rich and the powerful, including the establishment within the Democratic Party, the Liberty community greeted Sanders with a certain admiration. For his part, Sanders has actively campaigned in the American South. He has been sensitive to the plight of the southern poor and working class. He has taken the time to sit down and talk with them, regardless of their political beliefs. He has displayed a willingness to speak to those typically scorned and mocked by liberals.

Against the backdrop of mutual respect, Sanders' visit to Liberty marked a rare encounter between the traditions of American Evangelical Christianity and American Democratic Socialism. The first represents the marriage between Christianity and capitalism. The second represents an opposition to capitalism and all of its depravities. The first is positively hostile to feminism and homosexuality. The second embraces the fight for social justice and equality. The fault lines between the two sides could not be clearer.

Sanders opened his speech by acknowledging the stark differences between the Liberty community and himself. He declared at the outset his resolute commitment to women's rights, gay rights, and marriage equality. He acknowledged the disagreement between the Liberty community and himself on social issues. But that disagreement, he insisted, should not obstruct the fostering of dialogue for common ground. In the spirit of democracy and civil discourse, Sanders stressed the necessity of speaking across the divide, of the vital importance "for those of us who hold different views to be able to engage in a civil discourse."[5] He lamented the toxic nature of political discourse in America today, saying, "Too often in our country . . . there is too much shouting at each other. There is too much making fun of each other." It is too easy, he observed, to speak to those with whom we agree. It is much more challenging "for us to try and communicate with those who do not agree with us on every issue" and to see if "we can find common ground."

To that end, Sanders began by asking a very basic question framed in the Evangelical language of "morality." As he put it,

> You are a school which . . . tries to understand the meaning of morality. What does it mean to live a moral life? And you try to understand, in this very complicated modern world that we live in, what the words of the Bible mean in today's society. You are a school which tries to teach its students how to behave with decency and with honesty and how you can best relate to your fellow human beings, and I applaud you for trying to achieve those goals.

Sanders is not exactly known to be a religious person. Nonetheless, he attempted to communicate with his audience by invoking a religious framework, albeit a rather generic one. As he put it,

> Let me take a moment . . . to tell you what motivates me in the work that I do as a public servant, as a senator from the state of Vermont. And let me tell you that it goes without saying, I am far, far from being a perfect human being, but I am motivated by a vision, which exists in all of the great religions, in Christianity, in Judaism, in Islam, and Buddhism, and other religions.

Sanders quoted Mt. 7:12, which expresses the Golden Rule: "So in everything, do to others what you would have them do to you, for this sums up the war and the prophets." He quoted Amos 5:24, which says, "But let justice roll on like a river, righteousness like a never-failing stream." Sanders made it clear he took this second verse to mean treating others, "no matter their race, their color, their stature in life, with respect and with dignity." Thus, through a moral framework taken from the Bible, and using the rhetoric of "morality," Sanders proceeded to articulate his critique of America, a society he judged to be lacking in morality and justice.

Sanders went through a long list of serious problems in America, problems he routinely addresses in his political oratory. But unlike his general oratory, Sanders framed each of these problems as instances of immorality and injustice. He began by saying, "Now, when we talk about morality, and when we talk about justice, we have to . . . understand that there is no justice when so few have so much and so many have so little." Sanders then proceeded to criticize the immorality and injustice of obscene wealth at the very top, the low wages of the poor and the working class, the vast and deepening levels of income inequality between an ultra-elite class of millionaires and billionaires and the growing ranks of the poor. He criticized the immorality and the scandal of childhood poverty in America, especially among African American children. He criticized the injustice of Americans who die because of a lack of health insurance. In words of righteous indignation, Sanders said, "I think that when we talk about morality, what we are talking about is all of God's children. The poor, the wretched, they have a right to go to a doctor when they are sick."

Sanders invoked "family values" to condemn the injustice of poor and working mothers being forced to return to work shortly after giving birth because of a lack of paid family and medical leave. He called out the injustice of high youth unemployment, especially among African American youth. He further criticized mass incarceration, pointing out that America has a higher prison population than China. Sanders rounded out his critique of America by quoting a particularly poignant line from Pope Francis's *Evangelii Gaudium*: "We have created new idols. The worship of the ancient golden calf has returned in a new and ruthless guise in the idolatry of money and the dictatorship of an impersonal economy lacking a truly human purpose."[6]

Agreeing with Pope Francis, Sanders said we live in a world "which worships not love of brothers and sisters, not love of the poor and the sick, but worships the acquisition of money and great wealth." Returning to his opening remarks about the importance of dialogue and the search for the "the meaning of morality," Sanders implored his audience to join him to "have the courage to stand with the poor, to stand with working people and when necessary, take on very powerful and wealthy people whose greed . . . is doing this country enormous harm."

By speaking to Evangelicals on their own terms, by using the Evangelical idiom of "morality," by passionately criticizing grotesque social injustices in America, injustices widely ignored in conservative discourse, Sanders accomplished something unexpected: he forced his audience to acknowledge the strength of his critique and the ugly realities of economic inequality and institutional discrimination in America. Although he did not persuade his audience to embrace democratic socialism, Sanders nonetheless demonstrated the possibility of two very different traditions coming together to engage in a civil and reasonable grassroots dialogue.

In a very real way, the event was a rebuke of the logic of the culture wars and our increasing proclivity toward cynicism and incivility. It defied the kind of superficial dialogue, petty bickering, and sensational pseudo-debates that have become familiar features of our public sphere. It defied the instrumentalism of establishment politicians who conspicuously lack a meaningful and substantive political vision and who therefore play the game of demonizing other politicians to compensate for that lack. Lastly, the Liberty event was a tangible case of the power of face-to-face dialogue in the age of social media. It serves as an admirable example of reason as resistance against modern capital's assault upon civility and the bonds of social solidarity.

Right-side up in the upside down

In February 2019, Sanders again announced his candidacy for the presidency. Unlike his previous campaign, in which he was the clear underdog, Sanders has emerged this time as a clear frontrunner, giving him a very real chance at winning the Democratic nomination and facing off against Donald Trump in 2020. As of this writing, Sanders is scheduled to appear in a Fox News town hall event, despite the Democratic National Committee's (DNC) decision not to partner with Fox News for the 2020 election debates. In the face of criticism and ridicule from his Democratic rivals, Sanders has defended his decision by stressing the need to speak to the other side.[7] As he put it during an appearance on *The Daily Show with Trevor Noah*, "I think it is important to talk to Trump supporters and explain to them to what degree [Trump] has betrayed the working class of this country and lied during his campaign."[8]

In making this remark, Sanders drew a sharp line between two very different political games. The first game is what can be called *polemics*. Michel Foucault brilliantly describes the polemicist as a kind of holy warrior who, out of exaggerated self-righteousness, refuses to speak to the other side. As Foucault observes, to a polemicist, "the person he confronts is not a partner in search for the truth but an adversary, an enemy who is wrong, who is harmful, and whose very existence constitutes a threat." For the polemicist, "the game consists not of recognizing this person as a subject having the right to speak but of abolishing him as interlocutor from any possible dialogue."⁹

The second game is what Foucault calls "the serious play of questions and answers" and "the work of reciprocal elucidation." In a dialogue, "the rights of each person are in some sense immanent in the discussion." As Foucault puts it, "Questions and answers depend on a game—a game that is at once pleasant and difficult—in which each of the two partners takes pains to use only the rights given him by the other and by the accepted form of dialogue."¹⁰

The difference between Sanders and his Democratic rivals is the difference between dialogue and polemics. Whereas the DNC and the other Democratic candidates are predictably falling back upon the standard model of gladiator politics, which treats fellow citizens with opposing points of view as enemies to be shunned, Sanders has steadfastly defied that model by keeping a line open to the other side, by choosing to play a different game, one that encourages citizens of differing points of view to come together to reason with each other. In our increasingly toxic public sphere, Sanders's decision to speak to the other side is an admirable attempt at preserving dialogue, civility, and social solidarity against the universal acids of trolling and polemics. If this book serves a purpose, it is to show how MacIntyre can help guide that preservation.

Notes

1 MacIntyre, *After Virtue*, 27–28.

2 Terry Moran, Emily Taguchi, and Claire Pederson, "Leslie Jones' Twitter Troll Has No Regrets over Attacking the 'Ghostbusters' Actress," *ABC News*, September 1, 2016. https://abcnews.go.com/Entertainment/leslie-jones-twitter-troll-regrets-attacking-ghostbusters-actress/story?id=41808886 (accessed April 10, 2018).

3 Angela Nagle recounts the glee with which certain liberal Twitter trolls reacted upon hearing of the suicide of cultural theorist Mark Fisher. See Nagle, *Kill All Normies*, 117.

4 Sherry Turkle, *Reclaiming Conversation: The Power of Talk in A Digital Age*. New York, NY: Penguin, 2016.

5   Bernie Sanders, Remarks at the Liberty University Convocation, https://berniesanders.com/remarks-at-the-liberty-university-convocation/ (accessed January 17, 2019).

6   Ibid.

7   Benjamin Fearnow, "Democrats Ridicule Bernie Sanders over Fox News Town Hall Plans, Conservatives and Moderates Offer Rare Praise," *Newsweek*, April 3, 2019, https://www.newsweek.com/fox-news-bernie-sanders-dnc-loyalty-controversy-town-hall-democratic-2020-1385160 (accessed April 10, 2019).

8   Bill Scher, "Bernie Sanders Is Right to Go on Fox News," *Real Clear Politics*, April 8, 2019, https://www.realclearpolitics.com/articles/2019/04/08/bernie_sanders_is_right_to_go_on_fox_news_139986.html (accessed April 13, 2019).

9   Michel Foucault, *The Michel Foucault Reader*, edited by Paul Rabinow. New York, NY: Pantheon, 1984, 382.

10 Ibid., 381.

INDEX

4Chan 73–5, 84
8Chan 73

ABC xi
Accelerationism 79
ACLU 180
acquisitiveness 203–4
Adorno, Theodor 11, 109
advertising 86
aesthete 31–2, 35, 40
aesthetics 28, 55–6, 81, 167, 182–3, 198
affirmative action 69, 72
African-Americans xiv, 25, 69, 209–10
African-American Vernacular English (AAVE) 90, 197
Age of Reason 47
agonistics 15, 125, 130–1, 135–6
Ailes, Roger 70
Albert, Gerrard 113
Alex Fields, James 92
alienation 4–5, 32, 59
Alliance for Defending Freedom 69
Allman, Jamie xiii
Althusser, Louis 69
Alt-Right 74, 77, 79–83, 92, 94
Amazon.com 34
American Conservative, The 70
American Family Association 69
American Israel Public Affairs Committee (AIPAC) 26
American Spectator, The 70
Amnesty International 4
anarchism 14, 21
anarchist-hacktivist 74
Anderson, John 150–1
Anderson, Perry 6
Anglophone 2
Anonymous 74
Anscombe, Elizabeth 10
Antifa 21

anti-foundationalism 129
anti-realism 138
anti-war movement 127
apolitical 33
  LGBTQ movement 72
Arabic 196
Arendt, Hannah 138, 141
aretê 155
argumentum ad antiquitatem 165
Aristotelianism 12, 47, 153, 181, 188
  physics 188–9, 191–2
Aristotle 3, 10–12, 45–7, 102, 155, 188, 203
  metaphysical biology 46
  Nichomachean Ethics 45
Arizona 34
Asian-Americans 84
Aurelius, Marcus 160
Auschwitz 109
Australia 27
authoritarianism 117, 155–6, 165, 172
authority 32–3, 48, 54, 68, 74
Ayer, A. J. (Freddie) 28–9
  Language, Truth, and Logic 28

Bakhtin, Mikhail 81
Bannon, Steve 77
baseball 153–6, 164
Bataille, George 81
BBC Radio 7
behaviorism 159–60
Benjamin, Walter 69
Bennett, William J. 71
Bentham, Jeremy 56, 58
Berlin, Isaiah 60
Bernays, Edward 35
Bernstein, Richard J. 138, 178
  Beyond Objectivism and Relativism 138
Bezos, Jeff 34

Bhabha, Homi   69
Bible   209
Black Lives Matter movement   76
Black Power movement   68
Black Vernacular English   90
Blair, Tony   130
Blanchot, Maurice   81
Bloch, Ernst   35
Bloom, Allan   69
   The Closing of the American Mind   69
Blumenberg, Hans   132
Blumenthal, Richard   26
Boycott, Divestment, and Sanctions
   (BDS)   26
Branson, Richard   34
Breitbart News   21, 75, 77, 79, 82
British Columbia   164
Buchanan, Pat   79
Buckley, William F.   68, 76
bureaucratic individualism   13
Burke, Edmund   165
Bush, George W.   xiv–xv, 40, 72, 194
Bush, Jeb   xiv
Buzzfeed   73

Canada   27, 164
Cancer Research UK   86–7
capital   13–16, 67, 71, 73, 86–7, 126, 159, 203–4, 206, 211
capitalism   1–2, 6–7, 9, 14, 70–2, 79, 87, 126–8, 159, 208
capital punishment   168
Cardan, Paul. *See* Castoriadis, Cornelius
Carnap, Rudolph   28
Castoriadis, Cornelius   9
Cato Institute   70
Cavell, Stanley   180
CBS   xi
Central America   38
Cernovitch, Mike   78
Chapo Trap House   2
Charlottesville, Virginia   92
Chen, Anna   84
Cheney, Dick   193–4
Cheney, Mary   194
China   83–4, 210

Chomsky, Noam   1, 14
Christianity   5–6, 87, 107, 207–8
ChronicleVitae   161
citizenship   108, 136
civility   1–3, 93–4, 108, 203, 205–6, 211–12
class   1, 53, 72, 83, 87, 105, 126–8, 152–3, 196, 209
classism   63
Clinton, Bill   76, 130
Clinton, Hillary   xv, 26, 36–8, 71, 76, 78
CNN   xi
Cold War   7, 130
colonizer   58
Commentary   70
common good, the   61, 102, 117, 119, 132
common ground   134, 195, 208
common sense   50, 128
communication   16, 103, 106, 109–10, 119, 171, 182–3, 203, 206
communicative action   109–10, 118
communism   14, 130
Communist Party of Great Britain   5–7
communitarianism   103, 131
comparative reason   190
Conant, James   144
Concerned Women for America   69
consensus   13, 52, 107–9, 117, 133, 135, 151, 156–7, 199
   ethics as   116
   justice as   108
   political   125, 151
   rational   109, 135
conservation   105
conservative   xii–xiv, 4, 14–15, 23–6, 62, 67–72, 76–80, 82, 194, 207
conspiracy theories   78
consumption   32, 35, 40, 54, 57
Continental philosophy   63
contingency   129, 132, 166, 170
continuum of knowledge   155
conversation   29, 156–7, 206
   reflective   156
conversions   136, 167, 181–4, 187–8, 194, 199

Cooper, Alice   81
Coulter, Ann   25, 76
counterculture movement (1960s)   67–8, 71, 80–3
counter-hegemonic   128–9, 131
counterrevolutionary movement   68
criminal justice   85
Cromwell, Oliver   50
Cruz, Ted   207
Cubism   81
culture   xv–xvi, 2–3, 10, 23, 31–6, 40, 50, 55, 63, 73–5, 81, 83, 110, 112, 118, 140, 190, 192–3
culture wars   2, 11, 14–15, 24, 45, 48, 63, 67, 69, 71, 77, 79, 81–2, 101, 125, 140, 149, 178, 199, 203–4, 206, 210
Current Affairs   2

Dadaism   81
Dahrendorf, Ralf   160
Daily Show with Jon Stewart, The   71
Daily Show with Trevor Noah, The   211
Dakota Access Pipeline   164
Dark Ages   2
Dark Enlightenment   79
Daum, Keziah   83
Davidson, Donald   179, 195–6
Davis, Angela   14, 68
DDoS attacks   74
Dean, Jodi   2
de Benoist, Alain   79
DeBord, Guy   9
Declaration of the Rights of Man and Citizen   56
DeGeneres, Ellen   xv, 72
deliberation   101, 103, 107–8, 119–20
  conception of   108
  models of   119
  public   108, 114, 120, 133
  rational   104, 171
deliberative democracy   101–3, 119–21, 125, 132–5, 199
democracy   xiii, 15, 36, 79, 101–2, 107, 119, 133–6, 139, 143, 204, 208
Democratic National Committee (DNC)   212

Democratic Party of the United States   4, 39, 207, 211
Democratic Socialism   208
Democratic Socialists of America   2
deontology   110, 170–1
Depression Quest (video game)   75
Derrida, Jacques   69, 126, 129, 132
Descartes, Réné   48, 186–7
desert   75
desire   6, 8, 11, 23, 29–30, 48, 50, 56, 63, 73–5, 105, 119, 142, 152, 154–5
dialectics   3, 169–70
  conception of history   8
  critic   12
  critique   91
  engagement   12
  mode of critique   6
dialogical deliberation   103
dialogue   119–20, 194, 197–8, 210–12
  for common ground   208
  democracy of   119
  model of communication and   194
  rational   206
Diderot, Denis   47–8
Di Fiore, James   36
  "Stop Treating Political Parties like Sports Teams"   36
disagreement   9, 13, 28, 110, 128, 142, 154, 166, 171, 179, 192, 195, 208
discourse ethics   116–18
Discourse Principle (D)   110
Discovery Institute   70
Dissent   2
Dolezal, Rachel   89
Drudge Report   70
D'Souza, Dinesh   25, 69
Duchamp, Marcel   81
  Fountain   81
Dukes, Josh   21
Duke University   77
duty   54–5, 104, 155

Eagleton, Terry   2
ecology   118, 164

economy   xiv, 8, 105, 157
  gig   1, 157–9, 162
  market   117
Ellen DeGeneres Show, The   xv
Emancipation Park, Charlottesvill, VA   92
emotivism   29–31, 35
  core of   30
  culture of   32, 40
  ethos of   31
  logical culmination of   40
  nature of   94
Encounter   7
Engels, Friedrich   1, 6, 8–9, 53, 57
  The Communist Manifesto   1
  The German Ideology   53, 57
England   51
English Bill of Rights   56
English bourgeois culture   57
English imperialism   140–1
English language   196
Enlightenment, the   3, 11, 47, 54, 79, 165
Enlightenment project, the   47–8, 54–5
epistemic norms and commitments   171
epistemological crisis   171–2, 184, 186
epistemology   126
equality   4, 62, 72, 84–5, 105, 132, 192–3
ESPY awards ceremony (2015)   89
ethics   3, 13, 30, 46–7, 107, 133, 154–7, 206
  under capital   14–16, 67, 203
  as consensus   116
  cultural shifts in   194
  environmental   116
  Kantian   155
  philosophical   120
  rational   47, 152
  teleological   47
  virtue   11, 16
ethnic cleansing   77, 92
eudemonia   46, 155
Eurocentrism   101, 118
Europe, medieval   47
Evangelical Christianity   207–8
Evola, Julius   79–80
existentialism   54, 160

experience   81, 112, 160, 168–9, 184–6, 189
  conversion   181, 187–8
  practical   159, 168–9
exploitation   4, 113
  capitalist   71
  as self-discovery   159

Facebook   27, 78, 84, 90, 92, 204
fairness   104–6, 119, 139
  concept of   105
  and equality   119–20
  ideals of   119
  principles of   105
Fairness Doctrine   70
fallibilists   186
false universals   143, 199
falsity   110, 145, 167–8
Falwell, Jerry   207
Fanon, Franz   69
fascism   21, 79, 109
Federal Communications Commission   70
Federici, Silvia   2
Feminine Mystique, The   68
feminism   69, 71, 74–5, 78, 103, 208
Feyerabend, Paul   180
Fields, James Alex   92
finance
  capital   33
  globalized   127
Financial Crisis (2008)   xiv, 1–2, 85
First Nations   184
first principles   166, 170–1
Fish, Stanley   69
Fisher, Mark   87, 92
  "Exiting the Vampire Castle"   87
Florida   27
Focus on the Family   69
forms of life   134
  democracy as a   133
Foucault, Michel   69, 81, 126, 129, 141, 211–12
foundationalism   132, 138, 177
Fourteenth Amendment   61
Fox News   xiv, 70, 211

Francis, Pope   210
  Evangelii Gaudium   210
Frankfurt School   109
Fraser, Nancy   71
freedom   4, 7, 24, 59, 80, 104, 144, 160, 194
free market   2, 4, 14, 58
free speech   11, 24–6
Free Speech Movement   68
French civil society   59
French language   196
French Revolution   58
Freud, Sigmund   32, 63
Friedan, Betty   68
FrontPage Magazine   70

Gadamer, Hans-Georg   10, 132
Galilean physics   181, 191–2
Galileo   188–9, 191
Gamer culture   74–5
Gamergate   74–5, 92
Garden of Eden   23
Gass, William   31
Gates, Bill   34
Gawker   73
gay liberation movement   68, 193
gay rights   xv, 208
Gekko, Gordon   203
gender   4, 69, 85, 87, 89, 91, 126
generalized interest   112
genesis   166
Genette, Gérard   9
genocide   86
Georgian demonstrations (1956)   6
Germany   109
Gibson, Leslie   xiii
Giddens, Anthony   130
gig economy   1, 157–9, 162
Gillibrand, Kirsten   26
Gilligan's Island   152
Gingrich, Newt   207
Gödel, Kurt   28
Golden Rule   209
Goldmann, Lucien   7–8, 10
González, Emma   xiii

goods
  common   61, 102, 117, 119, 132
  internal   153–4, 206
  public   108
  social   61, 117
Gorgias   26–7, 35
government   26, 74, 102, 104, 113, 164
Gramsci, Antonio   80, 128–9
  Prison Notebooks   128
Gramscian organic intellectual   137
Gray, Briahna Joy   88
Great Britain   27
  Communist Party of   5
Great Recession   xiv, 1
Greenwich Village   68
Guantanamo Bay   xiv

Habermas, Jürgen   15, 101, 103, 108–12, 115–21, 132–4, 139, 149, 152, 178, 199
Habermasian democracy   115
Hall, Stuart   6
Hannity, Sean   28, 70
Hannity & Colmes   70
happiness   58, 62
Hardt, Michael   1
Harris, Kamala   88
Harvard Business Review   157, 162
Harvey, David   1
hate speech   24
Heartland Institute   70
Hedges, Chris   14
Hegel   3, 10–12, 170
hegemony   128–9, 131, 135
  conception of   128–9
  counter-   129
  political   113
Heidegger, Martin   109
Heraclitus   149–51
Heritage Foundation   70
hermeneutics   138
Herrnstein, Richard   69
Hesse, Mary   137
Heyer, Heather   92
Hilton, Paris   31

hipsterism 73, 78, 87
historiographical power 190
Hitler Youth 108
Hobbes, Thomas 59
Hogg, David xiii
Hollywood 4, 71
homophobia 88, 126, 192, 193
Horkheimer, Max 11, 109
   Dialectic of Enlightenment 11
Horowitz, David 25
Huckabee, Mike 207
HuffPost 36, 73
Human Rights Campaign 35
Hume, David 47–51, 53, 186–7
   An Enquiry Concerning the Principles of Morals 49
   A Treatise of Human Nature 48
Hunter, James Davison 14
Hurricane Katrina xiv
Hypatia 89–92

Iacoca, Lee 34
identity 38, 83, 85–7, 89, 127, 129, 136, 152, 160
ideologues 1, 69
ideology 1, 68, 70, 83
immigrant 1, 71, 79, 137
immorality 209
impartial 52, 56, 110–11, 120, 141, 144
impossibility of communication 194
incivility 2, 204, 206, 210
incoherent 6, 55, 142–3, 159, 162, 187
incommensurability 26–7, 178–82, 190
   thesis 178–9
incommunicability 183–4
independence 32, 144
indeterminacy 132, 171
India 33
Indigenous
   communities 14, 141
   culture 4–5, 140
   lands 164
   traditions 119, 164
individual 6–7, 30, 54, 56–61, 86, 88–9, 102, 104–5, 108, 117–18, 159, 185

individualism 4, 204
inequality 4, 129, 139
   income 51, 71–2, 85, 209–10
   social 139
Ingraham, Laura xiv
InfoWars 78, 82
injustice 4, 26, 104–5, 141, 209–10
Instagram 204
instrumentalism 36, 61, 211
   of the Democratic Party 39
   moral 37–8, 55, 61–2, 67, 81
Intellectual Dark Web 4
intelligibility 129, 160, 186
intentionality 105, 152, 160, 163, 194
interests 102, 111–12, 115–17, 128, 159
   class 53, 128
   economic 71
   human 116
   individual 117
   social 117
International Socialism 7, 9–10
Internet Relay Chat (IRC) 75
interpretation 4, 23, 115, 171, 185, 195
   contradictions and conflicting 166
Iowa State Fair (2011) 61
IQ 105
Iraq xiv, 40
   War xiv
Irish 140
irony 73, 76, 90
irrationalism 15, 35, 54, 165, 182–3
ISIS xiv
Islam 78, 107
Israel 26
Israel Anti-Boycott Act (S. 720) 26
iTunes 78

Jacobin 2
James, Henry 31–2
   Portrait of a Lady 31–2
Jameson, Fredric 2, 12–13, 69
Japan 27
   image boards 73
Jenner, Caitlyn 89–91
Jim Crow 85

Jobs, Steve   34
Jones, Alex   78
Jones, Leslie   76
Judaism   107
judgment   15, 30, 32, 46, 52–3, 89, 138, 144, 152–3, 155, 205
judiciary   108
justice   12, 24, 56, 61, 85, 103–6, 108, 114, 185
justification   117, 170, 172, 186
   modes of   166
   rational   170–1

Kaepernick, Colin   25
Kairos   1
Kant, Immanuel   30, 47, 51–3, 103–4, 110, 171
   The Groundwork of the Metaphysics of Morals   52
Kardashian, Kim   31
Kautsky, Karl   127
KDNL   xiii
Kierkegaard, Søren   47, 54–5
   Either/Or   54
Kimball, Roger   69
   Tenured Radicals   69
Kinder Morgan Pipeline   164
King Jr, Martin Luther   68
KISS   81
Klein, Naomi   1, 14
Königsberg, Prussia   53
Krebs, Angelika   116
Kuhn, Thomas   10, 136–7, 167, 179–84, 187, 189–90
   Structure of Scientific Revolutions   136, 179–80, 183, 189
Ku Klux Klan   92
Kupe   112

labor   5, 126–7, 159, 203
   exploitation   159
Labour Review   7
Laclau, Ernesto   125–30
   Hegemony and Socialist Strategy   125, 127, 129–30, 143
   On Populist Reason   136

Lakatos, Imre   10, 190
Lam, Jeremy   83–4
Land, Nick   79
language   4, 37, 60, 91, 104, 109, 140, 163, 183–4, 187, 196–8
   emotivist theory of   28
Latin   196
Latinx community   38
LeFort, Claude   9, 132
legislature   108
legitimacy   102, 135, 138
   political   102–3
Lenin, Vladimir   7, 14, 128
Leninism   128
   crisis of   13
Levant, Ezra   25, 78
Levellers   50
LGBTQ movement   69, 72, 76, 127
liberalism   xiii–xv, 4, 14, 25–6, 28, 62, 67, 71–3, 76–9, 83–5, 87, 117–19, 131, 205, 207
liberation   62, 101
   animal   14
   gay   68
libertarianism   xiv, 103
liberty   58–9, 104, 115, 119–20, 193
Liberty University   206–8, 211
Limbaugh, Rush   70, 76
linguistic communication   109, 142
linguistic frameworks   142
linguistic practice   169
LinkedIn   204
Listener, The   7
literary criticism   197
literary theory   69
Locke, John   56, 59, 102, 104
Lost   152
Lukács György   7
lumpenproletariat   128
Lutheran Pietism   53
Luxemburg, Rosa   9, 14, 127
Lyotard, Jean-François   9

McCarthy, Thomas   111
Machiavelli, Niccolò   39, 102, 132
McInnes, Gavin   78

MacIntyre, Alasdair xv–xvi, 2–16, 22–4, 27, 29–33, 45–58, 50–63, 67, 80, 93, 101, 117, 125, 140, 149, 151–5, 159–61, 163, 165–73, 178, 184–92, 194, 196–9, 203, 206, 212
   After Virtue 3, 5, 10–12, 22, 30–1, 55, 67, 93, 117, 203, 206
Maine xiii
Major League Baseball 153, 156
Malcolm X 68
Malkin, Michelle 25
manager, the 31, 33–5, 40
Manchu Qing 84
Manson, Marilyn 81
Manzoni, Piero 81
Māori 112–15, 119–20
   argument 101
March for Our Lives xiii
Marcuse, Herbert 7
Marjory Stoneman Douglas High School xiii, 27
marriage equality 208
Marx, Karl 1, 3, 5–6, 8–10, 12–14, 53, 57–60, 62, 76
   Capital 1
   The Communist Manifesto 1
   The Declaration of the Rights of Man and Citizen 58
   The German Ideology 53, 57
   On the Jewish Question 58
Marxism 5–6, 10, 13, 63, 103, 107, 120, 128
Massachusetts 156
maxims 52–3, 55
Mead, George Herbert 111
   Mind, Self, and Society 111
mechanistic conception of history 8
medieval 180
   Europe 47
Medium.com 84
memes 73–4, 80
memory 1, 22, 168
   public xv, 207
Mencken H. L. 78
Men's Rights Movement 78
mental illness 32, 78

Middle East xiv–xv
Mill, John Stuart 56–8
Mills, C. Wright 7
minorities 1, 38, 69, 71, 92, 102, 130, 137
Misfits, The 81
misogyny 72
mode of production 126, 203
modernity 126, 132, 134, 203
monarchical rule 59
Monbiot, George 14
monological reason 103, 106, 116, 171
Moore, Michael 27
moralism 12, 23
morality 6, 10–12, 23, 28, 45, 48, 51–3, 55–7, 61, 79, 115, 119, 133, 209–10
Mouffe, Chantal 15, 125–43, 149, 151–2, 178–9, 192, 199
   For a Left Populism 136
   Hegemony and Socialist Strategy 125
   The Return of the Political 131, 137, 141
MSNBC xi
multiculturalism 69, 72
Murdoch, Rupert 70
Murray, Charles 69
   The Bell Curve 69
Musk, Elon 34
mysticism 79

n+1 2
NAACP 2, 4
Nagle, Angela 74, 80–1, 83, 84–5
   Kill All Normies
narrative 11, 77, 79, 149, 152–3, 159, 162–3, 186, 191–2
National Equality Award 35
National Interest, The 70
National Review, The 70
National Socialism 109
Nazism xiii, 78, 92
Negri, Antonio 1, 14
neo-Confederate League of the South 92
neoliberalism 4, 72, 130, 136, 137, 139
neo-masculinist 78
neo-reactionary 79–80

Netflix xi
Neurath, Otto 28, 77, 177, 180
  Empiricism and Sociology 177
  The International Encyclopedia of Unified Science 180
New Criterion, The 70
New Reasoner, The 2
Newsletter, The 7
Newsmax Media 70
New Statesman, The 7
New York 68, 156
New York Times 84
New Zealand 112–15
  Wars 113
NFL 25
Ngāti Hau 112–14, 117
Nietzsche, Friedrich 3, 11–12, 79, 81, 126
nihilism 69, 76, 84
Nike 25
Nixon, Richard 70
Nobel Prize xiii
non-violence 113
no-platforming 24
North Island of New Zealand 112
North Korea xiii
Nouvelle Droite 79
NRx, the neo-reactionary movement 79
nuclear disarmament 7
Nuremberg trials 109
Nussbaum Martha 69

O'Reilly, Bill 28
O'Reilly Factor, The 70
Obama, Barack 72–3, 88
Obama, Michelle xv
Obamacare 36
objectivism 138–9, 190, 199
objectivity xii, 144, 191
obligation 112
  duty and 54–5, 155
Ocasio-Cortez, Alexandria 2
Oliver, Kelly 90–1, 93–4
ontology 126
original position (Rawls) 105–6, 117, 119, 152

Orwell, George *1984* 143–4
  "Literature and Totalitarianism" 143–4
Osmond, Gilbert 31, 40, 54
Otherkin 85
overlapping consensus (Rawls) 107

Paerangi, Ngā 112
paleo-conservatism 79
Palin, Sarah 207
Pankhurst, Sylvia 14
Pannekoek, Anton 14
paradigms 45, 48, 56, 75, 84, 180–4, 187–91
parliament 135, 143
partisan politics 7
passions 24, 48–51, 131, 134–5, 205
  political 134–5
paternalistic reasoning 116
patriarchy 11, 85
patriotism 25
Pavlov, Ivan 159–60
peasantry 128
petit bourgeoisie 128
Phil, Dr. 33
philosophy of science 134, 137, 187
phronêsis 155
physics 8, 189
  Aristotelian 188–9, 191–2
  Galileo's 188–9, 191–2
  model of 188
Piketty, Thomas 1
  Capital in the Twenty-First Century 1
Pizzagate 78
pleasure 48, 50, 56–8
Plekhanov, Georgi 127
pleonexia 203
pluralism 107, 127–8, 132–3
  agonistic 125, 136, 178, 199
polemics 211–12
politics xi, 2–3, 11, 13–16, 36, 68, 72, 91–2, 107–8, 126–7, 129, 143, 177
Pope Francis 210
popular culture xv
popular music 81
popular representation 50
popular sovereignty 131

populism 70, 136-7
pornography 73-4
postcolonialism 69
postcolonial theory 63
post-foundationalist 133, 137
postmodernism 77, 126, 132, 179, 194, 196
post-revolutionary 59
poststructuralist 129
post-truth xii, 40
poverty 8, 164, 209
power xii, 1-3, 31-4, 39-40, 57, 59, 61-3, 68, 70, 74, 84-5, 87-8, 101-3, 111-12, 118-19, 135, 140-1, 162, 171, 182, 191, 204, 211
practice 3, 7, 10, 23, 29, 50, 81, 143, 152-7, 163-4, 166-7, 169-70, 190, 206
practice-based community 156, 196
pragmatism 138
    American 186
praxis 13, 15
Price, Huw 142-3
privilege 51, 84-5, 119
    class 87
    white 38
proceduralism 199
production 127, 129
    capitalist mode of 126, 203
    means of 4, 104, 120
    relations of 128
progressivism 36, 39, 63, 71, 88, 205
proletariat 8, 10, 128
proof 49, 182
    formal 182
Protestant Reformation 47
Proud Boys 78
psychoanalysis 32, 63
psychology 38, 58, 86
    human 56, 105
public communication 2, 10, 14-16
public deliberation 107-8, 114, 120, 133
public discourse 93
public good 27, 108
public intellectuals 68
public opinion 102
public radio 70
public reason 103, 108, 114
public sphere 125, 133, 152, 211-12
Putnam, Hilary 190

Qin, Amy 84
Qing dynasty 84
Queen Gertrude (*Macbeth*) 185
Queen Mary College, University of London 5
queer theory 69
Quine, Willard Van Orman 177
    Word and Object 177
Quinn, Zoe 75

race 126
    war 74
racism 26, 63, 88, 126
Rancière, Jacques 2
rationality 109, 136-7, 165, 170-1, 183, 190
Rawls, John 15, 101, 103-9, 114-15, 117-21, 132-4, 139, 149, 152, 178, 199
    The Idea of an Overlapping Consensus 107
    The Idea of Public Reason 107
    Justice as Fairness 103
    A Theory of Justice 103
Reagan, Ronald 70-1
Reagan Battalion 82
realism 138
reason 28, 40, 48-9, 52, 54-5, 106-8, 114, 133, 141, 151-3, 198
Rebel Media 78
reciprocal role-taking 111, 198
Reddit 73, 75
reductionism 129
Reed, Adolph 72, 91
reflection 32, 168
    explicit object of 186
reformation 171-2
    Protestant 47
Rehg, William 110
relations of production 128
relativism 69, 138-9, 190, 195, 199

religion   120, 181, 204
    Wars of   47
republican democracy   101, 103
Republican National Convention
    (2016)   xiv
Republican Party, The   38–40, 193, 207
    campaign rhetoric   37
rhetoric   xii, 16, 37, 51, 72, 209
rights   105, 108, 114, 185, 212
Robin, Corey   82
Rogan, Joe   82
Roman Empire   93
Romney, Mitt   61, 207
Rorty, Richard   69, 141
Rousseau, Jean-Jacques   102, 104
Roy, Arundhati   1, 14
Ruaka   112
rural white America   70

Sabo, Kevin   xiii
Sade, Marquis de   81
Said, Edward   69
St. Benedict   2
St Louis   xiii
Salon   73
same-sex marriage   73
Sanders, Bernie   2, 38–9, 76, 206–12
Sandy Hook Elementary School
    massacre   78
Sartre, Jean-Paul   7, 160
Schlafly, Phyllis   68
Schlessinger, Laura   70
Schlick, Moritz   28
Schmitt, Carl   58, 80
Schroeder, Gerhard   130
Schumer, Chuck   28
science   22, 180–2, 189
Screamin' Jay Hawkins   81
Second Amendment   26–7
Secretary of Education   71
secularism   48, 51, 71, 81, 120
selfhood   32, 111
self-interest   52, 59
semantics   181–2, 198
Serrano, Andres   81

sexism   88, 126
Shakespeare   31
    As You Like It   31
    Hamlet   185–6
Shapiro, Ben   25
Sidgwick, Henry   56, 58
Sierra Club   4
Simon and Schuster   82
Situationism   81
skepticism   28, 30
Skinner, Quentin   132
slavery   11
Smith, Adam   47–8
Smith, Barbara Herrnstein   69
socialism   2, 7, 36, 129
Socialisme ou Barbarie   9, 132
Socialist Labour League   7
Socialist Review   7
social science   179–80
Socrates   35
    Gorgias   35
solidarity   7, 205
    counter-hegemonic   131
    social   5, 126, 211–12
Sorel, George   127
Soros, George   76
Southern, Lauren   78
Spencer, Richard   77, 82, 92
Spengler, Oswald   79–80
spontaneism   9. *See also*
        Luxemburg, Rosa
Stalin, Joseph   6, 76
Stalinism   6
Stevenson, Charles L.   28
Stewart, Jon   71
Stonewall riots   68
Stranger Things   xi
strategic alliance   128, 129, 135, 152
subjectivism   138
Super Bowl   36
Supreme Court   61
Surrealism   81
syllogistic reasoning   133
Syrian Refugee Crisis   xiv
systemic oppression   126

Tamakehu   112
Tamatea   112
Taylor, Charles   6, 47, 191
Te Ika-a-Māui   112–13
teleology   45, 47
telos   46–8, 58, 154–5, 162
therapeutic   33, 58
Third Reich   130
Third Way   130–1
Thompson, Dorothy   6
Thompson, Edward   6
totalitarianism   127, 143–4, 178
Townhall.com   70
trade union movement   8
tradition   3, 11–12, 14, 68, 112, 118, 141, 151–2, 155–7, 163–7, 170–3, 194–8, 208
transcendental reason   51–3
transgender identity   91
transgression   76, 80–2
trigger warnings   24–5, 86
trolling   xi, 2, 76–7, 80, 212
Trotsky, Leon   3, 7
Trump, Donald   xi–xvi, 21, 25, 37–40, 77, 79, 84, 206–4, 211
Trump, Melania   40
truth   xiii–xiv, 24, 35, 39–40, 46, 52, 94, 107, 110, 131, 136, 138, 141–5, 154, 167, 169, 172, 178, 186, 211
truthfulness   46, 154, 165, 206
Tumblr   84–8, 92, 204
Turi   112
Turkle Sherry   206
Tuvel, Rebecca   89–91
   "In Defense of Transracialism"   89
Twitter   xiii–xiv, 38, 73, 75–8, 82–4, 86–7, 92, 204

Übermensch   79
United States   26, 33, 35, 37, 56, 156
   Bill of Rights   56
   Democratic Party of the   4
   First Nations   164
   President of the   xiii
Unite the Right Rally   92

universalism   52–3, 110, 132–3, 138, 149, 152
unmasking   63, 76
Utilitarianism   56–8, 107
utopianism   13

values   56, 68, 102, 163
vanguard party   9, 128
Vanity Fair   89
Varoufakis, Yanis   14
Vice   73, 78
videogames   74–5
Vienna Circle   28
Vietnam War   68
Village People, the   76
virtue ethics   11, 16
Vox   73

Wall Street   2, 39, 71
Washington, DC   77–8
Washington Post, The   xiii
WeChat   83–4
Wedderburn, Dorothy   6
Weekly Standard, The   70
Welch, Jack   34
Welfare state   7, 127
West, Cornel   14, 69
Whanganui River   101, 112–15
White House   xvi, 38–9, 72
   Correspondents Dinner (2018)   xiii
Williams, Raymond   7
Winkler, Adam   61
   We The Corporations How American Businesses Won Their Civil Rights   61
Wittgenstein, Ludwig   132–4, 136, 141, 179–80
   On Certainty   179
Wolf, Michelle   xiii
women   38, 58, 68–9, 71, 74, 83–4, 205, 207
   rights movement   60–1, 69, 127, 208
   working-class   84
workers   4–6, 8, 34, 58, 157–9, 162, 203

working class   7–10, 126–8, 207, 209
World Net Daily   70
Wyden, Ron   26

Yarvin, Curtis   79
Yiannapolous, Milo   21, 25, 75–7, 79–83, 205
Yijun, Zhou   84
yoga   33
Young Turks, The   2
YouTube   2, 73, 78, 204

Žižek, Slavoj   1, 14
Zuckerberg, Mark   34

www.ingramcontent.com/pod-product-compliance
Lightning Source LLC
Chambersburg PA
CBHW050327020526
44117CB00031B/1831